HISTORY OF NORTHUMBERLAND

THE HISTORY
OF
NORTHUMBERLAND

BY
CADWALLADER J. BATES

**SANDHILL
PRESS**

Originally published by Elliot Stock, 62, Paternoster Row, London. 1895.

Reprinted in 1996 by Sandhill Press Ltd., 17 Castle Street, Warkworth, Morpeth, Northumberland, NE65 0UW.

ISBN 0 946098 42 5

Cover illustration: *Bamburgh Castle* : an original watercolour by Fred Stott.

Printed in Great Britain by Martins the Printers, Berwick upon Tweed.

CONTENTS

Publishers Note to 1996 edition

Cadwallader J. Bates, the well known and distinguished historian and antiquary, was born in Northumberland on 14th January, 1853. Educated at Eton and Jesus College, Cambridge, his studies were interrupted by eyesight problems. After travelling extensively in Europe he returned to live at Heddon Banks, and work in the Heddon Colliery office. Here he began a special study of castles resulting in his excellent book 'Border Holds of Northumberland'.

Following his father's death he purchased Langley Castle which he saw restored and furnished. His authoritative 'History of Northumberland' was written at the request of Elliot Stock, the publisher, for their series of county histories. A Northumbrian to heart, he was vice-president of the Newcastle Society of Antiquaries and contributed frequently to the Proceedings of same, many of his articles being printed in the Archaeologia Aeliana. He was also closely associated with the preparation of the 15 volume History of Northumberland issued under the direction of the Northumberland County History Committee.

He occupied several public positions throughout his life; a J.P. in Hexham, Governor of the Shaftoe Charity, President of several agricultural societies, and in 1890 held the office of High Sheriff of the County.

Cadwallader Bates died suddenly at the early age of 49, in March 1902 and was buried in the grounds of his home, Langley Castle. The obituary notice in the Newcastle Courant describes him as "one of Northumberland's most distinguished sons. On historical and antiquarian subjects he was a recognised authority. His letters to the press, like his books, revealed at once the scholar and the thinker. In this way he has enriched local literature as few authors have done."

PREFACE

THE Rev. John Hodgson intended that his great
'History of Northumberland' should consist of
three parts. The annals of the county as a whole were
to be followed by a description of the several parishes,
and an appendix of original documents was to complete
the work. Experience soon proved that, however just
this conception of an ideal county history, the order
adopted was the exact reverse of that called for in the
practical work of composition. The parochial history
required to be based on the documentary, while until
archives had been ransacked and localities viewed, the
crowning task of writing the general history could not
successfully be achieved.

Two generations since Hodgson have now been engaged
in collecting and publishing the records of Northumberland. So much material was ready to hand in 1890,
that a Committee was formed for the completion of the
parochial history, and thanks to the ability and industry

of our first editor, Mr. Edward Bateson, this vast undertaking has been auspiciously launched. Similar considera-
tions have led me to prepare the present volume. The
time for giving the final touches to the general history of
Northumberland is far distant, but the unused evidence
which has accumulated during the last half-century
may well be given to the public in an accurate form,
without waiting for theoretical perfection.

I fail to see why the work of writing the history of the
Counties of England demands less careful treatment than
that accorded to the Provinces of the Roman Empire.
To my mind, there is no difference of kind between
parochial, provincial, national, and universal history; but
prejudices die hard, and probably the historian whose
greatest service was the vehemence with which he insisted
on the unity running through all history, would have been
astonished at a proposal to treat the history of Somerset
in the same scholarly manner as that of Sicily. I have
given to Northumberland the same serious study that
I still hope to give to Poland, and in my first nine
chapters, at any rate, have traced every rill of history to
its fountain-head.

Original research must necessarily often lead to original
conclusions, and it is perhaps a little unfortunate that in a
popular series I have had to forego those footnotes of
reference and explanation that the subject often demands.
The present venture is, indeed, an epitome of a much
larger one which has long been in the course of preparation. In my anxiety to produce a Guide to Northumbrian

History that the Quaysider from Newcastle can really carry on his bicycle, and the countryman afford to read under the shadow of his bastle-house, I have had recourse to compression almost hydraulic. My road, no doubt, is sometimes too royal: results are given in a few words, without the fatigue of following long trains of close reasoning. Few things can afford more genuine pleasure than re-establishing the connection between architectural relics and the main stream of history; but I have only been able to touch slightly on our towers and castles, and have had to leave out my readings of the great monastic fabrics of Hexham, Tynemouth and Brinkburn. I am among the first to recognise shortcomings that can be made good in the three volumes of my dreams.

Of one advantage that attends a smaller work I have made the most: I have kept as far as possible to a rigid chronological proportion that enables one to judge of the flight of time and the influence that each successive period may have exerted on custom and character.

The history of Northumberland is essentially a drum and trumpet history from the time when the *buccina* of the Batavian cohort first rang out over the moors of Procolitia down to the proclamation of James III. at Warkworth Cross. It is a history of battles of kites and crows from the apparent raid of the Britons of Corbridge on the Britons of Windermere, down to the first County Council elections on North Tyne and Rede. I have not attempted to alter its character by discussing matters, like the village land tenure, common to all Aryan nations, which can equally well be studied in counties whose history is less full of action.

Once, and once only, have I allowed myself to stray into the by-paths of controversy, and that in the defence of my old friends, Mr. John Clayton and Dr. Bruce. All their conclusions as to the Roman Wall may not be capable of absolute proof, but they were the unwearied pioneers of its exploration, and it is to the charm of their characters that it owes no little of its interest.

This abstention from controversy and criticism does not argue any ignorance of the way in which Northumbrian history has been treated by southern writers, most of whom have thought it superfluous to catch their facts before proceeding to jug them. I will only instance one essay in Professor Freeman's ' English Towns and Districts,' that on the Percy Castles, the *leitmotif* of which is the allegation that there never was a real Percy in our Northumberland—as if Harry Hotspur were not our ideal incarnation of a real Percy, and any shadowy interest we take in the Norman Percies were not wholly of a reflected order. Not to mention many minor errors, we are gravely told that Jocelin of Louvain assumed the name of Percy; that he and all his race down to Jocelin, eleventh Earl of Northumberland, were male descendants of Charles the Great, and ought to have called themselves Karlings; that the Tudor chapel of the Percy College in Warkworth Castle is an Early English cross-church of the Claverings; and that Alnwick itself is a pure Norman castle of the Vescis.

To some extent the first part of Hodgson's scheme was supplied already by the Rev. Philip Ridpath's 'Border History,' a most admirable work to have issued from a Scottish manse, though rather encumbered with diplomatic details.   Recently, too, the information relating to Northumberland inserted by Mr. Bain in his excellent 'Calendar of State Papers relating to Scotland' forms an *amende honorable* for many a Border raid.   In our own Record publications, unfortunately, Northumbrian matters are dispersed haphazard, according to the whims of successive editors, through the Domestic, Scottish, Border, and Foreign series.   At Belvoir the Historical Manuscripts Commission did signal service in calendaring the Manners collection of Border papers; but it is difficult to speak calmly of their perfunctory treatment of the archives of Alnwick, Sion and Ford.   With a few brilliant exceptions, the volumes of the Rolls Series of English Chronicles which deal with Northern affairs deserve to be placed two or three shelves below the Delphin Classics.

In the vexed question of spelling Old English names, I have been guided more by their ordinary modern pronunciation than by the sign-manuals of their original bearers.   Nothing has done more to widen the rift at the Norman Conquest than the fashion of posting Eadwards and Ælfrids on one side of it, and Edwards and Alfreds on the other.   It is evident that contortions like Ædwini, Vtrede, Qwoenburh, and Ecgferth can never be intended to be on the lips of the nation.

It would be invidious to mention any of the numerous kindnesses I have received in relation to special points, without giving the whole list of my literary obligations. In the general work of passing through the press, I have received most valuable aid from my old college friend, the Rev. A. C. Jennings, and only in a somewhat lesser degree from Mr. Thomas Hodgkin, the Rev. F. J. Foakes Jackson, Mr. J. Crawford Hodgson, and Mr. A. B. Hinds.

C. J. B.

LANGLEY CASTLE,
May 29, 1895.

HISTORY OF NORTHUMBERLAND.

CHAPTER I.

INTRODUCTORY—THE FOUR DYKES.

THE very name of Northumberland is enough to make anyone inquire how it happened that the great kingdom which once stretched north from the Humber to the Grampians shrivelled and shrank till it came to be lineally represented by the present administrative county. The names of other sovereign members of the Heptarchy—Kent, Essex, Sussex—are also perpetuated in existing counties, but these counties are practically conterminous with the ancient kingdoms. Burgundy probably affords the only other example in Europe of geographical contraction such as Northumberland has undergone.

The present county is often popularly described as the land between Tyne and Tweed. This is, however, far from being strictly accurate. A very large district south of the Tweed and east of the central mountain range of our island is comprised in Scotland, while a considerable tract of Northumberland lies south of the Tyne. Then too, Berwick Bounds, from a point on the coast a little beyond Marshall Meadows, some three miles north of the town of Berwick, to Gainslawhaugh, four miles up the Tweed, are now included in Northumberland, so that the

Tweed merely forms the boundary of the county from Gainslawhaugh to Riding Burn, a distance of only some eighteen miles, including all the bends of the river. From the corner where Riding Burn enters the Tweed, there are no physical features capable of forming a natural frontier southwards, until we come to the Cheviots; the actual boundary was consequently a matter of perpetual dispute. Northumberland got much the worse of the final settlement, losing the upper valley of the Bowmont. From Steer Rig, as far as Thirleshope Pike, the delimitation scientifically follows the water-parting, the highest point on which, King's Seat, near Cheviot, rises to 2,419 feet above the sea-level, Peel Fell, at the head of North Tyne, being 444 feet lower. After ceding to Scotland the left bank of the Bells Burn, a tributary of North Tyne, Northumberland takes in the east side of Kershope Burn, though this flows by the Liddell into the Solway.

At Lamyford, Scotland, Northumberland, and Cumberland all meet. The boundary between the two counties keeps pretty well to the sky-line of the hills, one of them bearing the odd name of Horse Head, as far south as the source of the Gair Burn, and then follows the course of that stream, which after its junction with the Troutbeck assumes the name of the Irthing. On the Cumbrian side, the streams and hills are all becks and fells, on the Northumbrian, burns and moors. Flowing first south, then west, the Irthing continues to be the boundary till the Poltross Burn joins it from the south, though in the fourteenth century Denton in Gilsland was in the rural deanery of Corbridge and the county of Northumberland. Ascending the Poltross and crossing Blacklaw at 1,952 feet, the boundary should, geographically speaking, have given the whole basin of South Tyne to Northumberland; but the upper part of the valley of the Hartley Burn (opening out opposite Featherston, and including the small lake called Tindale Tarn), as well as the extensive parish of Alston at the head of South Tyne, cut off by the Gilder

Burn on the west and the Ale Burn on the east, are in Cumberland.

From Kilhope Moor, at the head of the West Allen, where Durham meets Northumberland and Cumberland, the boundary keeps along the hill-tops, of which that of Kilhope Law attains an altitude of 2,206 feet, as far as the burn which falls into the Derwent near Riddleham Hope. The Derwent would then take up the boundary till it joins the Tyne near Blaydon, were it not that the parish of Ryton, though on the northern bank, is in the county of Durham. As it is, the boundary turns north from the Derwent up the Milkwell Burn, and from it follows mere hedges and ditches to the Stanley Burn. From Wylam, where the Stanley Burn flows into the Tyne under the station platform, the latter river separates Durham and Northumberland down to the sea; but Newcastle has been a county of itself since the reign of Henry IV., though the enclave of the Moot Hall, including the space formerly occupied by the Great Hall, King's Chamber, and Half-moon Battery of the Castle has been preserved to Northumberland for the assizes and other public business.

Thus it will be seen that some Northumbrian water flows down Liddesdale, some past Carlisle; while Scotland and Cumberland both contribute their runlets to the great waterway of Newcastle. There is a Scottish field south of the Tweed near Wark, a fragment of Northumberland south of the Derwent; while on the Tyne both landings of Ryton Ferry are in Durham, both abutments of Newburn Bridge in Northumberland. It may seem superfluous to go into such details, but all these variations from the natural boundaries of the county have their origin in historical events of greater or less importance.

The basin of the Tynes and their tributaries, the Derwent, the Rede, and the two Allens, includes about one half of Northumberland, and is separated from the basin of the Till, which extends from the Tweed right

down to the latitude of Alnwick, by that of the Coquet;
these three being the only river-basins that extend to
the hills on the west side of the county, though the Aln,
the Wansbeck, and the Blyth are considerable streams.
Between the Tweed and the Aln a score of little streams
run direct into the sea, of which the Waren is the only
one of much historical importance. This tract along the
coast is separated from the Till by a range of bleak
moors that rise to over 1,000 feet in Rose Castle, the
great central beacon of north Northumberland. The
moors of Rothbury Forest, reaching nearly 1,500 feet in
Tosson Hill and Simonside, cut the county practically in
two.

The lakes of Northumberland are small, all being surpassed in size by the artificial reservoirs of Colt Crag
and Hallington. In the north are those of Paston and
Pallinsburn, the latter famous for its gulls. At Eglingham and Sweethope are larger sheets of water, but
the name of the Northumbrian lakes is specially given
to the five near the Roman Wall: Greenlee Lough or
Wigglesmere, Crag Lough, Broomlee Lough, Hallypike
Lough, and Grindon Lough.

The islands along the coast are Lindisfarne, or Holy
Island; the group of the Farnes, whose quaint names—
the Wedoms, the Knokys, the Walms, the Langstane, the
Cromstane, the Oxcarrs, and the Megstanes—appear in
medieval manuscripts; Coquet Island, near Warkworth;
and St. Mary's, or Bates Island, a little to the north of
Tynemouth.

No traces of palæolithic man have been found nearer
than the Yorkshire Wolds, but stone implements of the
neolithic period are of frequent occurrence in Northumberland. The celts are formed of the greatest variety of
materials: greenstone, porphyrite, flint, honestone, whinstone, and metamorphic rock. The examples in porphyrite from Burradon and Doddington are especially fine,
as are those in whinstone from Ponteland and Hetton;
but the finest of all is, perhaps, an ochreous-coloured flint

from Burradon-in-Coquetdale. A trimmed flake-knife from Ford, and a magnificent perforated axe-head from Seghill, are also important relics of the Stone Age. The twenty stones found together on Corbridge Fell, and the curious sink-stone from Percy's Cross, are possibly of comparatively modern origin.

Hoards of bronze implements, though not on a scale to suggest a manufactory, have been discovered at Alnwick, Wallington, and Thrunton near Whittingham. At the last-named place the swords and spearheads were sticking in the moss, arranged in a circle with their points downwards. One sword had, at the pommel end, very remarkable curved horns with projecting cones. Another fine sword, long and leaf-shaped, with seven rivet-holes, was found in the Tyne near Newburn. The bronze celts which deserve especial mention are a beautiful flanged one, ornamented with an interlaced pattern, from near Chollerford Bridge, and a trumpet-mouthed one of octagonal section from Newham. A curious sandstone mould for casting celts and rings was found at Cambo.

The barrows of Northumberland have hardly received the investigation that might have been expected. A very fine one at Dewley, near Newburn, is in process of being rapidly levelled by the plough; there is also another that deserves exploration, on the line of the Wall, between Brunton and St. Oswald. Nests of barrows occur in the Cheviots. The centre of the county contains comparatively few, though there is a tempting one at Trewhit. The Rev. W. Greenwell opened a barrow at Broomhill, near Ford, raised apparently in memory of a child of two years old, and containing remains of six attendants, probably killed at the funeral. His fine collection contains a cinerary urn with two series of figures raised in relief, and a drinking-cup ornamented with a notched piece of bone or wood, both taken from a cairn near Rosebrough, as well as other drinking-cups from Smalesmouth, Bewick, and Old Rothbury. In jet, we have a fine necklace from Blawearie and a button from Great Tosson; in gold, which is something extremely rare in prehistoric finds, a necklace from Chesterhope Common.

Of the many circles of upright stones that formerly existed, only those at Three Stone Burn, near Yevering Bell, and to the north of Duddo, can still be fairly traced. The fine circle at Nunwick, on North Tyne, described by Bishop Gibson, has long since disappeared. The King's Stone, on Crookham Moor, and the Standing Stones at Swinburn and Matfen, are examples of rude monoliths. The two stones at Percy's Leap, and the Mare and Foal near the Roman Wall, to the north of Haltwhistle, are probably remains of cromlechs.

Hill-forts are much more numerous in the region near the Wall, and to the north of it, than in the more southern parts of the county. Among the more remarkable are Yevering Bell, near Cheviot; the triple town at Greaves Ash, near Linhope; Rose Castle, above Chillingham; Spindleston, near Bamburgh; Old Bewick, Harehaugh, Old Rothbury, the Moot Hills at Elsdon, Gunnar Peak, Wardon and Shildon. The Rev. G. Rome Hall and Mr. R. C. Hedley have done much to aid the study of individual camps, but a great deal remains to be done in comparing their outlines and making the most of the few clues that may bring them into touch with known history. At Rowting Linn, Old Bewick, Morwick, and elsewhere we find those mysterious cups and rings that were first prominently brought into notice by the late Mr. George Tate, and as to the origin and signification of which it were still folly to be wise. It is well to remember that the popular term 'prehistoric,' in relation to British antiquities, covers two periods — the first before the arrival of the Romans, the second after their departure. Several of the camps may ultimately prove to be English, Danish, or even early Norman, earthworks.

Much might be said to justify the addition to this list of prehistoric antiquities of the lines of earthworks, stretching from the Tyne at Newcastle to Dykesfield near the Solway, known in popular archæology under the name of 'The Vallum.' The historian of Northumberland is confronted at the outset with the triple problem presented by the remains of the Roman Wall, and however earnestly he may wish to treat his subject in a manner that may commend it to the general reader, runs the greatest risk of being at once engaged in one of the most complicated of controversies. It is as if the history of England were necessarily to be prefaced with a dissertation on the authorship of the 'Letters of Junius,' or that of France with a laborious identification of the Man in the Iron Mask. The evidence afforded by the remains themselves, and by the references made to them by historians, is not only too meagre to warrant any definite conclusion as to their origin, but is often apparently contradictory. Instead, then, of attempting to bolster up by special pleading any dogmatic assertions as to the date or dates of the construction of these lines of earthworks, of the stone wall following the same course on the north, and of the forts connected with both, it seems better at once to declare that the whole question is still an open one; and, instead of playing the part of an advocate, to sum up the evidence, such as it is, in as judicial a spirit as possible. For this purpose, however, it is necessary, all the same, to adopt a hypothesis of some sort in order to marshal the facts of the case. That the hypothesis to be followed is not one hitherto suggested, nor perhaps the one most likely ultimately to prove true, appears to make it all the safer medium for exhibiting, in an unbroken sequence, the information we do possess, and at the same time impressing upon us the danger of hastily drawing any conclusions from this.

The earliest detailed account of the Roman Wall after the new birth of letters is to be found in a communication from Christopher Ridley, Vicar of Haltwhistle, in about 1572. He there calls it 'one wall builded betwyxt the Brittons and Pightes (which we call the Kepe Wall), builded by the Pightes,' thus giving expression to the current tradition of the neighbourhood in his

time that the Wall was the work, not of the Romans, but
of the Picts.   It seems incredible that writer after writer
should have disregarded this tradition, and declare that
the local name of ' The Picts' Wall ' was derived from
the fact that it was believed to have been erected not by,
but as a defence against, that mysterious nation.   The
value of traditions in general may be gauged by the way
in which we see all memory of the Romans and their
works had been locally lost in Northumberland by the
time of Elizabeth, though the name ' Murus Roman-
orum ' occurs in the Black Book of Hexham, at the end
of the fifteenth century.   There may, however, be a grain
of truth lurking in this particular tradition if, instead of
applying it to the stone wall, we restrict it to the earthworks, ' the four great ditches builded within it all the
way,' as Christopher Ridley calls them.   Equally incredible does it seem that it is only in 1892 or 1893 that
the fact of these earthworks consisting of four dykes or
mounds—two of them, it is true, being more or less
intermittent—has again been brought under notice.   A
great ditch, about 8 feet deep, 32 feet wide at the top,
and 9 feet across its flat bottom, was their central and
main feature.   The importance attached to this ditch
may be seen in the enormous labour expended in cutting
it through the basalt at Limestone Bank, west of Chollerford, and the little care taken to remove the basalt blocks
when once lifted out of it.   Generally speaking, where
the ground rises immediately from this ditch, either to
the north or to the south, there is a mound on the opposite
edge, so as to make the actual ditch higher ; and the
same principle of disposing the excavated earth in a way
that should make the whole work as wide and deep an
eternal gulf of separation as possible has been carried
out by forming two great mounds, placed 24 feet back
from either side of the ditch, so as to render it difficult
for it ever again to be filled in either by intention or
accident.

The excavations initiated by Mr. Thomas Hodgkin

at the Great Hill, a little east of the village of Heddon-on-the-Wall, in June, 1893, fortunately struck on a section of these Four Dykes where the central ditch had been cut in a bed of fire-clay. This circumstance not only enabled the original shape of the ditch to be distinctly traced, but, since the fire-clay was found deposited in both the principal mounds and the northern marginal one there present, proved them all to have been constructed of the upcast at the time the ditch was dug. A few hours of spade-labour thus disposed once for all of the ingenious conjectures attributing different epochs and different functions to the several mounds, which represented years of theoretical pondering. The great mound on the south side was at this point abnormally large, owing to the stones where the ditch was cut through the rock on the top of the hill, having been pitched upon it. In one place these stones seemed to have been arranged to form a sort of kerb to the mound, but further investigation proved this idea to be fallacious. It is not to be supposed that the several mounds ever had any regular dimensions ; these varied according to the requirements of the ditch, to which they seem to have been entirely subsidiary.

That these earthworks—now carried along the southern slope of a hill as at Harlow Hill and to the east of Halton, now overhung by crags or declivities on the south, as at the Chapel Hill, near Housesteads, and most remarkably so between Great Chesters and Walltown—could ever have been designed as a defence against either a northern or a southern enemy, is an idea undeserving of serious consideration. No military signification can be attributed to them, for whichever side of the ditch we take, the great mounds, or palisading upon them, would often require to be carried up to the height of 30 feet or so in order to command the bottom of it, which would otherwise have served as a lurking-place for assailants. This self-evident principle was properly attended to in the case of the Wall ; and to suppose that this was built within a cen-

tury of the ditch between the Four Dykes having been
dug, is, on this showing, to suppose that an entire revolution in the art of fortification must have taken place in
the interval, and of such a revolution there is neither
sign nor symptom in any Latin or Greek military writer.
The builders of the Wall appear to have carried
their military road along the northernmost dyke when it
suited their purpose, but the little importance they
attached to it is shown by their having apparently levelled
it near Halton in order to carry the road through it.

It is obvious that the Four Dykes, as they have been
described, can neither be called a ' Murus ' nor a ' Vallum,'
not that for purposes of frontier defence there was in
Roman times any real technical distinction between these
interchangeable terms, which should once for all be
discarded, considering the great additional confusion
that has been gratuitously imported into the puzzle by
their employment. Nor, again, were any of the com-
ponent mounds ' cespititious,' that is to say, built of turves
laid brick-fashion one over two others, as has now clearly
proved to be the case with the wall along the line of the
Clyde and Forth. The Four Dykes would appear to have
constituted purely and simply a boundary-line such as two
nations might agree to set out between themselves, the
strategic advantages of the frontier being equally balanced,
if they were taken into consideration at all. In any case,
the ditch was everything, and its course may have been
determined to a great extent by the ground being suitable
for its excavation.

Notwithstanding what Tacitus says about certain
British communities in this district having treated the
Romans on terms of equality up to the time of his father-
in-law Agricola, it seems impossible to believe that any
Roman general, however hard-pressed, would have agreed
to a delimitation so humiliating to the prestige of the
Empire. Similarly, we cannot conceive that any Roman,
least of all the Emperor most famous for his skill in
engineering and architecture, could have incurred the

enormous labour of carrying the Four Dykes across the island, without at the same time making them available for the protection of his province. Besides, if the Romans were in quest of a frontier hereabouts, it would seem natural for them, unless biased by some pre-existing boundary, to have followed the transinsular course of the Tyne and the Irthing, and to have erected their defensive works along the southern banks of those rivers. Why give up a line so strong and sheltered for a weak, imaginary one running over what, even if then better wooded, must have always been a series of bleak hillsides? The fertile Valley of the Tyne was no doubt a valuable source of supplies for the garrisons, but this would not counterbalance the strategic and climatic disadvantages that its inclusion entailed. Or if the Tyne Valley must be included at all costs, why not keep to the top of the basalt crags that form for miles a colossal wall of themselves, instead of digging a ditch through the marshy ground to the south of them?

It was just here between the two seas that the territories of the great nation of the Brigantes terminated on the north, without there being in nature any apparent reason for their so doing, so that it may easily happen that before the advent of the Romans the Four Dykes formed the boundary between them and the Selgoouai to the north-west and the Otalinoi to the north-east. Other prehistoric dykes of this description are by no means rare. Just over the Scottish border the Catrail, called also the 'Fossa Galwensium' and the Picts' Work Dyke, 'appears to have consisted of a fosse or ditch, nearly twenty-four feet wide, by about ten deep, and the earth thrown out on both sides was formed into ramparts'; immediately opposite the termination of the Four Dykes themselves, near the southern shore of the Solway, 'an earthen rampart and fosse' begin on the northern shore, and run across the upper part of the valleys of Dumfriesshire and Galloway, till they terminate at Loch Ryan; the so-called Offa's Dyke between the Dee and the Wye is much longer than our Four Dykes, and the tradition that that Mercian sovereign pitilessly slew every Welshman found to the east of it, illustrates the ancient use of a dyke, not as a military defence, but as a definite boundary that was not to be rashly overstepped; and, not to cite further examples, we have prehistoric earthworks on the Lower Danube in no less perplexing proximity to the fortified lines attributed to the Emperor Trajan than are the Four Dykes to our own Wall.

Nothing Roman has as yet been discovered in connection with the Four Dykes, but, in making the section near Heddon-on-the-Wall in 1893, a bronze axe-head, socketed and looped, was found in the great north mound, and although this may have been lying near the surface on the line of the ditch, and have been shovelled up at its making, still, it does undoubtedly suggest the possibility of its having been dropped while the mound was being raised, and that three or four centuries before the Christian era.

Another point worthy of attention is that, while the Four Dykes terminate to the west at Dykesfield, now separated from the Solway by more than a mile of marsh, the Wall is continued to Bowness, an extension that may be easily accounted for, if between the times of their respective construction a general elevation of the Cumbrian coast had taken place, which rendered it necessary to carry a line, whether limitary or defensive, further along the firm land before ending at the sea. Such an elevation is known geologically to have actually taken place prior to the Roman occupation. At their east end, again, the Four Dykes fall short of the Wall by the three miles between Newcastle and Wallsend, and here, too, it is only reasonable to suppose that the prolongation of the latter may be explained by the gradual silting up of the lower reaches of the Tyne, which consequently in that portion of its course did not afford the same security to their frontier that the Romans deemed to be sufficient between Wallsend and Tynemouth.

Whatever the ultimate verdict on the origin and significance of the Four Dykes may be, the line they follow
appears, as has been said, to have formed the northern
frontier of the Brigantes at the time when the country
beyond the Tyne first opens out in history. From the
Four Dykes to the Forth, the east coast was occupied by
the Otalinoi. Of the three towns which the 'Geographical
Guide' of Claudius Ptolemy places in their territories,
one only, Bremenion, at High Rochester in Redesdale,
can be positively identified, though it is probable that
the longitude of another, Alauna, should be slightly
rectified, so as to place it at Alnwick, or Alnmouth,
instead of in the very middle of the Firth of Forth. The
Alauna, or Aln, is the only river mentioned by Ptolemy on
the coast-line between the Wear and the Forth, but we
may be the less surprised at this meagre list of towns and
rivers when we remember that his work was expressly
intended to be a geography, or an account of the earth as
a whole, and not a chorography or description of particular places. The exact date of its publication in the
reign of Hadrian or Antoninus Pius is immaterial, as its
ethnographical value as an account of the position of the
several native tribes at the time of the Roman conquest
is little affected by it.

As to the line of separation between the Otalinoi and
the Selgoouai, whose name possibly survives in that of
the Solway, this mere tribal boundary may be represented
by the Black Dyke, which, with the ditch on the west
side, entered Northumberland in the extreme north-west
corner, near Black Knowe, and, after keeping roughly to
the water-parting between the Irthing and the North
Tyne, and passing the Wall and the Four Dykes at right
angles about two miles east of Housesteads, is said to
have been traced across the South Tyne as far south as
Allenheads. Both in the first vague allusions to northern
Britain in the Latin classics and in the later historians,
when a general term was required to apply to the part of
the island beyond the Roman pale, the Otalinoi and

Selgoouai appear to have been both included in Caledonia. It is just possible that the Otalinoi, whose name has often been misspelt Otadinoi, and another tribe of Tadinoi, or Gadinoi, manufactured out of it, may have given their name to the Watling Street, the road which led to and through their country, just as the Icknield Way is said to derive its name from the Ikenoi, the ancient inhabitants of Norfolk.

The portion of Northumberland to the south of the Four Dykes appears to have been divided by the Black Dyke among two tribes of the Brigantian nation: the Maiatai, whose chief settlement, Maia, with its temple of Mars Cocidius, would appear to have been near Keswick; and the Coroniatotai, whose name still lingers in that of Corbridge. It is remarkable that while altars to Cocidius abound to the west of the Black Dyke, even so close to it as at Housesteads and Little Chesters, not one has yet been discovered east of that line.

The Maiatai and Coroniatotai may have been among those Brigantian communities hitherto treating the Romans on terms of equality, whom Cnæus Julius Agricola, Vespasian's general, induced, by an alternation of sudden attacks and conciliatory measures, to agree to a truce and the delivery of hostages on his famous march north in the early summer of A.D. 79. Agricola proceeded, Tacitus tells us, to surround the territories of these tribes with *præsidia* and *castella*, and in so doing paid more attention and displayed more judgment than had till then been bestowed on any newly-pacified portion of Britain. We may, then, reasonably conclude that this fortified investment of the district was something more than an ordinary erection in it of camps and forts. It was clearly Agricola's object not to protect these semi-independent tribes from the raids of their northern neighbours, but to bind them to their promises, and prevent them from attacking him in the rear, while he was marching forward with the avowed intention of conquering the whole island.

In command of the Second Legion, and supported by a small fleet, he himself appears to have advanced from Chester along the ragged coast-line of Lancashire and Cumberland ; while the Ninth Legion pursued a parallel route from York, and a fleet sailed up the east coast to effect a descent on the Tay, so as to prevent the Caledonian tribes from moving down to meet him in mass, lest their own homes should be ravaged in their absence. Taking all this into consideration, it has been often surmised that many of the Roman forts on the line of the Tyne and Solway were originally founded by Agricola. If the Four Dykes represent the northern bounds of the Brigantian tribes he was desirous of encompassing, some of whom we know maintained their semi-independence for another sixty years, it would be natural for him to range his forts along the north side of these mounds, especially as he thereby gained the further object of protecting a short road across the island, so as to keep up communications with his York column and North Sea fleet.

The watchful eye Agricola kept over tribes that otherwise might have threatened his base of operations is one explanation of the remarkable fact that most of the forts on the Tyne-and-Solway Border front, not, as might be expected, the unsubdued north, but, on the contrary, the partially-subdued south ; for, with a devotion to red-tape more than worthy of a British Government department in our own days, the Romans laid out their encampments and the stone forts that succeeded them on certain fixed lines, from which they seldom departed. Their camps, which would otherwise have been squares with the corners rounded off, and a gateway in the centre of each of the four sides, were lengthened into oblongs in the direction of the enemy or the intended march. In this lengthened portion of the camp the main body of the troops was quartered. The gate by which they were supposed to march out was called the Prætorian Gate, that at the opposite end of the camp the Decuman. Between the two gateways in the side walls stretched the

Via Principalis, or High Street. The centre of the camp
was occupied by the Prætorium, the house of the commander, and the temple of his soldiers, opening on to the
Via Principalis. At the Decuman Gate, the back-door of
the camp, the market-people collected, and through it
the disgraced soldier was led to execution; the granaries
and storehouses were placed contiguous to it. The
great camp of the Saalburg on the German Limes,
which has been completely excavated, offers an excellent example of a Roman fort arranged on these stereotyped lines,
the Prætorian Gate facing the enemy's country. Along the
line of the Northumbrian Wall, on the contrary, the
Prætorian gates of the forts at Benwell, Rudchester,
Halton, Chesters and Carraw are turned towards the
south, as though that were the quarter in which danger
threatened. In the cases of Halton and Great Chesters,
the water was, originally at any rate, brought in aque-
ducts from a considerable distance to the north of the
Wall, and the other supplies must have been drawn from
the same direction, as there are no signs of any roads
crossing the Four Dykes, to reach the Decuman gates.

The southern aspect of these forts is especially apparent
when they occupy sites of great natural strength, as at
Birdoswald and Stanwix; the latter, dominating so
splendidly over Carlisle, can surely never have been
selected as a mere *tête-de-pont*. Even poor, despised
Gildas, in the fifth century, noticed that these forts had
not been designed originally as a line of defence against
the north, but had chanced to be built where they stand
as a defence against enemies in general.

One objection that naturally suggests itself against the
claim of Agricola to have founded these forts is the
absence among them of any inscription of his time.
This is, however, met by the fact that none have been
discovered in the chain of forts he is known to have
established between the Clyde and the Forth. Indeed,
there are very few inscriptions in Britain before the reign
of Trajan; the fashion of carving them did not begin

till that of Hadrian, nor become fully developed before that of Severus. A more serious objection is the fact that Bremenium (High Rochester) and Prima Statio (Risingham), and other stations on the Watling Street, also have their Prætorian gates on the southern side, which rather implies that some catastrophe like that which swallowed up the Ninth Legion at York—a general revolt of the Brigantes, no doubt—found the Roman legate of the day engaged with his army in a Caledonian campaign, just as Suetonius Paullinus was far away in Anglesey at the time of Boadicea's sack of Camalodunum, and that the whole series of forts rose during the war of re-conquest he was forced to undertake from the North.

Another illustration of the little importance the Romans attached to the Four Dykes as a military work is the way in which Watling Street crosses them at some considerable distance from the fort at Halton Chesters, which was the nearest fortified passage through them. That Watling Street was made before the building of the Wall may be surmised from its having crossed it, not through one of the gate-towers by which it was pierced at every Roman mile, but through a special gateway, half within, half without the Wall, with the ditch belonging to this latter carried purposely round it.

A very valuable, though much distorted, list of the names of native towns and Roman fortresses existing in the North soon after the time of Agricola has been fortunately handed down to us. The anonymous compiler of the geographical treatise in which this is preserved, *idiota ego hujus cosmographiæ expositor*, as, perhaps with some reason, he calls himself, was born at Ravenna, and wrote about the middle of the seventh century. Other countries he described according to their state in his own time; but Britain had so completely dropped out of the known world in consequence of the Saxon invasions, that for his account of it he avowedly had recourse to some ancient map or road-book, probably

originally written in Greek. This account gives the
names of 'cities' between the Clyde and the Forth, that
are evidently the same as the forts still to be traced there,
and probably founded by Agricola; and since, though
mentioning the Second Legion, styled Augusta, at Caer-
leon-upon-Usk, and the Twentieth, Victrix, at Chester,
it assigns no legion to York, it may be inferred that it was
originally drawn up in the interval between the disap-
pearance there of the Ninth Legion and its replacement
by the Sixth, on the Emperor Hadrian's arrival in the
island. This inference is very materially strengthened by
the string of names in question, not including that of
Pons Ælius (Newcastle-upon-Tyne), so called after the
bridge, doubtless, thrown across the Tyne under Hadrian,
a member of the Ælian family; while the forts usually
known as Borcovicium (Housesteads) and Amboglanna
(Birdoswald) appear under what seem the earlier names
of Velurtion and Banna. Then, again, we find in this
list of forts neither Alio (Whitley Castle), an important
post on the Maiden Way, nor Petrianæ (Old Carlisle),
the very centre of the elaborate network of Roman
defences on the west coast as finally developed.

Unlike the 'cities' between the Clyde and Forth,
which, according to this account, were joined together,
una alteri connexæ, as if already some sort of limitary rampart stretched across that isthmus, those between the
Tyne and Solway are merely said to have been in a
straight line from sea to sea. Their names, mostly
in the ablative case, are given under the corrupt
forms of:

SERDUNO ...	...	...	...	Wallsend.
CONDECOR	...	...	...	Benwell.
VINDOVALA	...	...	...	Rudchester.
ONNO ...	...	...	...	Halton Chesters.
CELUNNO ...	...	...	...	Chesters.
BROCOLITI ...	...	...	...	Carrawburgh.
VELURTION	...	...	...	Housesteads.
ESICA ...	...	...	...	Great Chesters.
BANNA ...	...	...	...	Birdoswald.

UXELLUDAMO	...	...	...	Ellenborough.
AVALANA ...	...	...	...	Papcastle.
MAIA	...	...	...	Keswick (?)
FANO COCIDII	...	...	...	Whitbarrow (?)
BROCARA ...	...	...	...	Brougham.

It will be noticed that this belt of forts leaves the line of the Wall after Birdoswald, and first reaches the western sea at Uxelludamum, near Maryport, following, no doubt, what always remained the great military route between the two seas. Carlisle, however, was already in being, as we learn from the following whorl :

VALTERIS ...	...	...	...	Brough.
BEREDA ...	...	...	...	Old Penrith.
LUGUBALUM	...	...	...	Carlisle.
MAGNIS ...	...	...	...	Carvoran.
GABAGLANDA	...	...	...	On Haltwhistle Burn (?).
VINDOLANDE	...	...	...	Little Chesters.
LINEOJUGLA	...	...	...	Settlingstones (?).
VINOVIA ...	...	...	...	Binchester.
LAVARIS ...	...	...	...	Bowes.

The two of these forts that are positively known to be in Northumberland, Magnæ and Vindolana, lie on the Roman road known in the Middle Ages as the 'Stanegate' or 'Carelgate,' from its being paved and leading to Carlisle, and which put Birdoswald in direct communication with Chesters, following reasonable gradients along the middle slopes of the hills on the left bank of South Tyne. There seems no more reason for confounding Gabaglanda with Amboglanna, the other name of Birdoswald, than with Glannibanta, which, as we shall see, was no doubt the same as Stanwix, near Carlisle ; many of these barbarous names have much the same ring about them, and the interesting camp that guarded the bridge by which the Stanegate crossed Haltwhistle Burn certainly deserved a name. A camp at Settlingstones, that may or not have been Lineojugla, is shown very plainly on Armstrong's map of Northumberland in 1769, but seems to have been since obliterated.

The very peripatetic geographer of Ravenna now leads us a dance down to the Moray Firth, and right across Scotland to Loch Ryan in Galloway, and then tempts us with :

EBIO	...	...	...	...	Ebchester (?).
CORITIOTAR	...	...	...	...	Corbridge (?).
CELOVION	...	...	...	...	Chesters (?).

These are just the places that were required to fill in his circular tour between Settlingstones and Binchester. Ebchester, though it cannot well be the Epiakon of Ptolemy, has no positive connection with the Northumbrian princess St. Ebba ; the name Coritiotar at once reminds us of the Coroniatotai, and Celovion comes quite as near Cilurnum (Chesters) as does Celunno, the form previously given.

A few more names follow, apparently of places in the North of Scotland, and then the Ravennas (as a native of Ravenna was called) comes out on the surer ground of :

TRIMUNTIUM	...	...	...	Melrose (?).
EBUROCASLUM	...	...	...	Netherby (?).
BREMENIUM	...	...	...	High Rochester.
COCUNEDA	...	...	...	Holystone.
ALAUNA	...	...	...	Alnmouth (?).
OLEICLAVIS	...	...	...	Ulchester (?).
EVIDENSCA	...	...	...	Derrydikes (?).
RUMABO	...	...	...	On the Tweed (?).

Eburocaslum seems to be a manifest blunder for Exploratorum Castrum, as Netherby, the first station on the Roman road north of Carlisle, was called, from the camp of the scouts there ; but the name may equally well have been applied to Risingham or other camps on the west branch of the Watling Street, north of Corbridge, along which *exploratores* were also quartered. The cross-road from Bremenium on the west branch of the Watling Street to the east branch at the Cove Burn can still be distinctly traced, but there are no traces of Roman remains now visible at Holystone, where this road crosses the Coquet, nor of the continuation of it towards Alnmouth. The fine camp at Ulchester, now corruptly called Outchester, seems to be Roman; that at Derry-dykes, west of Belford, is more doubtful. Nothing appears to be known with certainty as to how the eastern branch of the Watling Street terminated on the Tweed; and, except for the faint trace of Oleiclavis to be found in Ulchester, the passion of the Ravennas for circular tours is the chief reason for supposing him to have turned north again from the Aln.

CHAPTER II.

THE WALL.

THE Roman occupation of Northumberland with roads and fortresses would seem to have been well-nigh completed when the Emperor Hadrian landed in Britain in A.D. 121. He is usually credited with having favoured the resumption of the cautious policy of Augustus, who deprecated any extension of the Empire beyond the limits he himself had assigned to it. Hadrian certainly abandoned the provinces east of the Euphrates, but he retained Dacia, cutting it off from the rest of the Empire, and rendering an invasion of Mœsia more difficult by destroying the bridge his predecessor Trajan had thrown with so much labour across the Danube. Britain he also retained, though, by force of circumstances, perhaps, rather than of fixed policy, he appears to have relinquished all idea of subjugating the whole island, and to have fallen back for his northernmost frontier on the line of forts existing between the Solway and the Tyne.

Two fragments of a slab found in the church of Jarrow, but very possibly taken from Wallsend, notwithstanding that Jarrow itself had a Roman fort, seem to record the fact that 'troops stationed in the province of Britain in forts between the two shores of Ocean, were commended by Hadrian for having, under circumstances that tried the faith and loyalty of all, preserved intact the boundaries of the Republic, being only restrained by dire necessity from subduing the furthermost limits of the known world.'

A similar allocution, inscribed on the pedestal of a column in the camp of the auxiliaries at Lambæsæ, in Algeria, shows the pleasure it gave Hadrian to find masonry substituted for turf-walls. He there thanks the horsemen of the Sixth Cohort of the Commageni for 'accomplishing in one day work that others would have spread over many; for having constructed a long wall similar to those of winter forts with stones, large, heavy and unequal, in little longer time than it could have been built with turves, which, cut all of the same size, are easily carried and put together; and for having excavated a well-trimmed ditch through hard and rough gravel.'

In order to make the eastern portion of the new British frontier more accessible to his troops, the destroyer of the bridge of Turn-Severin threw over the Tyne the Ælian Bridge, commanded by a fort now obliterated by the city of Newcastle. His general policy of Imperial defence in places where the barbarians were marked off (*dividuntur*), not by rivers, but by *limites*, was to keep them out (*separavit*) by great stakes fastened together and fixed at the bottom like a mural fence. In Britain, we are told, as something exceptional, he first erected a wall eighty miles long, not so much for the purpose of keeping out the barbarians, as for that of marking them off (*divideret*) from the Roman citizens. Bowness, on the Solway, is almost exactly eighty Roman miles from Wallsend; but we might have expected to find a line of demarcation like the *limes* between the Rhine and Danube or the turf-wall between the Clyde and Forth, rather than a stone wall averaging 8 feet in width and 16 feet in height, with gate-towers every mile, and three or four turrets in each interval between them. The construction of this great Wall, mighty work of engineering though it is, seems to involve a confession of military inferiority to the tribes beyond that it seems hardly credible even the most pacific Emperor could have made in the second century. Still, we know the very theatrical turn of Hadrian's genius, and the imposing on the Empire of an artificial boundary of this enduring character may have been as much an example of it as is the extraordinary museum of buildings he formed in the neighbourhood of Tivoli. It is perhaps strange that a mimic Caledonian Wall does not figure in that collection.

As has been said, Hadrian's Wall, whether built of stone or turf, was designed for a dividing-line, and not an absolute partition. The ruined stone Wall, with its frequent gate-towers, bears out this description. Indeed, the Scottish historian Fordun was so struck by this aspect of it that he rendered its then current name of the Thirlwall by the Latin *Murus Perforatus*, as though these openings had been drilled through it. The gate-towers or mile-castles, as they are now usually termed, were about 60 feet square inside. That they are of the same date as the Wall itself, which formed their north wall, is shown by their other walls being of the same section and masonry; the east and west ones, indeed, are bonded into it. To the north as well as to the south were gateways about 9 feet wide, formed of more solid masonry. Sometimes the north gate of a mile-castle opens out into space over the brink of a precipice, suggesting that the Wall, though its general course is admirably adapted to the nature of the ground traversed, was in this particular subject to theoretical instructions transmitted from a distance. It is very improbable, therefore, that the work was personally superintended by Hadrian or any other emperor. Much wheeled traffic does not appear to have passed through these gate-towers, which, after all, may have been chiefly used for sorties to disperse any hostile force approaching to attack the Wall, or to readmit the Romans in case of defeat. Nevertheless, the unworn state of their thresholds is a strong argument in favour of their having been built at a very late period. Unlike the barbicans of medieval castles, these towers had both their gates opening inwards, and in this respect were better fitted for independent defence on all sides than for launching sallies on the enemy.

Identical inscriptions bearing the names of Hadrian and Aulus Platorius Nepos, his lieutenant in Britain, have been found in four nearly consecutive mile-castles, between Borcovicium (Housesteads) and Æsica (Great Chesters). There is a little difficulty about the only one of these that is quite perfect. Wallis, the historian, says it was found in the foundations of a mile-castle in an opening of the precipice by Crag Lake, called Lough-End-Crag, or Milking Gap, in digging stones for building a farmhouse belonging to William Lowes, to the north-east of Vindolana (Little Chesters). This house was that known by the name of Hotbank, and just between it and the outlet of the overflow from Crag Lough, now called Milking Gap, are the remains of a mile-castle. This was, however, not on the Lowes estate, as was the next castle to the west, at Steelrig, in the opening of the basalt precipice at the head of the lough. It is, no doubt, to the latter, situated to the north-west of Vindolana, that Wallis referred; otherwise he would not have so carefully noted the different direction of the farmhouse.

In a sparsely-inhabited country, the names of localities constantly vary, and the shepherds of Steelrig may easily have had their milking gap as well as the shepherds of Bradley. The slab was no doubt discovered, not in the actual foundations of the walls of the castle, but at the bottom of the débris with which the interior was filled, the fragments of the identical inscriptions in the Cawfields and Housesteads mile-castles being found in this position, one close beside, the other not far from, the respective south gateways. The presence of two inscriptions in honour of Hadrian in the same castle would not necessarily prove that one of them, and therefore possibly both, had been brought from some other place, as there may well have been an inscription over each gateway. These slabs, it may be fairly argued, did occupy some elevated position in the masonry of the walls; and even if used up again in subsequent restorations, there is no reason why they should not have been placed there originally by Hadrian's lieutenant.

On the other hand, the fact of the intended transportation of the Steelrig slab to the farmhouse on Hotbank, illustrates the long distance it was considered worth while to cart ready-dressed stones, even in the eighteenth century. The tombstone of Dagvald, a Pannonian soldier, found in the Cawfields mile-castle, where it had apparently been used for a hearth-stone, must have been brought a long way. Coins of Hadrian and Antoninus Pius were found in excavating the Housesteads mile-castle.

Other inscriptions of the time of Hadrian have been yielded by the forts of Æsica (Great Chesters), and Procolitia (Carrawburgh). At Magnæ (Carvoran), in consequence of a dream, Titus Flavius Secundinus, whose name occurs on a diploma of Trajan, dedicated in A.D. 137, as prefect of the First Cohort of Hamian Archers, an altar to Fortuna Augusta (whose golden image stood always in the Imperial chamber), for the recovery of Lucius Ælius Cæsar, Hadrian's adopted heir, whom the Emperor himself had prophetically described in the words of Virgil, as

> ' That youth the Fates but just display
>   To earth, nor let him longer stay.'

Hadrian's actual successor, Antoninus Pius, took land from the Brigantes, who had ventured to attack the allies of Rome. It is just possible that the Corionototai, the tribe of Brigantes round Corbridge, had indulged in a raid on the tribe round Windermere (Genounia, Vinonia). At any rate, Quintus Calpurnius Concessinus, prefect of horse, rendered thanks at Corbridge to the sun-god Mithras for assistance in slaughtering a number of Corionototai. The tribe was probably exterminated, and their lands given to a small military *colonia*. It is difficult to see how the Emperor, under the circumstances, could take lands from the Brigantes in any other way. The name of Corbridge still reminds us of the Corionototai, while the Roman walled town at the north end of the bridge by which Watling Street crossed the Tyne, and locally known as Colchester, preserves the memory of the *colonia*. The irregular walls of this town included about twenty-two acres, a third of the area of York, the capital of Britain, while Cilurnum (Chesters), almost the largest fort on the line of the Wall, did not occupy much more than five acres. Corstopitum (Colchester-on-Tyne) was thus the most important Roman settlement in the North, and signs of the high state of culture and civilization that prevailed in it are abundant. Two altars with well-turned inscriptions in Greek hexameter verse, one dedicated by the archpriestess Diodora to the Tyrian Hercules, the other by a man called Pulcher to Astarte, the Ashtoreth of the Book of Kings, recall the Greek schoolmaster, a native of Tarsus, whom Plutarch met at Delphi, returning from Britain.

The silver dish, or lanx, about 20 inches long and 15 broad, found here in the Tyne, probably represents, in the moulded bas-relief that has provoked so many learned dissertations, nothing more recondite than the Judgment of Paris. There are the three goddesses, Minerva, Juno and Venus, the last veiled and seated, as she is often depicted on Greek vases. To their right is Apollo, with his lyre laid down, as it had to be when the apple of discord was thrown into the marriage-feast of Peleus, and with the bow uplifted that was destined to slay Achilles. On their left stands Paris, in the costume he generally wears, with a bow and the fatal arrow. The roundlet on a pedestal in front of Paris appears to be the apple itself. The rest of the objects—the tree with ten birds in its branches, the temple entrance with its twisted columns, the pillar supporting a globe, and the hound, elk and griffin in the base—are mere decorative accessories.

Of even more delicate workmanship and truer art are the fragments of four silver pateræ, or saucepan-shaped

vessels, found at Capheaton, but probably part of the spoil
of Corstopitum.   The most interesting had its handle
ornamented with a bust of Hercules, and the symbols of
his six labours : the Nemæan lion, the Cerynian stag, the
Erymanthine boar, the apple-tree of the Hesperides, the
Hydra, and the Strymphalian birds.   From Corstopitum,
too, came the one vestige of Roman Christianity in the
North—unless we count a Gnostic gem recently found
at Æsica—in the shape of a silver basin for the priest to
wash his hands in, with the sacred monogram of the
Labarum repeated round its rim.   There is every probability that many of the carved stones of Corstopitum
were taken by Wilfrid to build his great church at
Hexham, but this does not of itself prove there was no
Roman settlement at the latter place.

The greatness of Corstopitum must belong to the period
when the country north of the Wall was also under
Roman rule.   Antoninus sent his lieutenant, Quintus
Lollius Urbicus, on a Caledonian campaign.   The names
of Urbicus occur on a slab carved by a cohort of the
Lingones, and found in the centre of Bremenium (High
Rochester) in close vicinity to a water-tank, adorned with
a representation of three long-haired nymphs at their
ablutions.   Urbicus drove the barbarians beyond the line
of the Forth and Clyde, along which he erected, if we construe the Latin strictly, a third wall built of turves (*alio
muro cespitaceo*).   We now know that this wall of Urbicus
was really built of turves overlapping one another like
bricks, and that the Four Dykes were not built of turves,
but were mere earth-mounds, possibly not Roman at all.
As has been already suggested, a turf-wall may have connected Agricola's forts between the Forth and Clyde
before the time of Hadrian, and Urbicus may have only
rebuilt this ; while Hadrian's Wall, though built on the
exact site of the present stone structure between the
Tyne and the Solway, may have also been composed of
turves.   It is much to be wished that the locality between
Birdoswald and Wallbower, where there are indications

of the stone wall having for once swerved from the line of an earlier one of turves or palisades, should be carefully examined.   The Second Legion, from Caerleon-on-Usk, was especially employed in building the Antonine Wall. Marcus Liburnius Fronto, one of the centurions, being at Condercum (Benwell), addressed his prayers for the safety of this legion to Dolichenian Jove, whose shrine was on the Aventine.

There was again trouble on the Border in the beginning of the reign of Marcus Aurelius, in A.D. 162.   The Caledonians seem to have burst through the northern wall, whose effective existence was thus limited to some twenty years.   Calpurnius Agricola took the field against the enemy.   During Agricola's lieutenancy in Britain, Aulus Licinius Clemens, prefect of the Hamian Archers, raised an altar at Magnæ to the Syrian Goddess.   Lest there should be any doubt as to who this divinity was, Marcus Cæcilius Donatianus, another prefect, recorded on a slab there a mystic exposition of her creed.   The original Latin iambics may be roughly rendered :

> ' There is a Virgin who above the Lion
>   Shines in the heavens.   She first gave us corn,
>   Justice established and founded cities.
>   Through Her grace we came to knowledge of the gods.
>   Styled thence Mother of the Gods, as also
>   Peace, Virtue, Ceres, and the Syrian Goddess,
>   She holds our lives and fate in the balance.
>   Syria sent forth this Her constellation,
>   Manifested to be worshipped in Libya,
>   Whence it is that we all are instructed.
>   In this Thy faith Thou didst initiate
>   Marcus Cæcilius Donatianus,
>   Prefect, with tribune's rank conferred by the Emperor.'

Marcus Aurelius admitted the unworthy Commodus to a participation in the Empire.   During their joint reign (A.D. 177-180) and the lieutenancy of Ulpius Marcellus, Tineius Longus, another prefect, who, with complacent vanity, describes himself as decorated, like Donatianus, with the broad stripe of a legionary tribune, and treasurer-designate in addition, placed an altar in honour of the god Anociticus in a small temple at Condercum (Benwell) with an apse at the south end. In the opposite corner, on the other side of the opening into the apse, stood an altar to the god Antenocitus, presented by Ælius Vibius, a centurion of the Twentieth Legion. Probably the divinity referred to on both altars was the Invincible Sun-god.

A British war was the principal military event in the sole reign of Commodus. The Caledonians broke through the wall that separated them from the Roman camps, and slew a general and a number of soldiers. Ulpius Marcellus was sent to stem their ravages.

On the murder of Commodus, Clodius Albinus, then lieutenant in Britain, attempted to seize the purple. He was defeated by Septimius Severus with the army of Illyria, at Lyons, in A.D. 197. Before hastening to Rome to reap the fruits of his victory, Severus put the affairs of Britain in order, and, with a view to prevent another governor following the example of Albinus, he divided it into two prefectures. A line drawn from the Humber to the Mersey or the Ribble probably now formed the boundary between the province of Britannia Superior, that nearer Rome, and the more distant Britannia Inferior. The comparatively small size of the northern province— for Chester-on-the-Dee was at any rate in the southern— points to a determination already taken by Severus to reduce the whole island to the Roman obedience. In a certain sense, then, Severus may be regarded as the creator of Northumberland. His northern province, with its central machinery at York, was destined to be of stunted growth, like the Plantagenet kingdom of Scotland with its chancery at Berwick. The idea of a Britannia Inferior stretching from the Humber to the Pentland Firth took ecclesiastical shape in the mission-schemes of Gregory the Great, and the origin of the two convocations of York and Canterbury may be legitimately traced to the *pronunciamiento* of Clodius Albinus.

Profiting by the transfer of British troops to the battle-field of Lyons, the Maiatai, who dwelt near the Wall in the plains and marshes of Cumberland, rose in revolt, and were naturally supported by the Caledonians from the mountainous districts to the north. In A.D. 207 Severus came in person to the island. He dismissed the barbarian envoys who came to sue for peace, and passing with a great army the 'rivers and mounds (*khomata*) that formed the defences of the Roman dominion,' entered Caledonia. The mounds in question can scarcely be other than the Four Dykes, but the special mention of them by an eye-witness like Herodian, notorious for his love of rhetorical effect, does not quite preclude the existence of a wall. During the first year that Severus was in the island, an extensive quarry was opened on the Gelt, near Lanercost, and before the close of it the fort of Prima Statio (Risingham), on Watling Street, north of the Wall, was re-occupied by a cohort of the Vangiones, the inhabitants of the most eastern part of Belgic Gaul. The south gateway, which had fallen into ruins, was now restored by order of Alferius Senecio, Governor of Britain, under the supervision of the Imperial procurator, Oclatinus Adventus, and the tribune Æmilius Salvianus. A quarry at Coome Crag, on the Irthing, appears to have been abandoned three years later. This, no doubt, points to very considerable building operations during the very time that, according to many historians, Severus built a wall across the island in order to protect the two provinces in Britain that he had recovered from Clodius Albinus. The length of this wall is variously given as thirty-two and a hundred and thirty-two Roman miles. If the former be correct, those who hold that this refers to the Tyne-and-Solway Wall may suppose that Severus reconstructed the works of Hadrian between Birdoswald and Bowness, the part most affected by the confederacy of the Maiatai and Caledonians ; if the latter, that he undertook a general fortification of the frontier, from Tynemouth to Ravenglass. It is remark-able that the Venerable Bede particularly insists on the fact that the wall of Severus was made of turves, with a palisade along the top. We now know that this was not at all the character of the Four Dykes, and what Bede must have had in mind was a turf-wall on the very same site as the stone wall, the construction of which he attributes to the fourth century.

On the whole, however, Septimius Severus is the very last man upon whom we should expect the Northumbrian Wall to be fathered. Like Julius Agricola and Edward Longshanks, he certainly contemplated the conquest of the entire island. After he had divided it into two provinces on the assumption that the whole would belong to the Empire, is it likely that he would open his Northern campaign by erecting a permanent barrier which would limit the size of Lower Britain to about a sixth both of Upper Britain and of its own intended extent? If he erected a wall at all, he probably rebuilt for the third time the turf one between the Clyde and Forth, where, indeed, Nennius does distinctly place his wall. This allocation harmonizes both with Bede's clear statement that the wall of Severus was a turf one, and with the account of the earliest writers, that its length was thirty-two Roman miles. The cool assertion of those who would have it of stone and place it between the Tyne and Solway, that neither XXXII. nor CXXXII., but LXXXII., is the correct number of miles, is a piece of unwarranted criticism. Possibly the idea of Severus having built a wall at all may have had its root in a misconception of the contemporary passage in Herodian, which mentions his division of the Roman portion of the island into two provinces.

Not only did Severus defeat the Caledonians, but he forced them to agree to a perpetual peace. Passing the Wall on his return, he discharged a certain Moor—there was a band of Moorish horse afterwards quartered at Abalabba (Papcastle)—from military service, perhaps in order that he might carry home the news of his successes to the disturbed frontier in Africa. Approaching the next posting-station, possibly Colchester-on-Tyne, the

Emperor kept turning over in his mind what omen would happen to him on this solemn occasion. The omen was a very black one : an Ethiopian ran out to meet him with a cypress wreath, shouting, ' Cæsar, thou hast been everything, be now a god !' Bassianus, the elder son of Severus, who longed for his father's death, may have arranged this funereal reception in the hope of giving the poor old man a fatal shock. Severus and his sons are commemorated on a slab in the roof of the crypt at Hexham, probably taken from Corbridge. After being longer in Britain than any other emperor, Severus died at York in A.D. 211.

Caracalla, as Bassianus is usually called, not only murdered his brother Geta, who was associated with him in the purple, but caused his name to be carefully chiselled out of every inscription throughout the Empire upon which it appeared. The slab from over the south gateway of Prima Statio (Risingham), and that in the roof of Hexham crypt, afford examples of this fraternal affection. The defence of the frontier, however, was by no means neglected during Caracalla's sole reign : the forts of Prima Statio and Bremenium (High Rochester) were both strengthened ; and the Rhætian spearmen of the former appear to have pushed further north. New mile-stones were placed on the military road along the Wall, and fresh works carried out at Alio (Whitley Castle) on the South Tyne. The personal crimes of the Emperors did not put a stop to progress in the provinces. There is a bare possibility that about this time the rough Illyrian giant Maximinus, who became Emperor in A.D. 235, erected a temple with a bas-relief of Jupiter near the mouth of the Tyne, while he was serving in the Sixth Legion.

While that Eastern voluptuary Heliogabalus was defiling Rome with his evil pleasures, a *balistarium* was built from the foundations on the west side of Bremenium in A.D. 220, and in the following year a building that had become ruinous through age was solemnly re-dedicated at Cilurnum on October 30. At Bremenium, too, Lucius

3

Cæcilius Optatus, tribune of the Vardulli, erected a temple to the Sun, whom Heliogabalus had associated with himself in the Empire.

The young Severus Alexander, the best of all who ever assumed the name of Cæsar, paid special attention to the state of the frontiers. He granted to the officers and soldiers stationed along them the lands that had been taken from the enemy, and these were to continue in their families, and never again become private property as long as their heirs continued to do military service. 'They would do their duties better,' he said, 'when the fields they defended were their own.' His lieutenant, Claudius Xenophon, restored the gates and towers of Vindolana (Little Chesters), and placed new mile-stones along the Carel Street. In A.D. 225 the Asturian cohort quartered at Æsica (Great Chesters) rebuilt an old granary there that had collapsed. Mile-stones of the succeeding Emperor, the rough Maximinus (A.D. 235-238), were set up just west of Corstopitum (Colchester), and at Crindle-dykes near Vindolana. During his joint reign with his son Maximus (A.D. 237), the first Batavians, and their prefect Burrius, appear to have strengthened the north-east corner of the fort of Procolitia (Carrawburgh).

Egnatius Lucilianus, the legate of Gordian (A.D. 238-244), inscribed an altar at Bremenium (High Rochester) to the Genius of the Emperor, of the first Vardullian cohort, and of the local band of scouts; while the prefect Agrippa restored at Condercum (Benwell) the temple of the Three Campestral Mothers and the Genius of the first Asturian horse. These three mother-goddesses of the plains are again commemorated on an altar found at Gloster Hill near the mouth of the Coquet. They are styled 'the Transmarine Mothers' on a stone at New-castle which portrays them seated in a triple arcade, and on the very ornate altar of Julius Victor at Risingham; and simply 'the Mothers' on the handle of a silver saucepan in the Backworth find. They seem to be again represented in a group of three figures seated on a bench, with cups in their right hands, from Borcovicium (House-steads). By the side of the burn to the east of this fort were three similar ladies ensconced in separate chairs.

In the reign of Gallus and Volusian, a sanctuary of the god Mithras, whose worship had spread from Persia over the whole Roman world, was cut out of the east side of a knoll to the south of Borcovicium. The front wall, with the entrance slightly north of the centre, was faced on both sides with dressed stone; the other walls were only lined with it. The interior would have been about 12 feet square, but the west part of it formed a recess, 7 feet long and 30 inches deep. In front of this recess stood a slab with a half-length figure of Mithras, in full relief, clasping a sword in one hand, a torch in the other, and set in a sort of oval band, ornamented with the signs of the zodiac. On either side of this was an altar to 'the Invincible and Eternal Sun-god.' That on the north was dedicated by Litorius Pacatianus, that on the south, erected in A.D. 252, by the centurion Publius Pro-culinus on behalf of himself and his son Proculus. Be-hind the slab with the zodiac stood a small statue of one of Mithras's attendants in Phrygian costume, with an uplifted torch. A great bas-relief, 6 feet high, represent-ing Mithras killing a bull (the protoplasm of all living things, according to Zoroaster), was probably inserted high up in the west wall of the building, below a low-pitched gable. This, at least, is the position occupied by the similar groups of Mithras and the bull carved on the rocks of Schoepheim, near the Rhine, and of Bourg-Saint-Andéol in the Rhone Valley. The faithful dog who guarded the bull and another attendant with an uplifted torch are among the remaining fragments of the taurine tablet of Borcovicium.

Another temple of Mithras, the Invincible Sun-god, on the brow of the hill outside the south-west corner of Vindobala (Rudchester), was restored by Tiberius Clau-dius Decimus Cornelius Antoninus, a prefect with almost as many names as a Spanish prince of the blood. In this temple Lucius Sentius Castus, of the Sixth Legion, placed an altar, with the simple dedication DEO, showing how the belief in a single supreme Divinity was surely gaining ground.   It was probably to Mithras that an altar was set up at Magnæ (Caervoran), in A.D. 258, for the health of the prefect Desidienus Ælianus. This is the last dated inscription we meet with ; after that milestones are the only things that afford any clue to the time of their erection.

The British Empire that existed for ten years (A.D. 287-296) independent of Rome, under Carausius and Allectus, terminated in the reconquest of the civilized portion of the island by the Cæsar Constantius.   In accordance with his general policy, Diocletian appears to have further subdivided the two provinces of Severus, so that while Upper Britain consisted henceforth of Britannia Prima and Britannia Secunda, Lower Britain comprised Maxima Cæsariensis, with a consular governor at York, and Flavia Cæsariensis, with a *præses* probably at Binchester.

The road-book possibly begun by the Emperor Marcus Aurelius Antoninus, whose care for the great routes of the Empire is specially recorded, and continued under the name of the ' Antonine Itinerary,' just as the ' Bradshaws,' ' La Chaixs,' and ' Hendschells ' of our own day bear the names of their original compilers, seems, in the form in which it has come down to us, to undoubtedly belong to the age of Diocletian.   Its value as a picture of Roman Britain depends on the time of the composition of the extant edition ; the question of when and by whom it was first compiled is one of comparative indifference.   The first route given in it, that ' From the Limes, that is, from the Wall to the Prætorium ' (apparently on the Humber), runs as far as York :

From BREMENIUM (High Rochester)
To CORSTOPITUM (Corbridge)   ...   xx. Roman miles.
To VINDOMORA (Whittonstall ?) ...   viii.   ,,
To VINOVIA (Binchester)   ...   ...   xviii.   ,,

To CATARACTO (Catterick)	xxii.	Roman miles.
To ISURIUM (Aldborough)	xxiii.	,,
To EBURACUM (York)	xvii.	,,
Leg. vi. Victrix (the Sixth Legion).		

This road seems to have been continued north to the Antonine Wall, but when this edition of the road-book was brought out, Bremenium was the last Roman outpost on it, as was Blatum Bulgium (Birrenswark) on the road leading north from Carlisle.

It is extraordinary to think that generation after generation of antiquaries should have racked their brains in vain over the tenth route, which seems to admit of a very simple explanation. We know from inscriptions that Bremetonacum is Ribchester, and Alo Whitley Castle, on South Tyne; from its position in the sequences of the Ravennas, and, as we shall see, of the Notitia, we may shrewdly suspect that Glanoventâ is the fort of Stanwix, overlooking Carlisle; while on the south side of the Tipalt, opposite Magnæ (Carvoran), is the camp of Gap Shield, eighteen Roman miles from Stanwix and twelve from Whitley Castle. We have only, then, to correct the distance between the latter and Overborough from xix. to xlix. miles in order to identify the central part of this tenth *Iter* with the Maiden Way, the steep raised road that leads over moor and fell from Overborough in Lonsdale, into the upper valley of the South Tyne.

Taking the recorded and actual distances in Roman miles, we thus get:

From BREMETONACÆ (Ribchester)			
To CALACUM (Overborough)	...	xxvii. (27)	Roman miles.
To ALO (Whitley Castle) ...	xix. (xlix.) (49)		,,
To GALAVA (Gap Shield)	xii. (12)		,,
To GLANOVENTA (Stanwix)	xviii. (18)		,,

In this, as in so many other moot points of antiquarian lore, writers generally lose themselves in clouds of exploded hypotheses, forgetting that these are only curiosities of antiquarian literature, and that raking them out again impedes rather than furthers a just comprehension of History itself.

Constantius, who became Emperor of the West in A.D. 305, carried a successful war into the woods and marshes of the Caledonians and other Picts. In A.D. 343, and again in A.D. 360, the Picts from beyond the Wall and the Scots from Ireland ravaged the outlying portions of the Roman dominions. Lupicinus, sent to Britain by Julian, could do no more than temporarily stem the torrent of barbarian invasion. In A.D. 364 the Picts and Saxons, and the Scots and Attacotti, fell on the unfortunate province. The Attacotti, a warlike race of men, were perhaps the same as the Otalinoi of Claudius Ptolemy.

A systematic defence had already been organized ; the troops along the northern frontier had been placed under the command of the Duke of the Britains, the forts along the south-east coast, from Portsmouth to Brancaster, under that of the Count of the Maritime Tract. The Count, Nectarides, was slain, probably by the Saxons ; the Duke, Fallofaudus, besieged by the Picts and Scots. The great general Theodosius, accompanied by his son, the future Emperor of that name, delivered the provinces of all these enemies, who had extended their ravages as far as London. His fleet chased the Scots to Ireland, the Saxons to the Orkneys. He conquered the Picts in a single campaign, bridled Caledonia with forts, and protected the frontiers with guards and watches. A province that had yielded to the enemy, and was now recovered, received the name of Valentia, in honour of the reigning Emperor Valentinian. Possibly this new province was Wales ; the idea that it was the country between the Walls of Hadrian and Antonine is one of the legacies we have received from the spurious Richard of Cirencester. We find about this time that the Attacotti were enlisted in the Roman army, not as auxiliaries, but as *fœderati ;* that is to say, not as natives dwelling within the Empire, but as barbarian volunteers from outside of it. St. Jerome met with some of them in Gaul, and declares that they preferred a rump-steak of shepherd or a cutlet of shepherdess to any delicacies of beef and mutton. Possibly their savage appearance gave rise to this charge of cannibalism, just as the first West Highland cattle exhibited in France were credited by the Parisian press with occasionally devouring their keepers.

In A.D. 383, Clemens Maximus, the commander of the Roman army in Britain, allowed himself to be proclaimed Emperor. He put firmly down an invasion of the Picts and Scots, but following the example of Albinus rather than that of Carausius, he crossed over to Gaul with all the troops available, including the Twentieth Legion. In Gaul he ruled, a half-recognised Emperor, for four years, and then, descending into Italy, was slain by Theodosius, son of the re-conqueror of Britain, under the walls of Aquileia. To Theodosius and his sons Arcadius and Honorius, recently raised to the rank of Augustus, an essay on military affairs was dedicated by an anonymous writer. In this curious tract the attention of the princes was specially directed to the state of the frontier in places where the barbarians were concealed by woods, assisted by mountains and protected by frosts (*pruinis*)—no doubt the Caledonian frosts (*Caledoniis pruinis*) of Hadrian's epigrams and Claudian's panegyric. The Roman soldiers were to wear a *thoromachus*, or woollen guernsey, under their cuirass or breastplate in travelling through these icy (*glaciales*) countries—Claudian, it will be remembered, speaks of icy Ireland (*glacialis Ierne*). The *thoromachus* would suffice against the cold, and protect the wearer from smaller darts without his being obliged to carry his shield, and this was of importance, since often the thick woods were inaccessible for heavy-armed soldiers, who found themselves weighed down and cut off in case of retreat. The best way of protecting a frontier, according to this writer, was to erect a series of *castella* at the distance of every mile, with a solid wall and strong towers. These fortifications might, he thought, be completed without charge to the State by the tenants of the adjoining lands, who would also keep watch and ward along them, and by their belt of garrisons ensure the immunity of the provinces from attack. His advice seems to have been eventually followed in a restoration, at any rate, of the Wall between the Tyne and Solway, with its mile-castles and turrets. The Picts and Scots were driven back by a legion (probably the twentieth) sent over by Stilicho, the minister of Honorius. Claudian represents this legion as spread out at the furthest extremity of Britain, which, strengthened by Stilicho, feared no longer either the Saxon or the Scot crossing from Ireland. Possibly the Roman *liburnæ*, or swift galleys that pursued the Scots, were furnished with paddle-wheels worked by pairs of oxen going round in gins, as recommended by the author of the tract dedicated to Theodosius and his sons. According to Gildas, it was at this time that a wall of turves was built across the island, a statement that must be supposed to refer to a restoration of the Antonine Wall.

In A.D. 402 the legion sent by Stilicho seems to have been again withdrawn. The Second Legion was moved from Caerleon-on-Usk to Richborough, on the coast most threatened by the Saxons, and it is just possible that the Sixth Legion may at the same time have left York for Carlisle, to defend the northern frontier. Gildas informs us that fresh troops were sent over by the Romans, and that the stone wall was built. It may have been reconstructed during the vicariate of Chrysanthus, who is stated to have executed many wonderful works in Britain. The Scots, who, with their oars and sails, contrived to circumvent the Wall, were again driven beyond the sea by the sudden onslaughts of cavalry patrols, that appear to have formed a new inner line of defence.

A very valuable list of the troops stationed in the north at about this time (A.D. 406), under the command of the Duke of Britain, is preserved in the *Notitia Dignitatum.*

In order to understand fully the general scheme of northern defence, it is best to give the entire list, especially as it is rarely met with, even in the most comprehensive works on the subject. The first portion seems to give the newer garrisons stationed between Danum, the 'Dancaster' of Leland, situated on Jarrow Slake, where the little river Don enters the Tyne, and Derventio, or Borough Walls, at the mouth of the Cumbrian Derwent, near Workington.

	NAME OF FORT.	RANK OF GOVERNOR.	GARRISON.	MODERN NAME.
1	...	Prefect	6th Legion	York ?
2	PRÆSIDIUM	Prefect	Dalmatian Horse	Binchester ?
3	DANUM	Prefect	Crispian Horse	Jarrow
4	MORBIUM	Prefect	Horse Cuirassiers	South Shields ?
5	ARBEIA	Prefect	Band of Tigris Bargemen	Tynemouth ?
6	DICTIUM	Prefect	Band of Dictian Nervii	Lanchester ?
7	CONCANGII	Prefect	Band of Watchmen	Chester-le-Street
8	LAVATRES	Prefect	Band of Scouts	Bowes
9	VERTERÆ	Prefect	Band of Guides	Brough
10	BRABONIACUM	Prefect	Band of Defenders	Kirby Thore
11	MAGLO	Prefect	Band of Solenses	Whitbarrow ?
12	MAGÆ	Prefect	Band of Pacenses	Keswick ?
13	LONGOVICIUM	Prefect	Band of Longovicani	Longthwaite ?
14	DERVENTIO	Prefect	Band of Petuerian Surprisers	Borough Walls ?

The second portion gives the older garrisons along the Wall, the Cumbrian coast, and the hills between Lancashire and Yorkshire. It is with this, containing as it does the names of a dozen garrisons in Northumberland—nine of them, Segedunum, Pons Ælius, Cordercum, Vindobala, Hunnum, Cilurnum, Procolitia, Borcovicium, and Æsica, incorporated in the Wall; two, Vindolana and Magnæ, situated on the Stanegate ; and one, Alio, on the Maiden Way—that we are chiefly concerned. It will be seen that this latter list follows pretty well the line of the Wall (*per lineam Valli*) from Wallsend to Birdoswald, and returns to it again from Bowness to Stanwix:

	Name of Fort.	Rank of Governor.	Garrison.	Modern Name.
15	Segedunum	Tribune	4th Cohort of Lingones	Wallsend
16	Pons Ælius	Tribune	1st Cohort of Cornovii	Newcastle
17	Condercum	Prefect	1st Ala of Astures	Benwell
18	Vindobala	Tribune	1st Cohort of Frisians	Rudchester
19	Hunnum	Prefect	Sabinian Ala	Halton
20	Cilurnum	Prefect	2nd Ala of Astures	Chesters
21	Procolitia	Tribune	1st Cohort of Batavians	Carrawburgh
22	Borcovicium	Tribune	1st Cohort of Tungrians	Housesteads
23	Vindolana	Tribune	4th Cohort of Gauls	Little Chesters
24	Æsica	Tribune	1st Cohort of Astures	Great Chesters
25	Magnæ	Tribune	2nd Cohort of Dalmatians	Carvoran
26	Amboglanna	Tribune	1st Ælian Cohort of Dacians	Birdoswald
27	Petrianæ	Prefect	Petrian Ala	Old Carlisle
28	Aballaba	Prefect	Band of Aurelian Moors	Papcastle
29	Congavata	Tribune	2nd Cohort of Lingones	Moresby
30	Axelodunum	Tribune	1st Cohort of Spaniards	Ellenborough
31	Gabrosentium	Tribune	2nd Cohort of Thracians	On the Waver
32	Tunnocelum	Tribune	1st Ælian Naval Cohort	Bowness
33	Glannibanta	Tribune	1st Cohort of Morini	Stanwix
34	Alio	Tribune	3rd Cohort of Nervii	Whitley Castle
35	Bremetennacum	...	Cuneus of Sarmatians	Ribchester
36	Olenacum	Prefect	1st Herculean Ala	Ilkley?
37	Virosidum	Tribune	6th Cohort of Nervii	Bainbridge

In A.D. 407 a certain Constantine, who had been proclaimed Emperor in Britain, withdrew the remaining legions from the island; in A.D. 410 Honorius wrote to the estates of Britain, advising them to undertake measures for their own safety, as the Empire was incapable of aiding them, and so the Roman domination came definitely to an end.

Although the occupation had lasted for a period as long as from the battle of Bosworth to the present day, and the forts along the Wall contain remains of three very distinct periods, it is extremely difficult for any student to regard the Roman civilization of the North otherwise than as a whole, especially when the memorials of its last two hundred years are comparatively meagre. There is therefore little to be gained by attempting to break up, chronologically, the vivid picture of this civilization that has been brought down to us on altars and monuments.

As we have seen from the army list of A.D. 406, very few of the soldiers quartered in the North were real Romans, although we need not conclude that all the auxiliaries were natives of the countries in which their regiments were originally raised. The figures of the soldiers themselves differ widely from our preconceived ideas. Flavinus, a standard-bearer of the Petrian horse, possibly killed in battle with the Corionototai, near Corbridge, at the age of twenty-five, is represented as a slim youth lightly clad, a plume of feathers for his head-dress, a dagger by his side, riding rough-shod over a hairy curled-up Briton, whose sword is pointed upwards as if to strike him in the moment of victory. His standard contains an image of the sun; his well-reined horse is furnished with martingales, and covered with a square-cut saddle-cloth. Manius Suilius Victor, an Asturian horseman of Cilurnum (Chesters), appears, on the contrary, almost nude, with a long sword in his hand and a jackal-like steed destitute of all trappings. Milenus, the bare-legged standard-bearer of the Batavians, at Procolitia Carrawburgh, again, is in full war-paint. His plain standard, with the figure of a bull on the top of it, is provided with three prongs to fix it in the ground. His loose tunic is gathered in round the waist with a belt, the long strap fastened by a round buckle; a short sword is suspended from over his right shoulder; the *umbo* of the small oblong shield in his left hand is ornamented with a hexafoil. An archer of Borcovicium, armed with a bow and quiver and a poniard, presents himself to us so full-faced that the crest of his helmet is a mere line. Poor Robin of Risingham, a rock sculpture, the upper part of which was blown off by a Northumbrian churl, as Sir Walter Scott calls him, in order to preserve from trespass his moor, worth a shilling an acre, never thinking of what he might have gained by showing it to strangers (an example which, alas! has not lacked imitators), also carried a bow with the quiver over his left shoulder, and seems to be bringing back from the chase a hare or rabbit. By far the noblest figure met with on the Wall, indeed the only one realizing our conception of a true Roman, is a helmeted spearman of Borcovicium, in a tight-fitting corslet reaching to his knees, with plates of armour on the shoulders, his oval shield turned inwards, revealing the handle contained in the central boss. Another life-like specimen from the same fort, with a high *galea* on his head, seems to have short sleeves and a sort of double-flounced kilt of plate armour. The oblong *umbo*, in bronze overlaid with tin, of the shield of Junius Dubitatus, a soldier of the Eighth Legion, found near the mouth of the Tyne, has an eagle holding an olive-branch on the central boss, and spirited figures of the four seasons—Spring struggling with a March wind, Summer with a scythe, Autumn with grapes and a fruit-basket, Winter donning his wraps— incised in the corners. A round umbo of the shield of a soldier serving in the century of Ruspus Quintus was found at Matfen.

Two small statues of civilians at Borcovicium, one in the fringed mantle of Roman Gaul, have lost their heads. Another civilian is setting out from Bremenium, probably on his last long journey, with a staff in one hand and a bag containing his viaticum in the other. The good man, now in the wall of the chapel at Dilston, is clad in his nightgown, and seems to have already helped himself to the food placed beside him at his burial. The figure of poor little Pervica, an Æsica child, is peculiarly quaint.

We are not left without some touches of the personal history of the strange collection of individuals from all nations who were cantoned along the Wall. From Pannonia, the land of the Drave and Save, came Dagvald and Cornelius Victor, both probably to Vindolana. The latter had enlisted as late as his twenty-first year, and died eleven days before his fifty-sixth birthday. Messius Magnus, a *duplaris* of the Sabinian ala, and his brother, left their home in the adjoining Noricum, which included the Salzkammergut, to defend the fort of Hunnum (Halton Chesters). Caius Valerius Tullus, a soldier of the

Twentieth Legion, born at Vienne on the Rhone, laid his bones at Magnæ (Carvoran), and at the same place Aurelia Itala, the faultless wife (*sine ulla macula*) whom the centurion Aurelius Marcus had brought from Salona in Dalmatia, was taken from him at the age of thirty-three. Terentius Firmus, master of the camps of the Sixth Legion, who dedicated an altar, now at Hexham, to Apollo, was a native of Siena. Quintus Petronius Urbicus, the prefect of the Gauls, who caused a quaint family of storks to be carved on an altar at Vindolana, belonged to Brescia; while apparently Rufinus, the husband of the 'very illustrious' Julia Lucilla, had served in both a Portuguese and a Bosnian cohort, and had been assistant-overseer of the Flaminian Way (the road from Rome to Rimini), when at the age of forty-eight years six months and twenty-five days death overtook him as tribune of the Vardulli at Bremenium on Watling Street. The monument erected near Cilurnum to a curator of the second Asturian horse, by his heir the decurion Æliomenus, points to some relationship between them and little difference in social standing. The curator appears to have attained to the temporary command of the regiment after fifteen years' service—the Caledonians no doubt considerably quickened promotion.

Family affection was very marked: Fabius Honoratus, tribune of the Vangiones at Risingham, and Aurelia Eclectiane, placed a tombstone at Cilurnum to the memory of Fabia Honorata, 'their sweetest daughter.' Aurelia Eclectiane was probably the lady referred to in the faulty hexameters on an altar found near a spring at Risingham, to the effect that

> 'Warned by a dream, a soldier to the Nymphs
> Bade Fabius's wife this altar raise.'

At Risingham, too, Dionysius Fortunatus wrote ' May earth lie light on thee ' over the grave of Aurelia Lupilla, his 'most pious mother,' while Blescius Diovicus did not neglect to commemorate his little daughter of a year and

three weeks.   Many of the settlers were killed no doubt
by the climate, while others fell on the field of battle.
One of them seems to have been struck dead by lightning
in a field near Hunnum (Halton Chesters).

Possibly it was the uncertainty of life that gave so very
religious a turn to the thoughts of the mural soldiery.   The
deities to whom they addressed themselves were various
in the extreme.   The Tungrians at Borcovicium having
had recourse in some emergency to the oracle of Apollo
at Clarus in Ionia, erected by his advice a regular
Pantheon to all the gods and goddesses.   In the same
state of perplexity, the tribune Julius Victor inscribed a
little altar at Risingham to the guardian gods of that
place.   The way in which this host of divinities became
reduced in nature-worship to one is illustrated by an
altar to the god Silvanus Pantheus at Bremenium.

Some of the images of the gods are no mean works of
art.   The Hercules of Vindobala (Rudchester), a fine
torso, holds a club in his right hand, the four apples of
the Hesperides in his left, with the skin of the Nemæan
lion thrown over one shoulder.   It is, however, difficult to
believe that the crude representations of this god on the
altar erected by Caius Vitellius Atticianus, a centurion of
the Sixth Legion, at Alio (Whitley Castle), can have inspired worshippers with any feelings of reverence.   In one
of these, a chubby infant, he is strangling the two serpents
sent by Juno to devour him; in another he is about to
leisurely smite the tree-like Hydra with his club.   The
Hercules that accompanies Mars on the tablet placed by
the Twentieth Legion over the east gate of Bremenium is
also repulsively coarse.   The Fourth Cohort of the Gauls
succeeded better with a gateway tablet at Risingham, on
which is a Mars of very delicate workmanship, and an
equally good companion figure of a winged Victory, her
right foot on the globe, a wreath in one hand, and a palm
in the other.   Borcovicium also had a splendid winged
Victory over the south gateway, and one holding a palm-
branch on the eastern.   At Hunnum, Victory was repre-

sented poised in the air (as on a Pompeian wall-painting) and at Rose Hill, near Gilsland, as issuing from a round native hut and hovering over the Roman eagle.

On the legions being entirely withdrawn, the Picts seized the country up to the line of the Wall, along the top of which was ranged a British force slow to fight, and frightened even to flee. With quaking hearts this senseless soldiery wore itself out with watches day and night, while there was no cessation of the barbed missiles, the Scottish *tela* of Claudian, with which the naked barbarians brought down the citizens from the walls of the forts. At last, leaving both the forts and the high wall, the Britons took to flight, and chaos followed.

While the past history of the Roman Wall presents so many difficult problems, it is unfortunately easy to predict that unless the island is conquered by some civilized nation, there will soon be no traces of the Wall left. Nay, even the splendid whinstone crags on which it stands will be all quarried away to mend the roads of our urban and rural authorities.

CHAPTER III.

THE Teuton had appeared with the Roman on the Border. The great victory of Julius Agricola over the Caledonians at Mons Grampius was won by a charge of his Tungrian and Batavian auxiliaries, and along the line of the Wall, Tungrians, Batavians, and Frisians settled down to garrison life at Borcovicium, Procolitia, and Vindobala, in the same geographical order that their tribes occupied on the German seaboard. At Borcovicium, two German citizens raised a shrine to Mars Thingsus, the Tuisco of Tacitus and original patron of our Tuesday, in conjunction with the two Valkyries, Beda and Filomena. Teutonic soldiers, too, frequently occur in cohorts first raised in other parts of the Empire.

The withdrawal of the last Roman legion from Britain leaves us in doubt as to the fate of these auxiliary troops, and it seems probable that many of them at least may have preferred to remain in the British homes to which they were attached by the ties of three or four centuries, and where they might still hope to overawe the native population, rather than either return to barbarism in their old recruiting-grounds, or run the chance of being butchered in Gaul or Italy.

For two hundred years, that is to say, from the abandonment of Britain by the Emperor Honorius at the beginning of the fifth century, to the arrival of the Italian missionary Paulinus at the beginning of the seventh, we have no certain knowledge of the affairs of Central Britain, but is that any reason for summarily rejecting what traditions we do possess, wild and incoherent though they be, under a lazy plea of antecedent improbability?

In the first place, a great wave of Cymric migration is said to have rolled down from beyond the Wall to the southern shores of Wales. Cunedda, 'a chief of lion aspect,' who had embraced Christianity, threatened Lugubalium (Carlisle) and Virosidum (Bainbridge) with his nine hundred horse, exactly the number, it is said, that were attached as auxiliaries to a legion:

> 'There is trembling from fear of Cunedda the Burner
> In Caer Weir and Caer Lliwilydd.'

This Guledig, or Celtic Imperator, seems to have been carried to his last battle on a hurdle by the men of Bryniech, or Bernicia, a kingdom of Celtic origin on the east coast north of the Tyne. To the south of the Forth the Jutes established a settlement soon after the middle of the fifth century, under the traditional leadership of Octa, son of Horsa, and his brother Ebusa. The three Lothians possibly represent the three 'lathes' into which Jutish districts were divided. Vortigern, it must be remembered, in calling Hengist and Horsa to assist him against the Picts and Scots, was strictly following the Roman precedent of enlisting the services of *fœderati*.

Another early Teutonic colony was established at Coldingham, the Caer Golud of the bards, and Urbs Coludi of Bede. The change of the English name of 'Coludesbyrig' to Coldingham is intensely interesting as proving that Colud, the ancestor from whom the Couldings claimed a common descent, lived himself on British soil, and we may infer that the same was the case with Eagulf and Eadulf, the progenitors of the Eagul-

4

fings and Eadulfings, whose 'hams' were at Eglingham and Edlingham, and with the other protoplasms of Northumbrian villages ending in the same two syllables. Certain tribal differences may be traced in the facts that while Coldingham and Chillingham are pronounced as written, Edlingham, and all the villages further south, like Ellingham, Bellingham, and Ovingham, end phonetically in 'jam,' while the ear could always distinguish Whittingham ('Whittinjam') on the Aln from Whittingham in Lothian even before the latter was given a final 'e.' The termination 'ton' belongs to a later period, when the Ovings of Ovingham had so increased and multiplied that it became necessary for them to throw off a colony at Ovington. Thousands of absurd derivations of place-names might have been avoided by taking the trouble to unearth their earliest forms, which are generally connected with some English settler or his descendants : thus, Burton in Bamburghshire was Burnulfeston, the 'ton' or enclosure of Burnulf; Pawston, Pollokston, the 'ton' of Pollok; and Farrowshields, Ferewithescheles, the shields or summer quarters of the shepherds of a certain Ferewith.

It has been conclusively proved that Napoleon Bonaparte was a solar myth, and it is of course equally easy to do the same with King Arthur. Of the twelve great battles in which Arthur is said to have been engaged previous to 516, the first may have been fought at the mouth of the Glen near Wooler, and the tenth at Trewhit, to the north-west of Rothbury, where there is a remarkable barrow. The memory of the Wall—the Northumbrian stone wall, of course — seems to linger strangely in the bardic minstrelsy. We are shown it lined with sixty centuries, the number that composed a legion :

> 'Three score centuries stood on the Wall :
> Difficult was converse with its watchman ;'

while Arthur, the Guledig, said to have arisen

'From the destruction of chiefs,
From the loricated legion
Around the old famous Border,'

is given

'His red purple,
His attack beyond the Wall,
His appropriate Chair
Among the patrol of the Wall.'

Legends of the court of Arthur held beneath the crags of Sewinshields were turned to political account by Thomas of Lancaster in the reign of Edward II., and were still current in the beginning of the present century, while one of the remarkable basalt rocks near the Wall in the same neighbourhood retains the name of the King's Chair. The forts on the Wall, especially Cilurnum and Æsica, exhibit remains of a third period of occupation, almost too barbarous to be Roman of the Lowest Empire, and yet very unlikely to be English. Particular ridicule has been cast on the stories of Arthur's victories over Gauls, Dacians, Spaniards, and Romans, but considering the polyglot character of the garrisons on the Wall, he may easily have fought and beaten all these, and Moors and Syrians into the bargain, without stirring more than twenty miles from what perhaps deserved in his day the name of Merry Carlisle.

Arthur's chief antagonist in his cycle of battles was Ossa Cyllelawr, or Ossa the Knife-man, whose son acquired the ominous name of 'Mug mawr drevydd' (Great Burner of Towns), while Ida, who founded the English kingdom of Bernicia in 547, was probably his grandson. A list of previous English leaders in Northumberland, commencing with a certain Hiring, seems a mere distortion of the Jutish traditions already mentioned. It is possible that Lindisfarne, and not Bamburgh, was the original English settlement on the Northumbrian coast. A genealogy of the kings of the Lindisfari, containing northern names like Beda and Biscop, does not seem to belong to Lincolnshire, which is usually credited with it. Ida's work, according to the earliest account, consisted in uniting the three states of Dinguayth, Guarth, and Berneich, which we may guess to be Bamburgh, Warkworth, and Berwick. The hackneyed passage describing how he 'timbered Bamburgh, that was first with hedge "betined," and thereafter with wall,' is an interpolation of a Kentish scribe in the eleventh century. All the same, there is no doubt that the acquisition by Ida of the great rock fortress that was known to the Celts as Dinguardi, and was to figure in Arthurian romance as Joyous Garde, marked the definite ascendancy of English interests between Tweed and Tyne.

Ida is said to have had twelve sons, six by his Queen Beornach, and six by his concubines. The frequent occurrence of the number twelve and its fractional parts in Bernician traditions makes it seem probable that the confederacies of Twelve Towns that we meet with on the Bowmont and South Tyne had their origin during the first period of English colonization, while the Ten Towns of Coquetdale and the Ten Towns of Glendale were somewhat later organizations.

The six legitimate sons of Ida—Glappa, Adda, Ethelric, Theodric, Frithwulf, and Hussa—figure one after another, in rather uncertain order, as kings of Bernicia. The crown, if there was such a thing, appears to have descended, not from father to son, but to the most able member of the royal house, and that possibly by a rough-and-ready form of election.

During the reigns of Theodric, Frithwulf, and Hussa (A.D. 572-592), Bernicia was almost reconquered by the celebrated Urien, prince of Reged, a Celtic state that appears to have long afterwards retained its semi-independence as the franchise of Redesdale. When we remember how completely the Celtic names of the country have been lost—how Medcaud, for example, has become Lindisfarne, and Dinguardi Bamburgh—little good can come of attempting to identify places named by the bards who sang the praises of Urien. One of his exploits was forcing the passage of the Garanwynion, possibly the Waren; and it was at this same ford, perhaps, that he had a bloody encounter with Frithwulf. Hussa, known to the Britons by the terrible name of Flamdwyn, or the Burner, advanced one Saturday morning with four hosts to overwhelm Reged and the neighbouring principality of Godeu (Kidland?). To his demand for hostages, Urien's son Owain retorted that his ancestor, Ceneu, would have raged like a lion if he had been asked to give hostages to anyone; while Urien himself bade his banner be unfurled on the mountain as a gathering signal for their whole clan to rush down to the slaughter of Flamdwyn and his Englishmen. The great Celtic victory of Argoed Llwyfain followed. Eventually, in alliance with three other princes, Urien had driven the English across the sands into Medcaud, or Lindisfarne, when, in the moment of what might have proved a final triumph, he was assassinated by the traitor Llovan Llawdivro, at the mouth of the Low (Aber Lleu), a little stream near Beal. A messenger escaped out of the battle with Urien's head, to bear the evil tidings to his capital of Erlleon. This was fated to become desolate, and the hearth on which wood provided by Reged was wont to blaze to be overgrown with nettles and brambles; nor was it long before Owain, 'the chief of the glittering West,' fell by the sword of Flamdwyn.

The conquest of Reged by the English of Bamburgh can hardly have been completed before Aedan, the king of the small Scottish state of Dalriada, appeared as the champion of the Celtic race. In A.D. 600 he revenged his defeat in the previous year by a victory in which Enfrid of Deira, brother-in-law of Ethelfrid, who had succeeded his uncle, Hussa, in the Bernician kingdom, was slain by Maelum mac Baodan.

Three years later, profiting by a Bernician rising in favour of Hering, the son of Hussa, Aedan advanced as far as Dægsanstan, most probably Dissington, the Digentun of the Hexham chroniclers, nine miles to the north-west of Newcastle, where he was utterly overthrown by Ethelfrid.　The victory, however, was purchased with the life of Ethelfrid's brave brother, Theodbald.

A year or two after Dægsanstan had secured him from the North, Ethelfrid, having married Acha, daughter of Ella, the founder of the English kingdom of Deira, between the Humber and the Tees, seized on that kingdom, driving into exile his wife's nephew, the boy-king Hereric, and her brother Edwin, then a young man of twenty.

In A.D. 607, already surnamed by the Britons Flesaurs, or the Destroyer, he extended his ravages across the island to the Dee.　The battle of Chester, won from Brochwel Gag-tooth, prince of Powys, and followed by the massacre of the monks of Bangor, drove an English wedge between the territories of the Cumbrian and Cambrian Celts.　Fearful of the exiled princes of Deira, Ethelfrid appears to have persuaded Cedric, prince of Elmet, near Leeds, to poison Hereric.　Redwald, King of the East Angles, at that time the Bretwalda, or chief-king of the Heptarchy, was only dissuaded by his wife from selling Edwin to Ethelfrid.

In A.D. 617, while Edwin was still in doubt as to his fate, St. Peter is said to have appeared to him in disguise, and, placing his right hand on his head, to have promised him a reign of unexampled glory.　In return Edwin engaged himself to follow the religious instructions of whoever should repeat that sign.　Soon after, Ethelfrid fell at the battle of the Idle, in Northampton-shire, overpowered by the superior forces of Redwald, and Edwin succeeded not only to his own inheritance of Deira, but also to Bernicia, the two together forming the kingdom of Northumberland.　Bebba, who seems to have been the second wife of Ethelfrith, possibly retained possession of the great stronghold of Dinguardi, which he had given her, and which derives from her its English name of Bamburgh (Bebbanburg).

In the eighth year of his reign Edwin married, as his

second wife, Ethelburg, a Christian princess from Kent. She was accompanied by the Bishop Paulinus, who, after Edwin's providential escape from assassination, and consequent defeat of the West Saxons, repeated the sign given by St. Peter, and persuaded the King to be baptized at York on Easter Day, A.D. 627. A wholesale conversion of the Northumbrian nation followed. St. Paulinus, who became Archbishop of York, spent thirty days with the King and Queen at Ad-gefrin, or Yevering, baptizing the people in the neighbouring river Glen. The royal town at Yevering (possibly the camp on the Bell), was, as Bede tells us, afterwards removed to the preferable site of Melmin, probably Kirknewton, where the dedication of the church to St. Gregory recalls the beginnings of English Christianity.

The glories of the reign of Edwin, the peace he established from sea to sea, and the imperial pomp he affected, belong to Deira rather than to Bernicia, where he must have been regarded as an intruder. At length, in A.D. 633, Penda of Mercia, a fierce adherent of the Northern gods, revolted against Edwin's authority, and, in alliance with Cadwalla, King of North Wales, defeated and slew him at the battle of Hatfeld. This battlefield, known to the Britons by the name of Meicen, was placed by them near the Severn.

The kingdom of Bamburgh now regained its independence under Enfrid, the eldest son of Ethelfrid. Enfrid had embraced Christianity, according to the Celtic rite, during his exile, but he now apostasized. Within a year, however, his head was struck off by Cadwalla, and his country laid waste by the Britons. Advancing, probably, from York to Corbridge, Cadwalla found Enfrid's next brother, Oswald, drawn up to oppose him at Hefenfeld, near the Roman Wall, on the high ground to the west of Watling Street. It is remarkable that, in the one battle in which the Wall plays a part, its site seems occupied as a position against a southern attack. Fortified, it is said, by a vision of St. Columba, the venerable

Apostle of the Celtic North, Oswald erected a wooden cross, the first in all Bernicia—for the mission of Paulinus in Glendale seems not to have led to the regular establishment of Christianity in that country—and, bidding his followers kneel before it, awaited with confidence the assault of the Britons. Cadwalla was strenuously repulsed, and forced to flee across the Tyne, where he was overtaken and slain, beside the Denisburn, a tributary of the Devils-water, now known as Rowley Burn.

In consequence of this victory, Oswald not only succeeded to his father's kingdom of Bernicia, but seized also that of Deira, his mother having been the sister of Edwin. He sent to Iona for a missionary to instruct his people in Christianity. The first one made no impression on them, and returned disconsolate. The work was taken up by Aidan, who offered the Northumbrians 'milk of milder instruction,' and settled on the island of Lindisfarne, where he became Bishop. Oswald himself acted as interpreter for Aidan.

One Easter Day, as the King and Bishop were seated at dinner, probably at Bamburgh, the attendants entered to say that the street outside was filled with starving poor. The King ordered not only the meat on his table to be given them untouched, but also the silver dish itself to be distributed among them. Upon this the Bishop seized Oswald's hand, and pronounced the blessing that it might never perish. Even from his enemies, the Britons, Oswald received the surname of Llangwyn, or Fair Hand.

After a glorious reign of eight years, Oswald became involved in a western war, and probably, like Edwin, hemmed in by an alliance between the Welsh and the Mercians, fell in the battle of Maserfeld, in A.D. 642.

The savage Penda proceeded to ravage Northumberland. The city of Bamburgh would have fallen a prey to the flames of the brushwood he had piled around it, if the prayers of Aidan on Farne had not diverted the wind. Oswi, brother of Oswald, succeeded to the Bernician throne ; but as he was probably the son, not of Acha, but of Bebba, Deira fell to Oswin, son of Osric. On the eve of a battle between these two Northumbrian kings, Oswin disbanded his army, and was put to death by order of Oswi. He was, it seems, buried at Tynemouth, on Bernician soil, for fear lest his own people should make political pilgrimages to his shrine. Aidan, who had been especially attached to Oswin, died twelve days after him, leaning against the west end of the wooden church in the village of Bamburgh. That same night a vision of angels bearing Aidan's soul heavenwards appeared to a shepherd named Cuthbert, as he lay, cross-like, in prayer on the ground, while watching his master's flocks on the distant mountains of Lauderdale. As the mantle of Elijah fell on Elisha, so a double portion of the spirit of Aidan seems to have descended on Cuthbert, who immediately resolved to embrace the monastic life.

There is no reason to suppose that Cuthbert was a Scotsman in the modern sense, any more than in the seventh-century acceptation of the term. At the age of eight he appears to have been taken into the house of a widow named Kenswith, in the village of Wrangham, near Doddington in Glendale, and we first meet with him joining other boys there in the not very edifying pastime of walking on their hands, with their legs in the air. Even thus early his serious turn of mind was remarked by his companions, and it was confirmed by a long affection of the thigh-joint. Relieved from this, and compelled to wander in search of a livelihood, he had the courage, while still a boy, to rebuke the heartlessness of the half-heathen countrymen at North Shields, who were enjoying the spectacle of five boats, manned by monks, who had just settled on the opposite bank of the Tyne, being swept out to sea in a strong westerly gale.

Cuthbert's intention of entering a monastery was deferred by the call of duty to serve as a soldier in defence of the Christian faith and Bernician monarchy. Oswi had done his best to live on friendly terms with Penda of

Mercia. His eldest son, Alcfrid, was married to Penda's daughter Cuneburg, and his daughter Elfled to Penda's son Peada. Preparatory to his marriage, Peada was baptized with his thanes by Finan, Bishop of Lindisfarne, the successor of Aidan, at Oswi's palace of Ad Murum, probably Heddon-on-the-Wall, the twelfth Roman mile-castle from Wallsend. It was perhaps this conversion of his son that roused the wrath of the fierce votary of Woden. In vain did Oswi give his eldest son by Enfled, a boy of ten, named Egfrid, to be brought up as a hostage at the Mercian court. In the strange company of Ethelhere, King of the East Angles, Ethelwald, son of Oswald, the ruler of some portion of Deira, and Cadwallader, son and successor of Cadwalla, with other British princes, Penda proceeded to lay waste the whole of Bernicia. The wooden stay against which Aidan had leant in his last moments was all that was left standing among the smouldering ashes of the church and village of Bamburgh. Oswi himself fled to Giudi, or Judeu, probably the Jutish stronghold that afterwards acquired the name of Edinburgh from some local Edwin. At any rate this fortress was considered more impregnable than even Bamburgh itself, and Penda and his allies allowed themselves to be bought off by the surrender of all the treasure Oswi had with him. During its march southwards through Lothian, Penda's host, forced to halt on the banks of the Winwæd (perhaps the Tweed), then swollen with heavy rains, found itself suddenly overtaken by Oswi and his eldest son Alcfrid. The Bernician forces numbered only a third of the Mercian, but actuated, perhaps, by religious scruples at the last moment, Cadwallader withdrew under cover of night, and Ethelwald deserted in the course of the battle. Penda himself fell with Ethelhere, and in the panic that ensued more of their followers perished in the raging flood than by the swords of the victorious Bernicians.

Before this battle, fought on November 15, 655, Oswi had vowed, if successful, to dedicate his daughter Elfled to the service of God, and to give twelve small townships, six in Bernicia and six in Deira, each containing ten families, for the purpose of erecting monasteries. It would appear also that Cuthbert received at this time a grant of twelve towns in the valley of the Bolbend (Bowmont), four of which, Eltheburne (Elterburn), Thorburnam (Thornington), Scotadun (Shotton), and Minethrum (Mindrum), are on the Northumbrian side of the present border. Returning from the south in the depth of winter, through the great waste that then stretched from the Tees to the Tyne, Cuthbert providentially found some sustenance for himself and his horse in the deserted shielings of some shepherds near Chester-le-Street. Although he was acquainted with the saintly monks of Lindisfarne, where at this time a young man of about his own age, named Wilfrid, was making astonishing progress in his studies, he was led to enter the monastery of Melrose through the great reputation of its Prior, St. Boswell. Two or three years later he was taken by the Abbot Eata, one of twelve boys confided by Oswald to Aidan, to be hosteller of a new foundation at Ripon.

Meanwhile Wilfrid was enabled to carry out his long-cherished wish of visiting Rome. Kneeling in the church of the monastery of St. Andrew, from which Augustine had set out on his mission to Canterbury, he devoted himself to the task of winning the whole of England for the Latin rite. On his return to Northumberland in A.D. 659, the storm that had long been gathering between the followers of Iona and Canterbury with reference to the date of Easter, the form of the tonsure, and other minor matters, broke out in full violence. The Celtic monks clung pertinaciously to the old Roman practice of fixing Easter as confirmed by Pope Leo the Great in A.D. 443, and refused to accept the change made by Pope Victor in A.D. 525, when Britain was cut off from the rest of the Western Patriarchate by the piratical fleets of the heathen Saxons. The conferences on the subject held between St. Ronan, a Scot who had studied on the Continent, and St. Finan,

Bishop of Lindisfarne, only led to more bitter estrangement, owing to the Bishop's hot and violent temper. Influenced by Wilfrid, Oswi's eldest son Alcfrid, who acted as Viceroy of Deira, ordered the monks of Ripon to either adopt the new Easter or leave their monastery, so Eata and Cuthbert returned to Melrose.

In the spring of A.D. 664, the Northumbrian Witenagemot, held at Whitby, definitely condemned the Leonine Easter. St. Colman, Finan's successor, withdrew from Lindisfarne to Ireland, taking with him some of St. Aidan's bones, and burying the rest in the cathedral sacristy. Eata and Cuthbert now conformed to the new usage, and, on Colman's parting recommendation, Eata was appointed Abbot over the English monks who remained on Lindisfarne. King Oswi had greatly loved Colman on account of his wisdom. The simple life of the monks in his time contrasted favourably with their extravagances in the succeeding age. A violent outbreak of the yellow plague carried off, among many other victims, Tuda, the new Bishop, and St. Boswell of Melrose. It was the custom in Britain to call churches after the saints who founded them, and the dedication of the church of Tweedmouth to St. Boswell was probably a memorial of his personal labours on the spot. St. Cuthbert succeeded him as Prior of Melrose.

The Northumbrian Witenagemot, presided over by Oswi and Alcfrid, unanimously elected Wilfrid to the vacant bishopric, the seat of which was to be transferred to York in compliance with the scheme of Gregory the Great for re-organizing the dioceses of Britain, probably on the same lines as they occupied during the Roman occupation. In order to be consecrated by bishops of the Latin rite, Wilfrid went to France ; during his prolonged absence Alcfrid died, and, a reaction taking place, Oswi promoted Chad, a bishop of the Celtic rite, to the vacant see. In A.D. 669, Theodore of Tarsus, the great Archbishop of Canterbury, obtained the substitution of Wilfrid, who continued to be Bishop of all Northumberland and the

Picts for nine years. It seems to have been on Tweed-side that a woman bringing her dead child to be baptized, with others, by Wilfrid, had her faith in its resuscitation fully justified.

In A.D. 670 Oswi died, after a reign of twenty-eight years. He was succeeded by his two sons, by Egfrid in Bernicia, and Elfwin in Deira. A formidable insurrection of the Picts followed. They came down from the mountains, and drove the English under-king Bernhith across the Forth. Egfrid marched to his assistance with a small army, and the whole country was reduced to complete subjection. As a thank-offering for an equally successful campaign against Mercia, Egfrid is said to have given Carham to St. Cuthbert, who appears to have been still at Melrose.

Egfrid, now about twenty-seven, had been married for twelve years to Etheldryd, an East Anglian princess nine years older than himself. Etheldryd's scruples had rendered this marriage a mere mockery, though otherwise the King and Queen lived not unhappily together. The royal house seemed on the point of extinction, and the kingdom might at any moment be shaken to its foundations for want of a direct heir. With exemplary patience Egfrid had waited till it was dangerous to wait longer. Wilfrid, to whom he appealed, was unable to overcome Etheldryd's unnatural obstinacy, and, as the best solution of the difficulty, aided her in becoming a professed nun, and so rendering the marriage void in canon law. Egfrid reluctantly consented to this course, and as his affection for Etheldryd was very real, he seems to have now given her the territory of Hagustaldesham, or Hexham, a petty state that some forgotten Hagustald had probably conquered from the Britons. Etheldryd, however, preferred to retire to Ely among her own people, and bestowed Hexham on Wilfrid, who founded there a monastery in honour of St. Andrew, like that at Rome, which had been the starting-point of Augustine's mission and of his own spiritual life. His church was the wonder, not only of that, but of the two succeeding ages. Stone foundations laid deep in the ground, with many well-finished crypts, supported a complicated superstructure of many aisles, with columns of various designs. The length and height of the walls were remarkable; the passages running round the different stories were approached by winding stairs. There is every reason to suppose that the high altar, as usual in basilicas of that period, was at the west end, above the existing crypt, while the present market-place occupies the site of the atrium, or entrance court. The whole was surrounded by a wall and towers of great strength and thickness. Free use was made of Roman friezes and altars, and the walls were covered with a coat of hard cement that excited especial admiration. Wilfrid was himself super-intending the work, when a boy named Bodhelm fell from a high turret on to the stone floor, but eventually recovered.

In reading of the magnificence affected by Wilfrid, we seem to hear the rustle of the robe of Wolsey. Irminburg, the new Queen of Northumberland, drew her husband's attention to Wilfrid's great secular wealth and his immense army of retainers. It was not only the King, but also the Metropolitan of Canterbury, whose dignity was completely eclipsed by the splendour of the Bishop of York. They therefore agreed to divide the great Northumbrian diocese by creating the separate sees of Lindisfarne and Hexham, the former extending from the Forth to the Aln, the latter from the Aln to the Tees. Hexham appears to have been intended for Wilfrid in case of his acquiescence in the scheme, but when he opposed it to the length of personally appealing to Rome, the administration of Hexham was intrusted, in A.D. 678, to Eata, Abbot of Melrose and Lindisfarne, in whose person the island-see was now revived. Eata appears to have compelled Cuthbert, who had been Prior of Melrose for some years, to leave that great centre of his missionary activity, and assume, as Prior of Lindisfarne, the charge of the cathedral-monastery. Cuthbert, however, continued his old practice of wandering about among the country people, instructing them in the faith. One day a prefect of King Egfrid, named Hildimer, came and begged him to send a priest to his wife, who was at the point of death, and to accord her sepulture on Holy Island. Himself accompanying Hildimer, on horseback, Cuthbert rightly conjectured that the lady had gone out of her mind, and comforted her husband with the assurrance that by the time they reached his house—possibly Ilderton, formerly called Hilderton—she would come out to welcome them cured in body and mind, and it was so. It was no easy task to persuade the brethren of Lindisfarne to change their old customs for the rule he framed for them himself, but Cuthbert was patience itself, and if the opposition was too strong in the Chapter one day, he calmly adjourned the meeting to the next. The dress prescribed by his rule was of undyed wool. He would often pass three or four nights together in prayer, warding off sleep by manual labour, or by walking round the island and examining everything on it. At last he obtained the permission of Eata and the brethren to adopt a solitary life. He retired first of all to Thrush Island, a rock about a hundred yards from Lindisfarne, and, like it, surrounded at high-water only. Here he constructed a 'thurs-house,' or hollow scooped out of the rock. Wishing, however, to withdraw still further from the world, he chose the island of Farne for his hermitage. Aidan had always had a companion during his stay there : Cuthbert resolved to brave the awful solitude alone. His *mansio* was a circular pit about twelve feet deep and fifty feet in diameter. The wall round it was carried up to a man's height with turf and rough stones excavated in the interior. Considerable protection was thus afforded from the wind, while the eyes and thoughts of the occupant were continually directed heavenwards. Within this enclosure were two huts, an oratory and a cell—the walls formed of natural earth, the roofs of rough beams and dry grass. Cuthbert dug a well in the middle of his cell, and this never went dry nor overflowed. He showed his practical sense as a sanitary engineer by erecting an out-house, supported on a twelve-foot beam, across the chasm known as St. Cuthbert's Gut. His well is now in the basement of the tower built at the end of the fifteenth century by Prior Castell, of Durham.

At first, St. Cuthbert accepted a small pittance of bread from Lindisfarne, but afterwards, recalling the text, ' He who doth not labour, neither shall he eat,' he asked the brethren to bring him some tools and seed-wheat. The wheat sown in the spring came to nothing by mid-summer, so Cuthbert begged for some barley, declaring that if that, too, failed, he would rather return to Lindis-farne than be supported by the labour of others. Although sown so late, the barley proved a splendid crop; but as soon as it began to ripen, the birds did a great deal of damage. ' Why touch ye that which ye sowed not?' inquired Cuthbert. ' Maybe ye have more need of it than I? If, then, God has given you leave, do His will; but if not, get ye gone, and do no more harm to another's property.' Whereupon the birds flew away, and never came near the barley again. Another day Cuthbert saw two crows pulling the thatch off the ' sailors' home' he had constructed near the landing-place. As they paid no attention to a slight waive of his hand, he solemnly adjured them to quit the island. They obeyed at once, but three days later one of them returned, and, its wings flapping and head abased, seemed with a pitiful caw to beseech Cuthbert's forgiveness. The saint willingly withdrew his ban, and the two crows speedily came back carrying a piece of hog's lard, which they deposited at his feet, and which he used to grease the boots of his visitors. After two or three years, however, of agricultural experience on this wild rock, Cuthbert shut himself up entirely in his ' monastery,' only communicating with the outer world by means of a window, and after a time he never opened the window except to bestow his benediction. His great reputation for sanctity brought many visitors to Farne from all parts of Britain.

Meanwhile, Wilfrid, whose tastes and character differed so widely from those of Cuthbert, had returned as the successful Apostle of the Frisians, armed with the decrees of Pope Agatho and the Lateran Council, commanding his restoration to the Northumbrian bishopric. King Egfrid and his Witenagemot, however, instead of deferring to the voice of Christendom, condemned Wilfrid to nine months' imprisonment. He was sent to Bromnis (possibly either the Roman Bremenium or Byrness), in a region of thick mists, and kept in a dark dungeon. This was said to be miraculously illuminated as he was singing his psalms, and he was credited with saving the prefect's wife there from death's door. He was transferred to the harsher custody of Tydlin, prefect of Dunbar, and it was only the illness of Queen Irminburg, after she had appropriated his small case of relics, that brought about his release.

Egfrid still had no son. In the spring of A.D. 684 his sister Elfled, the young Abbess of Whitby, prevailed on St. Cuthbert to meet her on Coquet Island. In answer to her anxious inquiries, the hermit-prophet declared that Egfrid had only a year to live, and would be succeeded by a king whom she would embrace with the same sisterly affection. 'Thou seest,' he continued, 'this great and broad sea, how it aboundeth in islands. It is easy for God to provide someone out of one of these to be set over the kingdom of the English.' Elfled at once understood him to refer to Aldfrid, a reputed son of her father Oswi, who was devoting himself to study on a Scottish island.

The following autumn Cuthbert was elected Bishop of Hexham in place of Tumbert, who had filled that new see since 681, and was now deprived 'for disobedience,' at a synod held at Twyford (probably Alnmouth), on the Aln, the boundary between the dioceses of Hexham and Lindisfarne. Egfrid was compelled to go to Farne

5

himself, with Trumwine, Bishop of Abercorn, and other dignitaries, and beseech the recluse to accept the proffered dignity. Even then Cuthbert made it a condition that the consecration should be deferred to enable him to pass the winter on Farne. This seclusion was interrupted by his visit to Eata, still Bishop of Lindisfarne, at Melrose. On the return journey he crossed the Tweed at Examford, a little above the great earthwork of Wark. Sibba, the lord of the 'wick,' that preceded the medieval castle, besought him to turn aside and bestow his blessing upon it. Accordingly Cuthbert entered the stronghold with solemn chant of psalm and hymn. One of Sibba's servants, who lay dangerously ill, recovered after a third draught of water blessed by the Bishop-elect.

At Easter, A.D. 685, Cuthbert was consecrated, and the same day he appears to have exchanged sees with Eata. The districts of Carlisle and Cartmel, recently taken from the Britons, were added to Cuthbert's diocese of Lindisfarne; the diocese of Hexham extended no further west than Wetheral. On Saturday, May 20, as Cuthbert was standing beside the Roman Well of Carlisle, he had a prophetic intuition of the slaughter of Egfrid and his army by the Picts, and hastened to advise Queen Irminburg to get ready her chariot to leave Carlisle for Bamburgh at daybreak on the Monday. His forebodings proved too true; Egfrid had fallen at Nechtansmere, the Mire of Dunnichen, in battle with Breide, King of Fortrenn. In consequence of this signal disaster, the Picts recovered the territory occupied by the English to the north of the Forth, while the Scots of Dalriada and Britons of Strathclyde renounced the suzerainty of Northumberland.

Aldfrid the Wise, having ascended the throne, soon restored the fortunes of the Northumbrian kingdom within its ancient limits. In the course of his episcopal visitation, Cuthbert came to the 'wick' of Hemma, a *comes* of the new King, situated probably at Greencastle in Kenterdale, the old name of the valley in the Cheviots behind Homildon. Hemma's wife, restored to health after being sprinkled with water blessed by the Bishop, herself offered him the 'loving cup.' He proceeded across the Tweed to Bedesfeld (now Bettyfield, near Smailholm), where he had shortly before afforded a refuge for some nuns who had abandoned their convent further north through fear of the victorious Picts. Turning back to Hexham in October, in order, probably, to be present at the burial of Bishop Eata on the south side of the cathedral (where a stone chapel was afterwards erected over his tomb), he set out for Carlisle, no doubt along the Carel-gate. Half-way between the two cities, he spent two days in a wild mountainous district, preaching and confirming at a place called Aehse, or Echse, which seems to be none other than the Roman fortress of Æsica. If so, it was then almost as desolate as to-day, for there was no church nor place large enough to receive the Bishop and his company, who took shelter in tents and shanties of boughs by the roadside. At Carlisle Cuthbert received the religious profession of Queen Irminburg, whose sanctity now won for her the title of ' Agna Domini.' There, too, he took leave of his friend, St. Herbert of Derwentwater. Passing through Hexham and Medoms-ley, where the plague was committing frightful ravages, he consecrated a church for the Abbess Elfled at Easing-ton, after which he received a splendid welcome from the Abbess Verca at South Shields.

Immediately after Christmas, A.D. 686, Cuthbert retired once more to the storm-lashed rocks of Farne. On February 27, Herefrid, Abbot of Lindisfarne, who had spent three days on the island, tapped at the window to receive his blessing, when he heard a deep groan. Cuthbert's reply led him, however, to suppose that it was an attack of an old complaint, and a great storm prevented his returning from Lindisfarne till five days later, when he found the Bishop in the guest-house near the beach, where he had lain the whole time since his departure. He became so ill that he allowed himself to be carried back to his oratory, and eventually permitted Herefrid to enter. Lying in a corner facing the altar, Cuthbert urged him to impress on the brotherhood of Lindisfarne the necessity of holding no communion with those who strayed from the unity of Catholic peace, either with respect to the date of Easter or monastic discipline. ' I would much rather have you take up my bones from the grave,' he concluded, ' and carry them with you wherever God shall appoint, than that you should on any consideration consent to the wickedness of schismatics and place their yoke upon your necks.' At the hour of nocturns, on March 20, A.D. 687, he received the sacrament, and then passed heavenwards. One of the brethren, waiting without, took a torch in each hand, and, ascending to a higher spot, signalled the news of Cuthbert's death across the sea to the watchman on the tower of Lindisfarne. The saint's body was placed on a ship, and, after being received at Lindisfarne with choirs of singers, was laid in a stone sarcophagus to the right of the altar in the cathedral which, built by Finan of sawn oaks in the Scottish fashion, with a roof of reed thatch, had been consecrated to St. Peter by Archbishop Theodore.

Wilfrid, who during his second exile had effected the conversion of Sussex, had been recalled by Aldfrid and reinstated in his monastery of Hexham. He was now entrusted for a year with the diocese of Lindisfarne, and appears to have consented to the consecration of John, generally styled of Beverley, from the monastery he afterwards founded, as Bishop of Hexham, on August 24, 687. This saintly Bishop was in the habit of withdrawing to a certain retired ' wick ' surrounded by a wall and a few scattered trees, about a mile and a half from Hexham Church, on the opposite bank of the Tyne, where there was a cemetery dedicated to St. Michael. One Lent he had a dumb youth with a sore head brought to stay in a cottage built on purpose within the enclosure, and on the second Sunday, making the sign of the cross on his

tongue, caused him to say first, ' Gae,' the vernacular for
' Yes,' then A, B, and the rest of the alphabet, and finally
syllables, words, and sentences. The youth, whose head
was also cured by the Bishop's physician, ungratefully
insisted on returning home, in spite of the saint's wish
to keep him in his household. The scene of this miracle
is laid at Erneshaw, near St. John Lee, which, however,
derives its name from the dedication of its church to St.
John Baptist, and in contradistinction to another Lee in
Hexhamshire.

His administration of Lindisfarne brought Wilfrid into
conflict with the monks, whose Catholicity was still
Celtic rather than Latin. Peace was only restored by
the appointment of the pious Edbert to the see in place
of Wilfrid, who now appears again as Bishop of York.
In 692 King Aldfrid and a synod of bishops once more
deprived the great Northumbrian of all his ecclesiastical
dignities except the abbey of Ripon.

Six years later the body of St. Cuthbert was found un-
corrupted at Lindisfarne, and placed in a raised shrine.
Bishop Edbert, who was in retreat on Thrush Island at
the time of the discovery, died soon after, and was buried
in the original grave at his own request. The miraculous
virtues of St. Cuthbert were again attested by the recovery of Bethwegen, the hosteller, who had been seized
with illness as he was washing the garments and mantles
of the guest-house in the sea. The island of Farne had
been occupied since Cuthbert's death by a recluse named
Ethelwald. In returning from visiting him one day,
Guthfrid, afterwards Abbot of Lindisfarne, was nearly
lost in a storm with two other brethren, when they saw
Ethelwald praying for them at the mouth of his cave, and
during a lull they were able to gain the mainland and
beach their boat. On Ethelwald's death, in 699, Edfrid,
then Bishop of Lindisfarne, restored the hermitage for the
anchorite Felgeld.

We should have a very false notion of the high civilization to which Northumberland attained in the Golden

Age of English Christianity if it were not for the splendid manuscript of the Gospels written by Edfrid. It seems incredible at the present day that a work exhibiting such high proof of living art could have been produced on the weird, waste island of Lindisfarne. The illuminations excel anything ever done by miniature painters, and must rather be classed among the masterpieces of the jeweller's craft; but the most striking feature of all is the extraordinary power of using quaint grotesques, without exciting the least feeling of comic incongruity; each of a string of birds, with blue necks and red tails, catches hold of the leg of the one above it with its beak, or two giraffes in red-dotted outlines get their long necks inextricably knotted together, without there being anything to provoke an irreverent smile. Each Gospel is prefaced by a cross set in a maze of microscopic ornament on one page, and a representation of an Evangelist on another. The figures of the Evangelists are intensely interesting, as conveying the illuminator's idea of the height of regal splendour. We have before us no Syrian tax-gatherer nor fisherman of Galilee, but an Egfrid or a Keolwulf, only the crowns replaced by aureoles, the sceptres by pens; while the articles of furniture enable us to conjure up some sort of picture of the interior of the great palace of Bamburgh. The Evangelists wear state dresses, the mantles always of royal purple, the tunics blue or pink or green. Their thrones are severally: a plain red stool, with a pattern of circles and triangles incised round the edge, and cross-pieces to the legs, that are painted blue on the inner side; two simple chairs in green and yellow, one with a plain blue cushion, the other with a pink one embroidered with gold; and an extraordinary settle that seems to have no bottom except a blue cushion. We are also shown a brilliant red curtain with six iron rings on a rod, a small round table, and a footstool inlaid with oblong designs. The florid full face of St. John is very striking, with his brown hair curled like a flowing wig. The angel of St. Matthew and the lion of St. Mark are blowing long horns.

St. Luke's ox, of a light cream colour, seems to belong to the breed still preserved at Chillingham. All four Evangelists have bare feet ; even this may be part of their regal state. The calendar attached to these Gospels is said to be the ancient Neapolitan one, a fact that would connect it with Archbishop Theodore's companion, the Abbot Adrian of Naples.

Meanwhile King Aldfrid had contracted an unhappy marriage with Cuthburg, sister of Ina of Wessex. A separation resulted, and, in spite of Cuthburg's subsequent foundation of the abbey of Wimborne, Boniface, the Apostle of Germany, beheld her in his Vision of Purgatory, the head and shoulders radiant, but the rest of the body bespeckled and sunk in a flaming pit. In 705, when Aldfrid died at Driffield, his son Osred was a child of eight. A certain Edwulf, possibly the husband of a daughter of Egfrid, was raised to the throne. Wilfrid advanced from Ripon to meet the new King, but was roughly ordered to leave the kingdom within six days, under pain of death to his followers. The Ealdorman Bertfrid now declared in favour of the child Osred, and, on being closely besieged on the rock of Bamburgh, vowed, in case of victory, to attend to the behests of the Holy See and procure the re-instatement of Wilfrid. A sudden change of feeling caused Edwulf to be deserted by his adherents ; the gates of Bamburgh were thrown open, and he was chased from the kingdom. With the consent of the young King, the three Northumbrian bishops and the rest of the Witan, Wilfrid was now restored to his abbeys of Hexham and Ripon ; and when Bosa of York died soon afterwards, John was translated to that see, and succeeded at Hexham by Wilfrid.

During his last journey from Rome, Wilfrid had nearly died at Meaux, when he had a vision, in which the archangel Michael promised him four more years of life, and enjoined him to build a church in honour of the Blessed Virgin. This he accordingly did to the south-east of his great church at Hexham, choosing an almost circular plan, for what was probably used both as a baptistery and a chapter-house.

A great victory won over the Picts by the Ealdorman Bertfrid in 710 conferred a certain lustre on Osred's reign; but the young King proved to be cruel and dissipated. Many of the nobles were put to death or forced to turn monks. Among the latter was Enmund, the founder of a monastery of St. Peter, which seems to have been situated at Heversham, in Westmorland, and the history of which was to form the subject of a Latin poem, by Ethelwulf, a monk of Lindisfarne, in the beginning of the ninth century. At last, in 717, Osred was ignominiously slain on the southern border of Northumberland near the coast, in his nineteenth year.

Kenred, a descendant of Occa, one of Ida's natural sons, filled the throne for two years, and was followed by Osric, possibly a younger brother of Osred. Osric was slain in 729. His successor, Keolwulf, brother of Kenred, in the double character of patron and censor, requested the Venerable Bede to send him his 'Ecclesiastical History of the English Nation' on its first appearance, and to 'Keolwulf the Most Glorious' Bede subsequently addressed the preface, extolling the King's own love of history and his desire of spreading the knowledge of it among his subjects. The troubled state of politics caused the great work to be very meagre in contemporary detail. In 731 Bede ventured to say that civil disorder was so rife that it was impossible to predict the turn events would take. Keolwulf was seized, shorn, and forced into a monastery, to be, however, speedily restored. Acca, the saintly successor of Wilfrid at Hexham, appears to have allowed himself to be implicated in this conspiracy, and fled the realm, while the leaders, Alric and Esc, were executed. Frithbert, a stanch friend of the reigning dynasty, was appointed to the deserted see. The good relations of the Northumbrian kingdom with the neighbouring states made Keolwulf's subjects unaccustomed to military service, while internal dissensions led them to seek safety for themselves and their children in the numerous monasteries. With the political insight of a true historian, Bede foresaw the dangers likely to arise from this neglect of the profession of arms. 'What will be the result,' he adds prophetically, 'the next age will show.' It is apparently to the monastery of Tynemouth, where Herebald was Abbot, that we owe the earliest portion of Symeon of Durham's 'History of the Kings.'

After the aspirations of St. Wilfrid had been realized, and the independence of the Northumbrian Church secured from the pretensions of Canterbury, by the bestowal of the archiepiscopal pallium on Egbert of York, the King's cousin, Keolwulf voluntarily resigned the crown in 737, and, becoming a monk at Lindisfarne, bestowed on that house not only the district of Warkworth, where he had built a church, and 'Bregesne' (probably Brainshaugh, near Acklington), but Woodchester (at the mouth of the Aln), Whittingham, Edlingham, and Eglingham. His fellow-monks are said to have now obtained a relaxation of the rule of St. Aidan that had restricted them to milk and water, and were permitted to drink wine and beer.

The prosperous reign of Edbert, brother of the great Northumbrian Primate, was not altogether free from dynastic troubles. St. Acca, the old enemy of the house of the Ocgings, died in 740, and was buried between two elaborate crosses at the east end of his former cathedral at Hexham ; but that same year Arwine, son of Edwulf— apparently of Edwulf, the two-months king of 709—was killed, after having, it seems, attempted to seize the throne during Edbert's absence on a Pictish campaign. Ten years later, after a second expedition of Edbert which added Kyle, in Ayrshire, to his dominions, another unsuccessful pretender named Offa took sanctuary on Lindisfarne. Bishop Kynewulf refused to surrender him, whereupon Edbert, after laying formal siege to the basilica, slew Offa and dragged Kynewulf a prisoner to Bamburgh. The administration of the Northern diocese was entrusted to the politic St. Frithbert, of Hexham, until the King's wrath was appeased and Kynewulf reinstated. The fame of Edbert was now so firmly established that the kings of all the nations round, English, Picts, Britons, and Scots, not only kept peace with him, but delighted to do him service; even Pepin le Bref of France concluded an alliance with him, and sent him many and diverse royal gifts. The zenith of his glory and that of Northumberland was reached when, on August 1, 756, in company with Angus, King of the Picts, he scaled in triumph the ancient British capital of Dumbarton, on the Clyde.

CHAPTER IV.

THE KINGDOM : CORBRIDGE.

ONLY ten days after the fall of Dumbarton had given the Northumbrian realm the widest expansion that it was destined to attain, the victorious host of Edbert was almost annihilated by a sudden onslaught of the Britons. The King, indeed, escaped, but this catastrophe in the heyday of triumph was fraught with consequences infinitely more disastrous for the future of Northumberland than those that, in the previous century, had resulted from the defeat and death of Egfrid at Nechtansmere. With all the success that had hitherto attended his arms, the Imperial sway of Edbert rested on a moral rather than a material foundation. His attack on the capital of Strathclyde weakened that confidence in his integrity and unselfishness which had led every nation in the island to delight in doing him honour. Neither the Britons, nor the Scots, nor even his own allies, the Picts, paid further deference to the royal fugitive. It was in vain that the other English kings promised to make good his losses in the North by cessions of their territories if only he would be persuaded to remain at the helm of State at Bamburgh. Struck down by the terrible blow that, at the end of a reign of twenty fortunate years, deprived him both of his moral prestige and his military fame, Edbert resolved upon abdication.

The Northumbrian crown, as has been said, seems to have been elective among the descendants of Ida, prefer-

ence being customarily given to the nearest capable
relative of the last monarch. In order to guard against
the dangers that a disputed election might occasion when
the State was left without a head, it became the practice
for the reigning King and the Witan to agree upon his
successor. To this official candidate, this selected heir-
presumptive, the title of Patrician was given in imitation
of the style assumed by Frankish princes, a title rendered
in English by the word Etheling. Unfortunately, like so
many other ingenious constitutional contrivances, this
preliminary solution served only to increase the very evils
it was intended to remove. A Patrician who saw himself
in danger of being set aside at the final election, if the King
should leave a son of sufficient age and popularity, was
tempted to possess himself at once, by open rebellion or
secret assassination, of what he had been led to look upon
as his absolute heritage.

Edbert had acknowledged as Patrician a certain Ethelwald Moll, probably resident at Catterick in Deira, and a
descendant of Ethelwald, son of Oswald, though by a
Celtic mother. Now, however, that his son Oswulf had
come to man's estate, Edbert deemed himself strong
enough, in abdicating, to secure that prince's succession.
In order to conciliate Ethelwald, he bestowed on him the
possessions of three monasteries in Deira, and incurred
in consequence the censures of Pope Paul. Then, as
nothing but the tonsure could, in those days, relieve an
anointed king of the burden of sovereignty, he became
a canon in his brother Egbert's metropolitan church of
York.

How far the actual border of Northumberland receded
southwards after the disaster that overwhelmed the host
of Edbert on the Clyde, it is difficult to determine. That
it did recede, and very considerably, is patent from the
fact that at this critical juncture the capital was removed
from the sea-washed rock of Bamburgh to the old Roman
city of Corbridge, in the golden valley of the Tyne. With
the loss of territory in the North, it became necessary to

seek a more central seat of government. Corbridge was
the chief town of the middle province represented ecclesiastically by the diocese of Hexham, just as Bamburgh,
while the capital of the whole monarchy, was also the
chief town of the province represented ecclesiastically by
the diocese of Lindisfarne.

As the Court was now largely affected by the classical
renaissance brought about by Alcuin, the Northumbrian
secretary of Charles the Great, there was something
characteristic in its being held in a city which, under the
Empire, had been the most northern centre of culture and
civilization. It is from Corbridge that the history of
Northumberland, during the two blood-stained centuries
that precede the final extinction of the kingdom, must be
viewed.

The young King Oswulf had not reigned a whole year,
when he was assassinated by the officers of his household
at ' Mechil Wongton,' or Great (Muckle) Whittington,
a village about seven miles to the north-east of Corbridge, on July 24, 759. The voice of the people placed
Ethelwald Moll on the vacant throne, but the Patrician
Oswin, possibly a brother of Oswulf, took up arms against
the new government. He probably relied on assistance
from the Picts, as the pitched battle in which he was
mortally wounded was fought, it seems, at Lilliesclive,
near Melrose. Party spirit continued to run so high that
a national assembly was convoked at Finchale on the
Wear, with a view to securing internal peace. The choice
of Finchale, south even of the Tyne, as the place of meeting, shows how the centre of gravity of the monarchy was
ever shifting southwards. In this national council, repre-
senting all Northumberland, and probably of a character
largely ecclesiastical, Moll was deposed, and Alcred, who
claimed descent from Edric, son of Ida, and was, therefore, clearly a Bernician, was proclaimed King in his
stead. The idea seems to have been to choose an independent prince, instead of the candidate of either of two con-
tending factions; but this policy, however sagacious in

itself, was destined to make confusion worse confounded by giving a third rival dynasty to Northumberland. To fortify his title, Alcred took to wife Osgeofu, daughter of the murdered Oswulf.

Writing to their friend Lullus, Bishop of Mayence, for the purpose of providing for mutual intercession in their prayers, King Alcred and Queen Osgeofu did not scruple to admit the critical condition of affairs, both in Church and State, but they were content to regard it as a Divine dispensation. In addition to a gold ring, they sent the Bishop twelve of those hooded cloaks called *sagæ*, that we see worn by the native peasantry on the Roman monuments at Treves, and which still form the characteristic garb of the Capuchin fathers. It says much for the skill and taste displayed in their manufacture that Northumbrian cloaks were so appreciated on the Continent.

At Easter, 774, the blow they had long calmly awaited fell on the royal fatalists. As the result of an understanding arrived at between his household and the ealdormen, the national Witan deprived Alcred of the throne, in virtue of the same power that had raised him to it. Archbishop Egbert, his wife's great uncle, was no longer alive, and Alcred had lost another of his chief supporters by the death of the High-Reeve Edwulf. After the removal of the court to Corbridge, Bamburgh appears to have been the seat of a line of High-Reeves, who claimed descent from a daughter of King Egfrid and were themselves the direct ancestors of most of the great Earls who were to rule Northumberland from the tenth far into the twelfth century. Contrary to the usage then obtaining in English families, each generation of these High-Reeves seems to have clung tenaciously to the name of Edwulf. The cradle of their race was probably the village of Edlingham (Eadwulfingham), which remained long after the Conquest a centre of English influence in the hands of their descendants. The abortive seizure of the crown by Edwulf on the death of Aldfrid in 709 does not seem to have checked the more slow and steady elevation of his house.

It was to Bamburgh that Alcred fled after his deposition. The ancient capital was so soon nearly forgotten, that the chronicler who relates this deemed it necessary to add a description of it by way of gloss. 'Bebba,' he says, ' is a most strongly fortified city, not very large, being of the size of two or three fields, having one entrance hollowed out of the rock and raised in steps after a marvellous fashion. On the top of the hill, it has a church of extremely beautiful workmanship, in which is a shrine, rich and costly, that contains, wrapt in a pall, the right hand of St. Oswald the King, still incorrupt, as is related by Bede, the historian of this nation. To the west, on the highest point of the city itself, there is a spring of water, sweet to the taste and most pure to the sight, that has been excavated with astonishing labour.' From this, we gather that the fortress of Bamburgh was then, as now, divided into three wards ; the entry was by a flight of steps near the west end of the rock, and from this you ascended through the two lower wards, occupied by the 'city,' to the deep well, now enclosed in the Norman keep, and to the inner ward beyond it, which contained a small basilica with a monastery attached. This church, according to St. Alred of Rievaulx, had at the time of King Alcred seeking shelter there been recently despoiled of one of its chief treasures, the head of St. Oswald. An old man praying before the shrine of St. Cuthbert on Lindisfarne, imagined he received that saint's commission to bring back there this head, which had been removed to Bamburgh, probably by Edbert. He proceeded to the basilica on the castle-rock on St. Oswald's Day, and found the head of the royal martyr exposed above the altar for the veneration of the faithful. The concourse of pilgrims obliged him to delay the execution of his plans till the following morning, when he lingered behind after Mass till everyone had left the church except the porter of the monastery. Seeing that this official kept a very strict watch on his movements, he dropped his belt and gloves near the altar and then went off to mount the horse his servant had waiting for him near the cemetery, possibly the cemetery among the sand-hills just east of the castle. Despatching his servant on an errand, he turned to the porter, whose curiosity had brought him out so far, saying, ' Just take hold of the horse, my good fellow, and let me get my belt and gloves which I left in the church.' Before the porter could say nay, he was off to the altar, hid St. Oswald's head under his arm, and with the gloves and belt displayed ostentatiously to allay suspicion, rode safely off with his sacred booty to Lindisfarne. He had the satisfaction afterwards to learn that the porter carefully locked up the church without ever looking inside again.

Bamburgh proved a sure city of refuge to the dethroned Alcred. Any chance of restoration, however, was, he found, so remote that he betook himself to the court of the Pictish King, Kenneth, whose espousal of his cause became no doubt the pretext for further and further encroachments on northernmost Northumberland. It was probably in consequence of his harbouring Alcred at Bamburgh that the High-Reeve, another Edwulf, was put to death the following year by order of the new King, Ethelred, the son of Ethelwald Moll. Ethelred endeavoured to give a special sanction to his election at Finchale by having himself crowned at York with a ceremonial of unprecedented magnificence.

Notwithstanding his solemn coronation, King Ethelred followed King Alcred into exile in 779, and then for nearly ten years the sceptre of St. Oswald was held by the direct heir of the Ocgings, Alfwald the son of Oswulf, and the grandson of Edbert. Styled for his justice and piety ' the Friend of God,' Alfwald had the honour of receiving in a synod at Finchale, George, Bishop of Ostia, the first legate of the Holy See ever accredited to Northumberland. At the time of the Legate's arrival at York, the King was absent in the Far North. It is worthy of notice that St.

Tilbert, prelate of the church of Hexham, signs the decrees of this synod immediately after the King, before the Archbishop, probably because Finchale was in the diocese of Hexham. In addition to the bishops, the Patrician Sicgan and the two high-reeves, Alric and Sigwulf, were present at what was more or less of a national Witenagemot. The growth of a considerable Northumbrian colony in the north-west of Ireland was emphasized by the consecration of Aldulf, Bishop of Mayo, in the monastery of Corbridge.

Neither virtue nor glory was capable of saving a Northumbrian King in the eighth century. On September 23, A.D. 788, Alfwald the Just was cruelly slain at 'Scythlescester,' near the Wall, by the wicked Sicgan. A long procession of monks and clergy, making the Vale of Tyne resound with their dirges, brought the King's body to Hexham. The monastery there, in which seven years previously the saintly Bishop Alcmund had been laid to rest beside his predecessor, St. Acca, still surpassed all others in England in size and beauty. The frescoes executed by order of Wilfrid were still bright on its walls. After all his travels on the Continent, Alcuin could assure St. Ethelbert, then the Bishop, that he knew no pleasanter place. A hundred more than a thousand years have now rolled by since Alfwald's burial, but his tomb, a thirteenth-century reproduction of an earlier one, is still shown in the priory church. Of the forty sovereigns of Northumberland, the Friend of God is the only one who has been given an enduring shrine. A light from heaven is said to have shone on the scene of his murder ; the church consequently built there, and dedicated to St. Cuthbert and St. Oswald, is probably represented by the ancient chapel of Halton, about three miles to the north-east of Corbridge.

As Alf and Alfwin, the two sons of Alfwald, were infants at the time of their father's murder, and as popular indignation made the succession of Sicgan, whatever were his claims, impossible, Osred, the son of Alcred and Osgeofu, was called to power. A year later, betrayed by his ealdormen and given the tonsure at York, Osred was glad to make good his escape to the Isle of Man. King Ethelred I. was now brought up from a dungeon to mount the unstable throne he had lost eleven years before. The learned Alcuin, that Northumbrian Erasmus, was at home at the time, and delayed his departure for France in consequence of the revolution, which, it may be suspected, he had some hand in bringing about. Queen Ethelhild, the widow of Ethelwald Moll, and now a nun, was his intimate friend and correspondent. Her son's restoration probably furthered the aims of the alliance subsisting between Alcuin's master, Charles, and the powerful Offa of Mercia. Alcuin, however, was not long in discovering that the character of the restored monarch ill accorded with his hopes. He was, it is true, able to effect some good by admonition and remonstrance, and continued to do his utmost to check the spread of a reign of terror. Though assisted by an influential party in the state, he was by no means successful. Ethelred thirsted for blood. The High-Reeve, Erdwulf, was led out for execution before the gate of the monastery of Ripon. The body, entrusted to the monks for burial, was borne into the church, but on assembling for matins, the brethren were surprised to find Erdwulf alive, and willingly accorded him sanctuary.

Less fortunate than Erdwulf, the young princes, Alf and Alfwin, were beguiled by Ethelred from York Minster, and drowned in Windermere. The horror this crime inspired led Osred to attempt the recovery of his crown. He landed from the Isle of Man on the coast of Cumberland, but was taken prisoner and beheaded by Ethelred's order, at 'Aynburg,' probably Alneburg, the old name of Ellenborough, near Maryport. His body, however, was buried near that of St. Oswin in the monastery of Tynemouth, the idea being, probably, to prevent any political pilgrimage to his tomb. After this destruction of both branches of the royal house of the Ocgings, Ethelred celebrated his marriage with Elfled, daughter of Offa, at Catterick.

The cup of Northumbrian wickedness was now filling rapidly to the brim. Repeated storms of thunder and lightning, accompanied by showers of dragon-like meteors, alarmed the national conscience. The High-reeve Sicgan, who had slain the good King Alfwald, laid violent hands on himself, and his wretched corpse was conveyed to Lindisfarne. Five weeks later a sudden descent of the Scaldings on the desecrated island caused all Christendom to tremble. Swarming like hornets and ravenous as wolves, the pagans, led probably by the celebrated viking, Ragnar Lodbrog, or Shaggy-breeks, landed on June 7, 793. They trampled with their unhallowed feet the sanctuary of what had come to be regarded as the mother-church of more than the half of England, and nearly the half of Germany. They dug up the altars and bore away all the treasures, even breaking off the upper limb of the great cross Bishop Ethelwald had set up before the church. Some of the monks they slew, others they dragged off in chains; many they jeeringly drove away naked; some they cast into the sea. Fortunate indeed was the priest Cudred, who contrived to slip out of the hands of his captors.

The fall of Constantinople can have scarcely caused more widespread terror in Christendom. If the power of St. Cuthbert could not preserve his own island, what place was safe? From the court of Charles the Great, Alcuin wrote to express his patriotic horror at the thought that the most venerable place in all Britain had been given over as a spoil to the heathen. He urged Bishop Higbald and the monks of Lindisfarne to take their chastisement to heart, and addressed similar moral warnings to the abbeys of Jarrow and Wearmouth. He promised to get his master Charles to do all he could to ransom the boys carried away into slavery. More practical still were his endeavours to provide for the national defence of Northumberland, by establishing good relations between King Ethelred, the Patrician Osbald and a certain Osbert.

The next year the pagans had already ravaged Jarrow, when their leader was put to a cruel death there by the English. Ragnar Lodbrog had been warned by his wife, Kraka, of the folly of sailing with large ships into a shallow slake like that of Jarrow. He is traditionally said to have been cast into a pit full of snakes, and as they gnawed at his vitals to have composed what (edited by Vigfusson and Powell), with its wild refrain,

'We hewed with the brand,'

is evidently in part the battle-song of Ragnar himself, in part the dirge in which his Queen gave expression to her grief. The fearless heathen, after his fifty-one battles, has no dread of death:

'I am willing to depart. They are calling me home, the Fays whom Woden, the Lord of Hosts, has sent from his hall. Merrily shall I drink ale in my high seat with the Anses. My life-days are done. Laughing will I die.'

The pangs of his torture are alleviated by prophetic confidence that

'The porklings would grunt
If they knew of the old boar's need,'

and that his death will be avenged by his descendants.

Many of the viking ships that escaped from the Tyne went ashore during a heavy gale, and the crews were mercilessly despatched by the English. Higbald and his clergy, seeing in all this the interposition of St. Cuthbert, returned to Lindisfarne, where they found that the body of the saint had not been disturbed.

The lesson of the sack of Lindisfarne, enforced though it was by the letters of Alcuin, failed to restore internal peace to Northumberland. On April 18, 796, the butcher King, Ethelred I., was murdered in his capital at Corbridge by the High-Reeve Aldred. This new crime, which lost him an ally, led Charles the Great to declare that the

Northumbrians were worse than the pagans themselves,
and Alcuin had some difficulty in restraining him from
giving them practical proof of his indignation. The
Patrician Osbald was proclaimed King by the ealdormen
of his own family, but, after a reign of twenty-seven days,
was deposed by the joint action of the royal household
and the other ealdormen. He had at one time taken
monastic vows, probably as a condition of his life being
spared, and, during the religious revival that the descent
of the Northmen at first occasioned, had promised
Alcuin that he would act up to his profession. He now
escaped to Lindisfarne with a few faithful followers,
and, taking with him some of the brethren, made his
way to the Pictish court. Alcuin did not fail to remind
him of his broken faith, and of the amount of blood of
kings, princes, and commons that he and his partisans
had shed.

Erdwulf, the High - Reeve whose life had been so
strangely preserved at Ripon, was now solemnly invested
with the royal diadem at York. Fresh troubles, however,
immediately began, through the new King repudiating his
wife and taking a concubine. The death of Ethelred was
avenged by the ealdorman Tortmund on its perpetrator,
Aldred the High-Reeve, no doubt of Bamburgh ; while St.
Alcmund, son of King Alcred, and one of the last scions
of the royal house of Ida, was seized by the frontier
guards of Erdwulf and put to a cruel death. Complications between Northumberland and Mercia gave the West
Saxon Egbert an opportunity for acting as mediator, and
so exercising a certain authority over both kingdoms. In
806 Erdwulf himself was driven into exile, and humbly
sought the Imperial presence at Neumagen on the Rhine.
He proceeded to Rome, and having been favourably received by Pope Leo, returned to Northumberland, accompanied by the Legate, the deacon Aldulf, and by the Abbots
of St. Amand and St. Omer, as envoys of the Emperor.
By means of this strange mediation, which, if it had been
undertaken by the Pope or the Emperor alone, would

infallibly have been construed into a donation or a commendation of Northumberland, Erdwulf was restored to
his throne, which a second Alfwald, who had occupied it
for two years, showed little reluctance to surrender.   The
year following this restoration, death closed Erdwulf's
career of adventure and vicissitude.

The thirty-two years' reign of Erdwulf's son and successor, Enred, owed its very exceptional length, not to the
virtues and talents of the King, but to the utter exhaustion
of Northumbrian politics.   It was sullied by two events,
that have much more in common than their bare mention
by the chroniclers at first sight discloses : the extinction
of the bishopric of Hexham in about 820, and the submission of the Northumbrians to Egbert, the West Saxon,
at Dore, near Sheffield, in 827.

Tidfrith, the last Bishop of Hexham, was consecrated in
814, and about seven years later the splendid Church of
St. Wilfrid is said to have fallen to ruin.   Hexham was
not the only Northumbrian bishopric that disappeared at
this period ; Baldwulf, Bishop of Whitherne, consecrated
at Harehaugh, on the Coquet, in 790, is last mentioned in
803, when he assisted at the consecration of Egbert of
Lindisfarne at Bywell.   The extinction of both sees,
Whitherne and Hexham, appears to have been the result
of a great Pictish revival.   Galloway was never fully recovered by the English, and probably at this time the
valleys of North and South Tyne re-acquired a Celtic
character.   We find soon afterwards Carlisle separated
from Lindisfarne by a district ominously called The
Waste.   Along the east coast the *Drang nach Suden* was
also strongly manifested.   Angus mac Fergus, King of the
Picts, is said to have been encamped in the Merse in 820,
when St. Andrew appeared to him in a vision, and it is
highly suggestive that at the very time when that apostle
ceased, on the destruction of Hexham, to be the patron of
Northumberland between the Tees and the Aln, the celebrated monastery destined to become the seat of the
primacy of Scotland was founded in his honour on the

coast of Fife. The dedications to St. Andrew of churches
at Corbridge, Bywell, Heddon-on-the-Wall, Newcastle,
Long Benton, and Bothal, and, with every probability, at
Shotley, Ovingham, and Bolam, are interesting memorials
of the lost middle bishopric, which seems at first to have
been held *in commendam* by Wulsi, Archbishop of York,
and his successor, Wimund.

The contemptible incapacity of King Enred, which had
been manifested in the base surrender of Northumbrian
independence to the West Saxon at Dore, left the defence
of the Border from the Picts to the Bishops of Lindisfarne,
and so laid the foundation of that palatinate jurisdiction
that was so long and honourably enjoyed by the successors
of St. Cuthbert. The great Bishop Egred, 831-847, founded
the two Jedworths as frontier strongholds in Teviotdale,
and strengthened Norham, which he gave to St. Cuthbert.
There, too, he dedicated a church, probably on the strong
position now occupied in part by the Norman castle, in
honour of St. Peter, St. Cuthbert, and St. Keolwulf, whose
shrine he removed thither. Nor did he forget the spiritual
needs of the great tract of territory with which that royal
saint is said to have endowed the cathedral monastery,
but built churches at Whittingham, Edlingham, Eglingham, and Woodchester, or Wooden, on the hill at the
mouth of the Aln. This seems to show that the forma-
tion of definite parishes proceeded very slowly in the
North, and is good evidence of the district in question
having been the actual property of the monks of Lindisfarne, since Edlingham at any rate was then in the united
diocese of York and Hexham. A still more southward
direction was given to the views of the island brotherhood by Egred's own donation to it of the great territory
of Gainford, probably his own family property, which
comprised also Cliffe and Wycliffe on the southern side
of the Tees, and Billingham, which, though on the north
side of that river, belonged in civil matters to York.

Advantage was taken of the sees of York and Lindisfarne being both vacant in 854 to readjust their bound-

aries. Wulfhere of York received the portions of the
diocese of Hexham that lay between the Tees and the
Tyne; Erdwulf of Lindisfarne, that between the Tyne
and the Aln, the Picts, no doubt, having lightened his
episcopal duties beyond the Tweed. These limits, as
will be seen from what has just been said respecting the
line of the Tees, must be taken in a general sense as
referring more especially to the coast; the whole of
Hexhamshire, including the parish of St. John Lee, north
of the Tyne, remained, no doubt, in the spiritual jurisdiction of York.

In these last days of its glory, during the nominal
reign of Osbert, who had succeeded the murdered
Ethelred II. in 849, the diocese of Lindisfarne comprised
not only all the churches between the Tyne and the
Tweed—those of Melrose and Teviotdale among the rest
— but also the churches west of The Waste, on the
Cumbrian coast to the north of the Derwent; while the
Church of St. Cuthbert reckoned among its possessions
Abercorn and Edinburgh, Tyningham and Coldingham,
and Culter and Carnwath on the water-parting between
the Tweed and the Clyde, all, probably, monasteries that
had lapsed to the diocesan, besides the wide district of
Kimmerghame lying to the north of the Tweed, between
the Leader and the Whiteadder.

The mysterious substitution of the Scots for the Picts
as the northern neighbours of Northumberland did not
long delay the continued dismemberment of the distracted kingdom. By 860 the Scottish King, Kenneth
mac Alpin, had burnt Dunbar and seized Melrose, thus
extending his dominions from the Forth to the Tweed.
These territorial losses naturally caused considerable
disaffection among the subjects of King Osbert, and
when, if ancient tradition is to be trusted, he carried off
the wife of the ealdorman Beorn, this disaffection ripened
into a revolution which replaced him on the throne by a
certain Ella. In the sequel the rival kings came to an
arrangement by which Osbert reigned over the country

north of the Tees, where he deprived the monks of Tilmouth and Warkworth, while Ella established himself at
York. Both of them were slain near that city during the
great Danish invasion of 867, and the same fate met the
high-reeves Bertwulf and Denwulf.

The country north of the Tyne was placed by the
Danish conquerors of Yorkshire under the government of
a puppet-king named Egbert. He was, however, driven
out, restored the next year, and then succeeded by Ricsig.
In 875 the fleet of the savage Halfdane entered the Tyne,
intending to winter at the mouth of the Team, and then
waste the hitherto spared province of Bernicia, and the
monks of Lindisfarne, where the sack of 793 was too
well remembered, dispersed in a panic. Bishop Erdwulf
in this extremity sought the counsel of the Abbot Edred
of Carlisle. Recalling the dying injunctions of St. Cuthbert, Edred recommended that the saint's body should
be removed to a place of greater security. The young
men who had been receiving their education in the
monastery proved of truer metal than their preceptors.
Seven of them took on themselves the especial guardian-
ship of the shrine, and, accompanied by the whole population not only of the island, but also of the district of
Lindisfarne on the mainland, they set out on their nine
years' wanderings, taking with them all their relics and
treasures, even the great stone cross of Bishop Ethelwald. Bishop Erdwulf had already paid great attention
to the isolated portion of his diocese on the west coast,
and the shrine was no doubt carried in the first instance
to Carlisle, where the Abbot came from. But the Danes
followed close behind, and the Bishop and people fled
southwards along the coast till they came to the extreme
boundary of the diocese of Lindisfarne, at the mouth of
the Derwent. Here the shrine was taken on board a
ship, with the professed intention of transporting it across
the Solway to Whitherne, where it may be supposed there
was still an English colony, and whither the faithful might
hope to follow on foot. No sooner, however, was the

anchor weighed, than the Bishop and the older men who were in his confidence gave the treacherous order to steer straight to Ireland. The despair of the deserted multitude on the shore can easily be imagined. Then suddenly the wind veered right round to the west, and a violent tempest arose. The magnificent Lindisfarne Gospels, written by Bishop Edfrid, were washed overboard. Erdwulf threw himself on his knees before the shrine, and was thankful to disembark again in safety. The storm having subsided, the Bishop and his company crossed to Whitherne, and great was their joy when they found the precious volume washed up on the sands there. The illuminations seemed to their delighted eyes more beautiful than ever. The slight injury done in three or four places by the sea-water directed their attention to most apposite passages. They must have applied the warnings of the destruction of Jerusalem to the fate of Lindisfarne and their own exile, and have derived singular comfort in reading on the blotched page, ' You shall be hated of all men for My Name's sake, but a hair of your head shall not perish ;' or, again, ' It is impossible that scandals should not come, but woe to him through whom they come.'

The car on which St. Cuthbert's shrine had been brought from Lindisfarne was no doubt left behind at the mouth of the Derwent, and it became necessary to search for fresh means of conveyance. The seven faithful guardians appear now reduced to four, and of these Stithard is said to have found a bridle or rope hanging on a tree in a wood, Edmund to have captured a colt, and Hundred to have come upon a cart. The three youths received in consequence, as sobriquets, the old English names of their respective discoveries—Rap, Colte, and Cretel. A yet wilder legend explains how Eilaf (called also, it would seem, Franco), the fourth bearer of the shrine, acquired the name of Tod. The faithful four were wandering by themselves—the Bishop and Abbot are lost sight of—in the waste territory of the Picts, and all the food they had with them was a horse's head and a cheese. As Stithard, Edmund, and Hundred began to think of dining, they found that the cheese was missing, and considering that it must have been stolen, they besought St. Cuthbert to signally punish the thief. Presently a fox, or 'tod,' came running towards them, trundling the cheese with its paws, and then they remarked that Eilaf was nowhere to be seen. They began to suspect that he was the culprit, and had been turned into the fox by the indignant saint, so they fell on their knees before the shrine and prayed for his pardon and restitution. Accordingly he resumed human form, but the name of Tod stuck to him and his descendants, some of whom became hereditary priests of Bedlington.

Most of the Lindisfarne exiles now settled down in the mountainous districts of Cumberland and Westmorland, and a fifteenth-century tradition ascribes to this the dedication of many of the churches in the west there to St. Cuthbert. The strange thing is that an English kingdom (with its capital no doubt at Corbridge), continued to survive north of the Tyne, where the population of Northumberland preserved its distinctly English character. King Ricsig was succeeded, in 876, by Egbert II. During the reign of this, the last English King of Northumberland, St. Cuthbert is said to have appeared to Alfred the Great, in Somersetshire, and to have assured him of a speedy victory over the Danes, whose leaders, Halfdane and Ingvar, were soon afterwards slain in a descent on Devonshire.

The extinction of the Bernician kingdom in the person of Egbert II. (878-879) coincides exactly with the appearance, in Scottish tradition, of the great hero Grig, or Gregory (879-889), who is said to have subdued the whole of Bernicia and nearly all England, the England of the Scots then consisting of the ancient Northumberland. The fact that Bamburgh weathered the storm raging all around, and survived as a stronghold of Northumbrian independence, is largely due to the diplomacy of the High-Reeve

Aldulf, who played off Scot against Dane, and became rather the ally than the vassal of the West Saxon. It was probably their reluctance to accept the assistance of the Scots, whom they regarded as schismatics, that caused the precipitate flight of Erdwulf and his monks from Lindisfarne. Their departure left Aldulf free in this respect, and the issue proved that the shrine of St. Cuthbert might, like the hand of St. Oswald, have remained safe in Bamburgh all the time.

As it was, after seven years' wanderings, the shrine was brought to the monastery of Craike, that occupied a strong position about ten miles north of York. The Danes, who were beginning to regularly colonize Yorkshire, were without any recognised leader. Abbot Edred of Carlisle came and told Bishop Erdwulf that he had had a vision in which St. Cuthbert commanded him to repair to the Danish army, and order them to ransom Guthred, son of Hardicanute, a young Dane of royal descent, from his captivity with a widow at Whittingham, and proclaim him King, clasping a gold bracelet on his right arm, on the hill of Oswi, by which Easington, in the county of Durham, is probably meant. This they accordingly did, in 884, and the shrine was then borne from 'Oswigesdune' to the old Roman fortress of Cunca-chester, or Chester-le-Street, to which the see of St. Cuthbert was definitely transferred from Lindisfarne. Out of gratitude for his promotion, Guthred bestowed on Bishop Erdwulf and his successors the land between the Wear, the Tyne, and the Derwent—the Durham Derwent of course—and thus formed an ecclesiastical buffer-state between his own kingdom, with its capital at York, and the country beyond the Tyne, which was more or less under Scottish protection.

With the consent of Alfred, the southern portion of the ancient diocese of Hexham was now taken from the Archbishop of York, and given to the Bishop of Chester-le-Street, whose diocese, though it lineally represented that of Lindisfarne, thus came far more to represent territorially

that of Hexham.   This transplantation of the bishopric
of Lindisfarne southwards is of itself sufficient evidence
of the great encroachments of the Scots.   In the end
Guthred is said to have repulsed the Scots from the hill
of ' Mundingedene,' near Norham, when their army was
engulfed in one of the morasses that then abounded in that
district.

On the death of King Guthred in 894, the claims of his
sons were disregarded by Alfred.   The disinherited
princes appear to have lapsed into heathendom, and on
reaching manhood to have established themselves as
roving vikings on the coast of Ireland.   They soon
crossed over to ravage Cumberland.   Erdwulf ' the prince '
had been slain there by Edred, the heir of King Ricsig,
who had ridden over the hills from the east and
carried off his wife.   Pursued by popular execration,
Edred sought the protection of St. Cuthbert, and was
located by Bishop Cutheard between the Wear and the
Derwent.   His example was soon followed by Elfred,
the heir of the High-Reeve Bertwulf, slain at York in
867, who, flying from the Danish pirates, crossed the
mountains and settled on the sea-board of Durham.
Another fugitive, Tilred, Abbot of Heversham, bought
South Yoden (Little Eden, near Hartlepool), and gave
half of it to St. Cuthbert that he might be received
among the brethren at Chester-le-Street, and half to the
cell of Norham to be Abbot there.   About the same time,
a priest named Berrard gave his estate of Willington, on
the north side of the Tyne, to be admitted into St. Cuthbert's Household, while Bishop Cutheard bought, no doubt
from the Danes, the township of Bedlington, between the
Blyth and the Wansbeck, with its dependencies of Neder-
ton (Netherton), Grubba (Gubeon), Twisle, Cebbingtun
(Choppington), Sliceburne (Sleekburn), and Commes
(Cambois).

Soon after the death of Edwulf of Bamburgh in 912,
Reginald, King Guthred's eldest son, came with a great
fleet and seized the land of Edwulf's son, Aldred, who was

as great an ally of Edward as his father had been of Alfred. He marched thence to the royal city of Corbridge. Aldred invoked the powerful assistance of Constantine of Scotland. In the battle that ensued the Scots were routed, and Aldred and his brother Uctred were the only English leaders who escaped. St. Cuthbert's tenants, Elfred and Edred, were both killed ; but the latter's sons, Esbrid and Elstan, after fighting bravely, submitted to Reginald in consideration of a grant of the lands their father had held of Bishop Cutheard. The victory won by the Scots at ' Tinemore,' possibly Tynemouthshire Moor, in 918, when they displayed the crosier of St. Columba as their standard, appears to have restored the rule of Aldred over the country north of the Tyne.

Reginald succeeded in surprising York in 923, but on the advance of King Edward to Bakewell in the Peak in the year following, all the combatants who were tearing Northumberland in pieces made their submission to him, Aldred of Bamburgh among the rest. The Northumbrians, it should be noticed, were already divided into English, Danes and Norwegians or Norsemen. Another roving fit soon afterwards seized King Reginald, who perished, with his sons and friends, at Chailles on the Loire in 925, ' taking with him nothing he had robbed St. Cuthbert of, except his sin.' His brother Sitric succeeded him on the throne of York, and received in marriage a sister of King Athelstan, but after a year's reign died mysteriously, ' accursed with hunger,' probably starved to death by his brother-in-law. Athelstan at once seized the kingdom for himself, driving out Sitric's sons, Guthfrith and Anlaf. At York, he received from Harold Fairhair, King of Norway, the present of a purple-sailed galley, accompanied by offers of armed assistance. That same year he took the hitherto inviolate fortress of Bamburgh, expelling Aldred, who was glad, with the other Northern chiefs, to make his peace at Dacre on the Eamont.

The government of Northumberland, we are told in the invaluable ' Egilsaga ' (which has recently been translated

from the Icelandic by the Rev. W. C. Green), was entrusted by Athelstan to two earls named Alfgar and
Godric, who, on hearing of an invasion by the Scots
under the leadership of Anlaf the Red—it is difficult to
distinguish the many Anlafs of the period—advanced to
oppose him. Godric was killed ; Alfgar fled. On this,
two earls of Bretland (Cumbria), named Hrings and
Adils, went over to Anlaf, who encamped his host near a
' burh' called Vinheide, or Weondune, in all probability
the place now called Wendon, or Wandon, between
Chatton and Wooler, and accepted Athelstan's challenge
to a pitched battle on a field staked out with hazel-rods in
the flat between the great ' Vinwood ' (Chillingham Park
and Hebburn Wood) on one side, and a river (the Till) on
the other, a piece of history that was to be nearly
repeated in the case of Flodden. Athelstan's men, who
were comparatively few, set up a great array of tents on
the high ground where the distance between the wood
and the river was least, and staved off the day of battle
till the King had reached a 'burh' (Bewick) at the south
end of the heath. At last Hrings and Adils made a
sudden dash forwards. Earl Alfgar and the Northumbrians
moved along the river bank to oppose Adils, but were
repulsed, and Alfgar, dreading a renewal of Athelstan's
indignation at his former defeat, fled past the southern
' burh ' to escape by sea from the west coast. Adils
returned from the pursuit to attack the two Norse brothers,
Egil and Thorolf, who had engaged Hrings on the woodside. Hrings was, however, slain, and Adils forced to
take refuge in the wood at nightfall. The next day
Athelstan himself advanced next the river to meet Anlaf,
while Thorolf again kept to the higher ground near the
wood. Thorolf was pressing forward, hoping to outflank
Anlaf, when he was overpowered and slain by Adils and
his followers, who sprang suddenly out of the wood. His
death was speedily avenged by Egil, who had been leading Athelstan's vanguard. The Scottish earls took to
flight, and in the end Anlaf himself was slain. Athel-

stan's presence in Northumberland is best remembered
through the rhyming grant he is said to have made of
Roddam and Heddon to Paulan, possibly the early
possessor of Pallinsburn :

> ' I Kyng Adelstan
> giffs here to Paulan
> Oddan and Roddan,
> als gud and als fair,
> as evyr thai myne war,
> and thar to wytnes
> Mald my Wiffe.'

Notwithstanding Athelstan's victorious compaign in
Scotland, King Constantine allied himself in 937 with
Anlaf, son of Sitric, who entered the Humber with six
hundred sail. The crushing defeat they experienced at
Brunanburh, wherever it was, has often been confused
with the battle of Wandon. Forgetful, however, of
Brunanburh, and undeterred by Eric Bloodaxe, son of
Harold Fairhair, who had been set over them as King,
the men of York called in Anlaf of Ireland. Anlaf
perished in the sack of the Church of St. Balthere at
Tyningham, while his followers on their way back to
York ravaged Lindisfarne with the sword.

After his re-conquest of Mercia, King Edmund received
the submission of Anlaf, son of Sitric, whom, on his
baptism, he made King of Northern England. In a few
months, the restless Northumbrians drove out Anlaf, and
Edmund stood sponsor at the confirmation of the young
King, Reginald II., son of Guthfrith. The next year,
however, Edmund was strong enough to seize the
Northumbrian crown for himself.

On Edmund's assassination, the Northumbrian Witan
swore fealty to his brother Edred, but revolting soon
afterwards, again raised Eric Bloodaxe to the throne.
Edred consequently harried all Northumberland, burning
even St. Wilfrid's minster at Ripon, and the Witan, aban-
doning Eric, made an entire submission. No sooner,
however, was Edred really gone, than Anlaf Cuaran

appeared on the scene as a pretender, while Malcolm of Scotland, the son of Donald, raided Teesdale, carrying off the Norwegian settlers and their cattle. Anlaf Cuaran was eventually driven out, and Eric Bloodaxe installed for the third time at York. In 954 this last King of a separate Northumberland perished on the wilds of Stainmoor. The blow, struck by the hand of a son of Anlaf, was directed by the crafty Oswulf, who appears to have been the son and successor of Aldred of Bamburgh.

CHAPTER V.

THE EARLDOM.

THE Kingdom of Northumberland had become in its latter days so much of an alien institution that its final overthrow must have been regarded at the time in the light rather of a restoration than of a revolution. Once again from the royal rock of Bamburgh, a prince of the race, if not of the lineage of St. Oswald, ruled the whole land between Forth and Humber—*provincias omnes Northanhymbrorum.*

Oswulf, it is true, purchased an increase of actual power by the surrender of his rights as a feudatory prince. He became the Viceroy of Edred, with the title of Ealdorman or Earl, and since this acknowledgment of the West Saxon monarchy took the form of a voluntary commendation, the Earldom of Northumberland, according to ideas then prevailing, became hereditary in his family.

It was not long before the loss of Edinburgh threw doubts on the loyalty or the capacity of the new Earl. Still English in 957, the city was evacuated and occupied by the Scots before 963. Three years later, the rule of Oswulf was restricted by Edgar, the successor of Edred, to the territory north of the Tyne. An Earldom of York was bestowed on Oslac, and the sea-board of Deira from the Tees, as far as Birdforth it would seem, or in other words, the district of Cleveland, was entrusted to Edwulf, surnamed Evilchild. The Bishop of Chester-le-Street probably claimed jurisdiction between the Tees and the Tyne. As might have been foreseen, this disintegration of the ancient Northumberland, prudent as it may have been in curbing the ambition of Oswulf, placed the whole country at the mercy of the Scots, whose ravages extended to Hartlepool and Cleveland. In their extremity, Bishop Elsig and the two Earls of Deira conceived a scheme that should buy off the Scots and at the same time still further impair the authority of the distrusted Oswulf. This was the cession of Lothian, or whatever was left of Northumberland north of the Tweed. The Scottish King, Kenneth, agreed to hold this of Edgar, and peace was established on the Border for upwards of thirty years.

The death of King Edgar was followed by a revulsion of Northern policy. Oslac was banished from York, and Northumberland from the Humber to the Tweed re-united to form the earldom of Oswulf's successor, Waltheof of Bamburgh. The sack of the old Bernician capital by the Danes, led by Guistin and Guthmund, in 993, completely shattered Waltheof's power, which was henceforth restricted to the north of the Tyne. Bishop Aldhun, who removed the see of St. Cuthbert from Chester-le-Street to Durham, appears to have taken this opportunity for appointing a bailiff of his own to the rule of Hexhamshire.

On the invasion of Northumberland by Malcolm, King of Scots, in 1006, the feeble Waltheof, instead of attempt- ing to meet the enemy in the field, shut himself up in Bamburgh. His son Uctred, who had married Bishop Aldhun's daughter, collected a force of Northumbrians and Yorkshiremen, then for the first time clearly distin- guished from each other, and gallantly raised the siege of Durham. On hearing of this exploit, King Ethelred con- ferred on Uctred not only the Northumbrian Earldom of his superannuated father, but also that of York, which had just fallen vacant. Upon this advancement, the young Earl repudiated Ecgive, the Bishop's daughter, and took to wife Sigen, whose father Styr, a rich noble, bargained that his son-in-law was to slay Thurbrand the Hold, his mortal enemy.

Uctred followed up his rout of the Scots from before Durham with other successes. There is every reason to believe that he recovered the greater part of Lothian, as, like his predecessor Oswulf, he held, we are told, the Earldom of all the provinces of the Northumbrians— *comitatum omnium Northanhymbrorum provinciarum.* His glory attained its zenith when, the Countess Sigen dead or not, he received for third wife Elgeve, the daughter of his sovereign Ethelred.

Returning from a foray into Cumberland in 1013, Uctred was overtaken at Brough-under-Stainmoor and eased of his booty by the Scots. Three years later, with the connivance of King Canute, he was treacherously murdered by Thurbrand, the very man he had bound himself to kill by the weird settlement made on his second marriage.

Uctred's brother Edwulf Cudel, the next Earl, placed in jeopardy between Canute on the one side and the Scots on the other, deemed it prudent to come to terms with the latter by giving them back the whole of Lothian. The church of Durham seemed likely to lose its vast estates beyond the Tweed; and in September, 1018, the people of St. Cuthbert living between that river and the Tees were led north by the clergy for the vindication of their rights. At Carham they were encountered by Malcolm and his vassal, Owen the Bald, the ruler of Lothian. No less than eighteen priests fell with the leading Northumbrians in the panic that ensued — a panic heightened by the fears inspired by the appearance of a comet for thirty nights previously.

The news of this disaster broke the heart of Bishop Aldhun. Earl Edwulf did not long survive him. The latter's nephew, Aldred, son of Uctred, inherited the Earldom of Northumberland only — *solius Northumbriæ comitatum.* This is perhaps the earliest instance in which the name of the ancient monarchy that stretched northwards from the Humber is restricted to the area, more or less, of the modern county of Northumberland.

Earl Aldred avenged the murder of his father Uctred by slaying Thurbrand the Hold, who therefore probably dwelt to the north of the Tyne. The blood-feud was taken up by Thurbrand's son Carl. He and Aldred laid wait for one another, Carl possibly supported by Siward the Dane, who seems to have been invested by Canute with the Earldom of York, if not of all Northumberland, in about 1023. The wandering minstrel Othere the Black apostrophized Canute in the lines (translated by Vigfusson and Powell) :

' Young King, thou madest the English fall near the Tees ;
   The dyke of the Northumbrians flowed deep over the bodies of the
      dead.'

It was not, however, until his return from a pilgrimage to Rome, in 1031, that Canute gave his full attention to the affairs of the Far North. He advanced in the first instance against Cumberland, then held by Duncan, grandson of King Malcolm through his daughter Beatrice. Duncan, like Earl Uctred, had refused to do homage to a Danish usurper. The mediation of certain bishops and elders led him to give way. It is probable that it was at this time that he received in marriage the sister or other near relation of Siward, whose dowry consisted of twelve towns in England. These may reasonably be identified with the Twelve Towns of South Tindale: Kirkhaugh, Knaresdale, Thirlwall, Wall Town, Haltwhistle, Plenmellor, Melkridge, Ridley, Thorngrafton, Whitfield, Ouston, and Elrington. It is curious to notice that the towns of Blenkinsop, Wyden, Featherston, and Lambley were not included in this grant, while Elrington formed an enclave separated from the rest by the territory of Langley.

This extension of the sphere of Scottish influence to

within a few miles of Hexham was followed there by a great revival of English national feeling, that found expression in the cult paid to the local saints. The church of Hexham had been given by Bishop Edmund to Alured, sacrist of Durham, and was served by two vicars named Gamel. A 'dregn,' or one of the lesser nobles of Hexhamshire, declared that St. Alcmund, the Bishop who died in 781, had appeared and bidden him tell Alured that he was to translate his body, which lay buried near the cross of St. Acca against the east wall of the church, to a worthy shrine in the interior. The relics were found at three o'clock in the afternoon of July 31, and, as it was then too late to celebrate Mass, they were deposited for the night in St. Peter's porch. Alured, a keen relic-hunter, took this opportunity to abstract a portion of a finger to carry back to Durham. All the next day it was found impossible to lift the chest containing the sacred bones. 'What? Would ye bear me into the church with my limbs mangled,' demanded St. Alcmund of the dregn that night, 'that, thus mutilated, I should wait on St. Andrew and his altar, which I served so long with a whole body and a sound mind?' On the third day Alured humbly restored the missing fragment; the chest was then easily raised, and borne solemnly into the basilica.

Perhaps it was this wild religious revival that led Aldred and Carl to lay aside their animosities and start together on a pilgrimage to Rome. A great storm prevented them embarking, and, taking this as a warning to defer their journey, they returned to Carl's house, possibly to Charlton, on North Tyne. The Earl was honourably entertained, and Carl made a point of 'setting' his guest on the way to Bamburgh. As they were passing through Risewood, perhaps the wooded valley of the Riseburn in Redesdale, the old hate seized Carl, who turned and slew Aldred at a spot still marked in the twelfth century by a small stone cross.

The pride of Aldred's brother and successor, Earl

Edwulf, is said to have caused him to terribly spoil the 'Britons,' possibly the Celtic population of North Tyne, as the words scarcely imply an invasion of Cumberland, or other Scottish district. It was in revenge for this persecution, no doubt, that Duncan, King of Scots, marched into Northumberland in 1040. He laid siege to Durham, but was signally repulsed.

In 1041, desirous of being reconciled to Hardicanute, Earl Edwulf presented himself at his court. In spite of the safe-conduct he had received, he was betrayed into the hands of Siward, who slew him as Thurbrand slew his father, Uctred. Siward now expected to enjoy undisputed sway in the Earldom of the whole province of the Northumbrians, from the Humber to the Tweed—*totius provinciæ Northanhymbrorum comitatum ab Humbra usque Tuedam;* but two years later he was compelled to assert his authority by force, laying waste the province in his charge. Again, in 1054, when he invaded Scotland by sea and land, and had succeeded in putting Duncan's grandson, Malcolm, in possession of Cumberland and Lothian, he was recalled from Dundee by the news of a Northumbrian insurrection, and the massacre of his son, Osbern Bullaxe, with his house-carls. The degradation of Bamburgh was now completed by the theft of the right arm of St. Oswald by Winegot, an enterprising monk of Peterborough, who, having mastered the ins and outs of the ruined church, found a favourable opportunity for abstracting the royal relic from its shrine.

In recounting this pious theft, Reginald of Durham breaks out into a patriotic lament over the fallen fortunes of the Northern capital, translated probably from some ancient poem. 'The city,' he says, 'renowned for the splendour of her high estate, is in these latter days burdened with tribute, and reduced to the condition of a handmaiden. She, who was once the mistress of the cities of Britain, *domina civitatum Britonensium,* has exchanged the glories of her sabbaths for shame and desolation. The crowds that flocked to her festivals are represented by a few herdsmen. The pleasures her dignity afforded are turned to naught.'

Siward endeavoured to render his rule popular in Northumberland by marrying the daughter of Earl Aldred. In 1055, he died on his bed at York, clad in the armour he insisted on resuming. His son Waltheof was a child of six or seven, so the Earldom was conferred by Edward the Confessor on Tostig, son of Earl Godwin, and brother of Harold.

Malcolm, King of Scots, took advantage of Tostig's absence on a pilgrimage to Rome, in 1061, to ravage Lindisfarne. The Earl's rule was very unpopular. In 1065 a monk named Edward had a vision, in which St. Oswin, the royal martyr of Deira, bade him raise his body that was buried at Tynemouth, and place it in a shrine in the church. Tostig refused to lend his assistance; but his countess, Judith, daughter of Baldwin of Flanders, begged Bishop Egelwin, who was going to the translation, to bring her one of the saint's hairs. The body was found with some difficulty, and the Countess of Northumberland satisfied herself of its authenticity by testing the incombustible nature of the hair brought her on the great hearth of the palace. Tostig had a residence at 'Tynemutheham,' which was the scene of many of those drunken bouts that the English delighted in. Returning intoxicated from one of them, the Earl's favourite chaplain did not scruple to prolong his debauch within the walls of the very church.

The anger of St. Oswin was kindled against Tostig, and the anger of a popular saint was a dangerous force in politics. In the autumn came the crisis: three Northumbrian thanes, Gamelbearn, Dunstan, son of Ethelnoth, and Glonicorn, son of Erdwulf, surprised York, and butchered Tostig's Danish house-carls. They declared the Earl outlawed for his oppressive laws, and obtained the Confessor's consent to the appointment of Morkere, brother of Edwin of Mercia, in his stead. It was agreed or implied that Oswulf of Bamburgh, the son of Earl

Edwulf, should be the actual ruler of the country north of the Tyne.

Alone among all the great nobles of the North, Oswulf of Bamburgh bowed not the knee to the Norman Conqueror. His Earldom was consequently given to Copsig, who had acted for a time as Tostig's lieutenant. Oswulf fled to the hills and woods, gathering round him a band of followers reduced to the same extremities as himself. A great feast was spread at Newburn on March 12, 1067, to welcome Earl Copsig across the Tyne. Suddenly the house of the revellers was surrounded by Oswulf and his friends. Copsig escaped to the church, but this was set on fire, and on his making to the door, Oswulf struck off his head. A few months later, Oswulf himself was killed by a robber whom he was pursuing, and in this obscure encounter the male line of the great House of Bamburgh came to an end.

According to the strict principles of hereditary succession, Waltheof, son of Siward by Elfleda, granddaughter of Uctred by his first wife, should have now been Earl; but Gospatric, son of Maldred by Algitha, daughter of Uctred by his third wife, purchased the rule of Northumberland from the Conqueror for a large sum of money. The next year, however, Gospatric took the lead in a general movement against the Normans in the North, and on its collapse withdrew with Edgar Etheling into Scotland. William entered York in triumph, and received from Ethelwin, Bishop of Durham, the submission of Malcolm of Scotland. He now thought himself strong enough to confer the Earldom of Northumberland north of the Tyne on one of his own followers, Robert de Comines. The new Earl and his Norman knights were, however, massacred in passing through Durham.

In the autumn of 1069, a great Danish fleet arrived in the Humber, and Edgar Etheling, Earl Gospatric, Waltheof, son of Siward, and the leading men of Northumberland, hastened to join the invaders in carrying

York by storm. This revolt, however, also collapsed in the usual way of English attempts at resistance. The Conqueror retook York, and marched north, devastating the whole country. By the advice of Gospatric, Bishop Ethelwin and his canons fled from Durham, taking with them the body of St. Cuthbert. The first night of their flight they spent at Jarrow, the second at Bedlington. On December 13 they reached Tughall, the property of a rich man named Gillomichael, who had boasted to one of the Tods, the hereditary priests of Bedlington, how he would worthily receive the saint in his hall hung round with golden shields. Instead of this, as Tod had half expected, the Family of St. Cuthbert with the shrine were relegated by Gillomichael to his barn, while he himself passed the night drinking with his friends out of jewelled cups of gold. On their way to Lindisfarne the next morning, the Bishop and clergy had the satisfaction to see the inhospitable homestead consumed by fire, with the exception of a portion of the barn.

Gospatric had taken advantage of the desertion of the cathedral to carry off the treasures of Durham. A terrible vision, related to him at Bamburgh, by the monk Ernan, described the torments which Gillomichael, just dead, suffered already, and which were in store for him, should he not repent. He accordingly set out on a pilgrimage barefoot over the sands to Holy Island.

Meanwhile William, having burnt the church of Jarrow, marched up the Tyne to Hexham, laying everything waste before him. Alarmed at his approach, the English broke up their camp on Lindisfarne, and fled across the Tweed by night. William pursued them to the banks of that river, and spent a fortnight in negotiations on the very Border. Having received the submission of Gospatric, who, however, did not venture in person into his presence, he returned to Hexham by a still wilder route, which no army had yet been known to traverse. From Hexham he marched back to York. The whole country from the Humber to the Tweed was turned by this terrible harrying into a desert, given over to wolves and robbers. York, Durham, and Bamburgh were the only inhabited towns left. For nine years all cultivation ceased.

In April, 1070, the shrine of St. Cuthbert was taken back to Durham; but sentence of outlawry was passed on Bishop Ethelwin, who escaped to Scotland with all the treasures of the church that he could readily seize. Soon after this, Malcolm, issuing from Cumberland, advanced down Teesdale into Cleveland, destroying everything that had escaped the Normans. As if to prove the sincerity of his renewed allegiance to William, Earl Gospatric profited by Malcolm's expedition to lead a foray into Cumberland, and returned in triumph with much booty to Bamburgh. On hearing of this, Malcolm swore that henceforth death or slavery should be the only choice left to the English. The most frightful outrages were committed, and Scotland was filled with English captives. One youth, immured by Malcolm in the Black Hole of Berwick, attributed his escape to Norham to the intervention of St. Cuthbert. Fortunately, the marriage of Malcolm to Margaret, sister of Edgar Etheling, entirely changed the position of the English in Scotland.

In August, Thomas of Bayeux was consecrated Archbishop of York, and as the whole of Hexhamshire lay waste without a husbandman, the bailiff, Uctred, son of Ulfkill, came to him and represented that he might easily take possession of it, especially during the vacancy of the see of Durham, as the successor of St. Wilfrid, the founder of the lapsed monastery. This the Archbishop accordingly did. The church of Hexham was restored about the same time by Eilaf, the hereditary priest.

A new Bishop of Durham was appointed in 1071 in the person of Walcher of Lorraine. The Conqueror assembled a great fleet and army to avenge the cruelties of the Scots. Crossing the Tweed, and advancing unopposed through Lothian and Calatria, he compelled Malcolm to do homage to him as feudal lord of Scotland at

Abernethy on the Tay.   On his march south he found the
Tyne so high that it was impossible to ford it, and there
was no bridge.   He pitched his tents near 'Monec-
cestre,' as the old Roman fort of Pons Ælius, now Newcastle, was then called, and waited for the water to fall.
Provisions ran short; fodder was urgently required for
the horses.   A band of scouts was sent to pillage the
monastery of Tynemouth, to which all the stores of the
district had been removed.   By the time, however, their
leader, a distinguished knight named Robert, caught sight
of the church-tower, he had acquainted himself with the
terrible fate of those who violated St. Oswin's peace, and
forbade any further advance.   Nevertheless, some of his
soldiery helped themselves to the forbidden forage.   The
horses, on eating it, were seized with a kind of madness.
Robert's favourite charger was among those affected, but
on his offering his best cloak at St. Oswin's shrine, it at
once recovered.

For some reason William now determined to remove
Gospatric from the Earldom.   He had been pardoned for
the part he took in the storm of York, so an older charge
of connivance in the murder of Cumin at Durham was
raked up against him.   He thought it prudent to withdraw to Scotland, where Malcolm granted him the lands
of Dunbar.   Northumberland was now confided to
Siward's son Waltheof.   The old blood-feud with the
race of Thurbrand the Hold proved too strong even for
the saintly character of the young Earl, and he had the
sons of Carl, his recent comrades in arms, put to the
sword as they were feasting at Settrington, near York.

The closest friendship subsisted between Waltheof and
Walcher.   The Earl sat in the synod, with his three
knights, Alwin, Wulstan, and Kenulf, and carried out in
his county whatever the Bishop deemed good for the
advancement of Christianity.   In 1073 Aldwin of Winch-
combe and two Benedictines from Evesham came to
York, and obtained from Waltheof's sheriff, Hugh, son
of Baldric, a guide to 'Munechecester' (Newcastle),

but finding no traces of monks there, yielded to Bishop Walcher's wish that they should settle in his own territory at Jarrow. As 'Earl of all Northumberland,' Waltheof gave to Prior Aldwin and the brotherhood of Jarrow the church of Tynemouth, with the body of St. Oswin. He entrusted them also with the monastic education of his young cousin, Morkere, who was taken by boat to Tynemouth. In an unguarded moment Waltheof joined the conspiracy formed against the Conqueror at the bride-ale of Exning, in Cambridgeshire, and, in spite of his instant confession and apparent pardon, was beheaded near Winchester on May 31, 1076.

The experiment of governing Northumberland through native princes having failed, it was next attempted to rule it under the sanction of the Church, and Bishop Walcher was advanced to the Earldom; while the franchise of Redesdale, that had belonged to Maldred, son of Akman, was given to Robert de Umfraville, with the charge to free it from the wolves and robbers who had infested Northumberland since the harrying of 1070. With Umfraville, better known as Robert-with-the-Beard, came Gilbert de Batail, who received from him a grant of Fawdon and Netherton, and Robert de Montnytt, who built a manor-house at Reveley and founded the church of St. Mary at Ingram. The English element continued, however, to predominate over the Norman in the councils of the Earl-Bishop, his chief adviser being Liulf, who had married Waltheof's aunt.

A third invasion of Northumberland by Malcolm, in the summer of 1079, appears to have been a mere raid, devoid of political significance. The inhabitants of Hexham, trembling at the approach of the Scots, were comforted by the report that St. Wilfrid had hastened on horseback from his tomb to their assistance, and that in passing Durham he had been joined in this aërial ride by St. Cuthbert. The Tyne suddenly rose in the night, and the Scots, losing their way in one of their own mists, left Hexham unmolested. The murder of Liulf, through

Norman jealousy, led to the massacre of Walcher and his followers at a tumultuous assembly of men from beyond the Tyne, held at Gateshead in May, 1080.

A prelate of very different mould, Odo of Bayeux, the Conqueror's brother, was commissioned to avenge the death of Walcher. This he did in the most relentless manner, laying the whole land again desolate. Nor were the offences of Malcolm overlooked; but the expedition that William's eldest son, Robert, led as far north as Falkirk was destined to be principally memorable from the fact of his founding the New Castle upon the Tyne during his homeward march.

The real conquest of Northumberland by the Normans now began. Gilbert Tison, said to have been William's standard-bearer at Hastings, acquired the vast estates that centuries of history had grouped into the barony of Alnwick. William de Merlay, said to have been also at Hastings, under the banner of Geoffrey, Bishop of Coutances, received Morpeth and Morwick, which latter he gave to St. Cuthbert; Hugh de Laval settled at Calverdon (Callerton); a Bertram obtained Mitford, and a Burum, Bolam. The small fiefs of Dilston and Chevington were held by knights of English origin, while the thanes of Halton, Callaley, Hepple and Roddam retained those manors and their dependencies by a less honorable tenure. Throckley, Whittingham, Eslington, Beadnel, Mousen, Roddam and the three Middletons, remained in the hands of smaller native proprietors. At Bamburgh, the gate-keeper, Canute, had his office made hereditary, while the tenants of Callaley and Yetlington were to cart thither the trunk of a tree for the King's hearth, every other day, between Whitsuntide and Lammas.

A certain Alberic, perhaps an Aubrey de Vere, was made Earl of Northumberland. He confirmed the monks of Jarrow in their possession of Tynemouth, and aided in transferring them to Durham. The activity of these Benedictines was exhibited in the foundation of a new church on Holy Island in 1082. Three years later

Alberic fell into disgrace, probably on account of diffi-
culties with Scotland. Setting out for the East, with
the wild idea of becoming lord of Greece, he was glad on
his return to Normandy to gain the hand of a rich lady
named Græcia.

On Alberic's disgrace, the government of Northumber-
land was entrusted to Geoffrey, Bishop of Coutances.
Geoffrey and his nephew, Robert de Mowbray, joined
William of St. Carilef, Bishop of Durham, in supporting
Robert of Normandy against William Rufus. A local
dispute subsequently arose between the two bishops.
William de Merlay appeared before the council of the
Red King, complaining that the men of the Bishop of
Durham, in his castle, had taken from his lord of Cou-
tances two hundred cattle that were under the King's safe-
conduct, and refused to restore them.

Bishop Geoffrey appears to have resigned the Earldom
in favour of his nephew Robert, who, mindful no doubt of
the cattle-lifting feud with St. Carilef, sent his servants,
Gumer and Robert Taca, to drive Prior Turchil and the
monks of Durham from Tynemouth, and to replace them
with Benedictines from St. Albans. The vast extent of
the estates still vested in the Earldom in Mowbray's time
appears from his grants to Tynemouth of Amble, Wylam,
and Coquet Island, together with the tithes of Newburn,
Ovingham, Bywell St. Peter, Bothal, and Woodhorn.
After a time Mowbray and St. Carilef became good friends,
possibly in consequence of their common antipathy to
Rufus, and agreed to an amicable partition of the manor
of Ros, claimed both by Bamburgh and Lindisfarne.

In May, 1091, Malcolm, King of Scots, invaded Northumberland for the fourth time. Intending to advance
into the heart of England, he pitched his camp at Chester-
le-Street, while the ravages of his followers extended up
to the city of Durham, which, with the Norman camp
immediately south of it, was reduced to the extremes
of want. Led by Nigel de Albini, the good men to whom
the keeping of the land was entrusted succeeded at last

in dislodging the Scots and driving them over the Border. The dearth of provisions at Newcastle was keenly felt by the victors, and they were constrained to turn aside to Tynemouth, which, enjoying the Peace of St. Oswin, was the great storehouse of the whole country. At their approach the monks came out to meet them in the gateway, bearing the shrine of St. Oswin, and charging them to respect his patrimony. Nigel de Wast, a near relation and great friend of Albini, paid the saint military honours, and, turning his horse round, was in the act of audibly vowing that he would not eat of the plunder till he was assured of his forgiveness, when a. less scrupulous knight cannoned into his horse, and sent both it and its rider over the steep cliff. In miraculous fashion both escaped unhurt.

The following autumn, Rufus himself, accompanied by his brother Robert, set out on an expedition to Scotland. Fifty of his corn-ships from the South of England put into the Tyne about Michaelmas. Their crews were accused of plundering the neighbourhood, and the vengeance of St. Oswin was discerned when most of the vessels were lost with all hands in a sudden squall off Coquet Island. Malcolm had defiantly advanced out of Scotland into Lothian to meet William, but the 'Scotte Watra,' a great river (probably the Tweed) was in flood, and the two armies were drawn up on the opposite banks. Through the strange mediation of Edgar Etheling and Robert of Normandy, a peace was concluded, the chief conditions being that Malcolm should do homage for Lothian, and that he should receive twelve towns in England, no doubt the Twelve Towns of South Tyndale which his grandfather Duncan had received as the dowry of his Danish bride.

The next thing, however, was for Rufus to seize on Cumberland, driving out Dolfin, and rebuilding Carlisle. Malcolm, who assisted in laying the foundation of the present cathedral of Durham on August 11, 1093, proceeded, in company with the bishop, William of St.

Carilef, to the English court at Gloucester. Rufus wished to refer the matters in dispute to his own council in England, whereas Malcolm's contention, that they could only be determined by men of both kingdoms on the marches, is evidence that the Border Laws were already in existence. In angry mood, the Scottish King returned home, and invading Northumberland for the fifth time, was met on the banks of the Aln by Morel of Bamburgh and Gilbert de Gulevant. In a battle, fought on St. Brice's Day, November 13, Malcolm himself was slain with 3,000 of his lieges. His eldest son, Edward, died of his wounds in the forest of Jedburgh, and both their bodies were conveyed to Tynemouth for burial.

Morel, who was the nephew of Earl Robert de Mowbray, and Sheriff of Northumberland, soon afterwards seized on the cargoes of four Norwegian vessels and refused to restore them; while the Earl, his uncle, elated with the defeat of Malcolm, paid no regard to a thrice-repeated summons to the Red King's court in the spring of 1095. William marched north to chastise the rebel. The castle of Tynemouth, then the strongest on the Tyne, was taken after a siege of two months, and apparently dismantled. The fortress of Newcastle and the Merlay stronghold at Morpeth were secured without much difficulty. William did much to strengthen the former, and is even said to have enclosed the town that had grown up around it with a wall. Earl Robert himself had taken refuge in impregnable Bamburgh, with his young bride, Matilda de Laigle. Finding it impossible to carry the castle by storm, William began building in front of it a wooden fort, called a *Malvoisin*, or ' Bad Neighbour.' He compelled the leaders of his army to assist the rank and file in pushing on the work. Dismayed at the progress it made, Mowbray called loudly from the ramparts of Bamburgh to the noble labourers who had sworn to join his rising, addressing each by name, and bidding him not be forgetful of his oath. These taunts of despair, and the fear and shame they engendered, contributed greatly to the amusement of Rufus

8

and those really loyal to him. At length, weary of the protracted siege, the King returned to the South of England, leaving Bamburgh to be watched by the garrison of the Malvoisin.

Provisions were beginning to run short in the castle, and Mowbray's spirits were depressed by the close blockade, when a secret message reached him from the warders of Newcastle, promising to throw open the gates if he appeared suddenly before it. Only too delighted with this prospect of retrieving his fortunes, the Earl slipped out of the postern one night, and, going on board a small ship, was carried by a favourable wind down the coast to Tynemouth, the monks of which were still grateful for the favours he had bestowed on their house. The garrison of the Malvoisin, hearing of his escape, set out in pursuit, and warned the captains of Newcastle. Mowbray made his attempt on Newcastle on a Sunday, but the treacherous warders had been replaced, and he was fortunate in being able to make his way back to Tynemouth. After a gallant defence of the monastery, inside the castle there, for two days, he was taken prisoner and conveyed to Durham. Bamburgh continued to hold out, under the brave Countess of Northumberland and Morel, the Sheriff, until the King, having returned from Wales in November, ordered Mowbray to be led before the castle, with the menace that both his eyes should be gouged out unless it instantly submitted. A wife and a nephew chose the latter alternative, but the preservation of his eye-sight could have been of little use to the Earl in the lifelong imprisonment to which he was condemned.

The Earldom of Northumberland was now suppressed. Liulf of Bamburgh, an Englishman, was made Sheriff in the room of Morel. The estates of the Earldom were taken for the King's use, and many of them granted to the barons who had assisted in Mowbray's overthrow. The barony of Bywell, comprising St. Peter's parish there, was conferred on the Balliols, as also probably the manor of Bothal, which seems to have passed from them by marriage to the Bertrams. By the scheme formulated by Rufus for the defence of his castle of Newcastle, the Balliols were to furnish thirty men for its ward, and eleven other barons, the grantees of Carham, Bolam, Callerton, Whalton, Ellingham, Hadston, Bothal, Dilston, Gosforth, Styford, and Morpeth, twenty-six. Besides this, these same barons, with the exception of those of Morpeth and Bolam, were bound to each keep up a house in the castle, the reason for these exceptions probably being that the barons of Morpeth and Bolam had already small castles of their own. The cornage, to the payment of which they were all subject, and which has begotten a whole tribe of wild theories, ancient and modern, was probably nothing more than an old crown-rent.

Scotland, after the death of Malcolm Canmore on the Aln, had been rent with civil wars, but in 1098 Edgar Etheling, marching under the banner of St. Cuthbert, and aided by the brave English captain, Robert, son of Godwin, succeeded in placing his nephew, Malcolm's son Edgar, on the throne. Grateful for the assistance of the church of Durham, Edgar founded Coldingham as a cell of the monastery, and gave Berwick to the bishop. In 1099, however, Ralph Flambard, who had succeeded William of St. Carilef in the see, sallied out and destroyed a castle that Robert, son of Godwin, was building near Berwick, whereupon Edgar resumed possession of the town. Flambard's grant of Allerden and Haliwarstell to the monks of Durham is a curious specimen of the English then spoken :

‘ Ralf biscop greteth well alle his theines and drenges of Ealondscire and of Norhamscire. Wite ye that ice habbe getythed (given) Ste. Cuhtberht that lond in Elredene. and all that thærto belimpeth (belongeth) clæne and clacles (strifeless) and Haliwarestelle. ic habbe getythed Ste. Cuhtberht his agen (own) into his cyrce. and hua soa braues (whoso spoils) thisses breve (brief).

Crist hine (Christ him spoil) thisses lives hele (health)
and heofne rices mirde (mirth).'

Henry I.'s alienations of the crown lands in Northumberland were very extensive. Gospatric, Earl of Dunbar,
received the barony of Beanley, to be held by the grand-
serjeantry of being, as it were, hereditary mediator
between the Kings of England and Scotland; Nicholas
de Grainvill obtained the barony of Ellingham; Robert
de Muschamps, that of Wooler; Hugh de Bolbec, Styford;
Avenel de Bradford, Bradford; Robert de Umfraville,
Prudhoe; Ralph of Worcester, Hadston; Walter Espec,
the justiciary, Carham; Siward, Gosforth; Odard, son
and successor of Liulf in the shrievalty, Embleton; and
Eustace-fitz-John, lord of Alnwick, Budle and Spindleston. The priory of Tynemouth had a grant of Graffard's
land and services, which comprised Monk's Seaton,
Whitley and Shields, and a confirmation of the two halves
of Eglingham that had been given to it by Winuth the
Fisher. During the early part of the reign (1100-1118),
and probably before Henry's grants of Carham and
Beanley, his queen, Matilda, as Regent of England
during his absence in Normandy, had bestowed the
church of Carham on Durham, and Archimill's estate
of Bewick on Tynemouth. Nigel de Albini was commanded by her to demand the restitution to Bishop
Flambard of the lands Robert de Muschamps had
occupied in contravention of the partition of Ros made
by Robert de Mowbray and William of St. Carilef.

In 1120 Lothian was definitely taken away from the
spiritual rule of Durham, and made subject to the see of
Glasgow. As if in dread of losing also his temporal
possessions in the North, Bishop Flambard founded the
castle of Norham in the following year. The same distrust of the Scots probably led Henry I. to undertake
a personal survey of Northumberland in 1122. Two old
monks of St. Evroud, in Normandy, who followed him to
present their newly-chosen Abbot, found the roads of
Northumberland in their normal state of wretched repair.

Henry proceeded to Carlisle, and apparently built there the first Norman keep on the Border. Various improvements were carried out at Bamburgh about 1130, under the direction of the master-mason Osbert. In his Honour of Carham, Walter Espec built a castle of great strength on a steep ridge, or *kaim,* some 60 feet above the Tweed. This received from the country-people the name of Werch, or Wark, it having been the great work at which they were compelled to assist. If Espec's fellow justice-itinerant, Eustace-fitz-John, who married Beatrice de Vesci, the heiress of Alnwick, did not actually found the castle there, he may reasonably be credited with building the earliest portions of it now remaining.

The pillage of the villages of Errington and Dissington, connected with the new Augustinian priory of Hexham, by Robert and Uctred, sons of Meldred, in 1133, seems a last echo of English resistance, and the first instance of the raids of the wild spirits of Tyndale and Redesdale that were to work such havoc in the more settled parts of Northumberland. The Austin canons of Nostell had been granted the churches of St. Oswald and St. Aidan at Bamburgh by King Henry, 1121-1129, and he now proceeded to strike a further blow at the authority of Bishop Flambard, by erecting the see of Carlisle and appointing thereto their prior, Alfwald. Signs were not wanting that Northumberland itself might be added to the new diocese. The churches of Warkworth, Corbridge, Whittingham, and Rothbury had been given to the King's chaplain, Richard de Aurea Valle for his life; the reversion of them, together with the churches of Newburn and St. Nicholas at Newcastle, was now bestowed on the canons of Carlisle.

Henry I. died in December, 1135. David of Scotland, who had married Matilda, the only child of Earl Waltheof, refused to recognise Stephen, and entered Northumberland as the champion of his own niece, the Empress Matilda. He took Wark, Norham, Alnwick, and Newcastle, but failed to reduce Bamburgh. His march on

Durham was checked by the arrival of Stephen. An agreement was come to at Newcastle by which David received Waltheof's Earldom of Huntingdon in right of his wife, and his son Henry the land of Carlisle as part of Cumberland, the old appanage of the Scottish heir-apparent. The castles of Northumberland were given up to Stephen, but it was understood that if ever he should determine to revive the Earldom, the claims of David and his son were to be carefully borne in mind. Nothing came of this vague promise, and during Stephen's absence in Normandy, in the spring of 1137, David again crossed the Border. The English earls and barons assembled at Newcastle to resist him, but an armistice was arranged at Roxburgh by Thurstan, Archbishop of York. The question of the Earldom was again mooted on Stephen's return in November, but David met with a decided refusal. Indeed, Stephen went so far as to bestow the coveted Earldom on David's stepson, Simon de St. Liz, the eldest grandson of Waltheof, whose only record in Northumberland is his grant of a salt-pan at Warkworth to the newly-founded Cistercian abbey of Newminster.

On the dark winter's morning of January 10, 1138, William, son of Duncan, once King of Scots, attempted to seize Wark by a *coup de main*. The castle had been greatly strengthened, and Espec's nephew, Jordan de Bussei offered a stout resistance. King David and his son appeared with reinforcements, and for three weeks the siege was vigorously prosecuted with *balistæ* and other engines of war. The defence was equally spirited, and after his standard-bearer had been slain in his sight, and many others killed and wounded, David broke up his camp. William - fitz - Duncan conducted a reconnaissance to Wardon, where two of his soldiers broke into the church of St. Michael, while the King and his son, after wasting Northumberland and burning among other places the abbey of Newminster, fixed their head-quarters at Corbridge. Hearing that Stephen had outflanked them, and was on his road to Scotland, they beat a hasty retreat to

Roxburgh. Stephen's raid over the Border from Wark was brought to a sudden termination owing to his distrust of his own followers, especially of Eustace-fitz-John. After Easter, David again harried Northumberland, and was in the act of entering the city of Durham, when a mutiny among the wilder portion of his troops compelled him to return to the Tweed, where he took and dismantled the castle of Norham. He then again invested Wark, the garrison of which had several times cut off his supplies, and had fallen on his son's escort, but again he was baffled. Eustace-fitz-John now openly joined David. As they were marching together past Bamburgh, which they had not intended to attack, the young men of the place began to jeer at the Scots from behind a wall erected in front of the castle, but the Scots broke in and slew nearly a hundred of them. Having destroyed the crops at Mitford and other places, whose owners sided with Stephen, David crossed the Tees and was utterly routed at the Battle of the Standard, near Northallerton, on September 22, 1138. He had left Wark blockaded by two of his barons, and he now returned to direct the siege in person with all the forces he could rally. His engines of war were often destroyed with similar appliances by the besiegers, only one knight of whom was killed, and that during an imprudent sally. At last, about Martinmas, the castle stores were exhausted; a live horse and a salted one was all that there was left to eat, when the Abbot of Rievaulx brought a message from Walter Espec, directing the garrison to capitulate. David allowed them to march out with the honours of war, and presented them with twenty-four horses. He then razed Wark to the ground.

By the mediation of the Papal Legate, Alberic, Bishop of Ostia, and Matilda, the queen of Stephen and niece of David, a treaty was concluded at Durham in April, 1139, by which the Earldom of Northumberland was made over to Henry-fitz-David. The castles of Newcastle and Bamburgh were excepted from this grant, but David afterwards took possession of them by force. At Bamburgh, in the presence of Alfwald, Bishop of Carlisle, and Adam the Sheriff, Earl Henry conferred a charter on the monks of Tynemouth, freeing the peasants of their demesnes from the obligation of aiding in the building of Newcastle, or any of his other castles. At Newcastle at Michaelmas, 1147, he further relieved them from all military service unless an army should attack him in ' Northumberland between the Tyne and the Tweed,' a limitation implying that his Earldom of Northumberland stretched beyond those rivers, and especially over Lothian, where the same sheriff Adam attested his benefactions to Coldingham. Earl Henry gave the fishery of Bradyare in the Tyne to the monks of Durham, besides confirming to them the grant of lands at Cramlington made by a certain Nicole. He gave a salt-pan at Warkworth to the priory of Brinkburn, and confirmed William, son of Aluric of Corbridge, in his possession of Dilston. He appears to have had mints both at Bamburgh and Corbridge. His seal represents him as a tall young man on horseback.

King David's occupation of Newcastle was destined to be of great importance in municipal history, as he adopted its customs in the organization of the burghs he founded beyond the Tweed. Newcastle thus became an authority in civic matters for Scotland, such as Magdeburg was for Poland. David had himself been in possession of North Tyndale, where he granted Thornton, Staincroft, Walwick, and Hethingeshalch (Henshaw) to Richard Cumin and his wife, Hextold, a grand-daughter of King Duncan. Hextold afterwards married Malcolm-fitz-Malcolm, Earl of Athol, and, as Countess of Athol, bestowed some of these lands on the monks of Durham. A man named Sproich, who lived at Bellingham, was employed by the almoner of Durham to repair the bridges on North Tyne. His daughter Eda, a brunette, would work at her fine dress instead of going to church on St. Lawrence's Day. Her fingers suddenly became contracted, and were only restored after a draught of water from St. Cuthbert's well and a whole night spent in prayer in his church there. When Eda was to be married, Eilaf, Earl Henry's bailiff, demanded a heavy fine from her parents, and, on their refusing to pay, drove off their cow to the stable of Elsi of Wark. Sproich again invoked the aid of St. Cuthbert; Elsi's house was struck by lightning and burnt to the ground, while the cow escaped and ran home to Bellingham.

The thirteen years of Earl Henry's rule must have long been regretted in Northumberland as an era of unexampled peace and prosperity. The cloister was at that time the great civilizing agency, and the foundation of the Austin houses of Alnwick Abbey and Brinkburn Priory must have exercised a very beneficent influence.

Earl Henry died on June 12, 1152, leaving by his wife Ada, daughter and heiress of William de Warren, three sons, Malcolm, William, and David. Rousing himself with difficulty from his grief, King David took Henry's second son, a boy of ten, to Newcastle, and caused the barons of Northumberland to do him homage as their Earl. Under the style of 'William de Warren, Earl of Northumberland,' the young Earl confirmed the Brinkburn canons in the possession of their salt-pans at Warkworth. The death of Eustace-fitz-John, the aged lord of Alnwick, in an ambuscade laid by the Welsh in the defile of Coleshill, in 1157, deprived the Scottish princes of one of their chief supporters in Northumberland. Henry II. marched on to Rhuddlan, and there confirmed Eustace's son, William de Vesci, in his father's estates.

William de Vesci obtained from the young Earl William the privilege of a market at Newbiggen, near the burgh of St. Valery. It should not be forgotten that as the breeze that at last wafted the Conqueror's fleet across the Channel was ascribed to the intercession of St. Valery, the Norman lords of Alnwick may have evinced their gratitude by dedicating to him the cruciform church that crowned the mound at the mouth of the Aln, which appears to have been known in earlier times under the varying names of Twyford, Woodford, Woodchester, and Wooden.

On Henry Plantagenet's return to Chester, the young King, Malcolm IV., did homage, and gave up to him the land of Carlisle, the county of Lancaster, and the castles of Newcastle and Bamburgh, all which he had received as the heir of his grandfather, David. He obtained as compensation the Earldom of Huntingdon. The two kings met again at Carlisle in the following year, but quarrelled so much that Malcolm returned home without receiving knighthood at Henry's hands. The ground of their quarrel lay, no doubt, in Henry's high-handed resumption of the Earldom of Northumberland, which was an easy matter when once he had gained possession of Newcastle and Bamburgh. Earl William's title was not very clear, and he was, at any rate, Henry's ward during his minority. The Earldom at its origin had saved Northumberland from the Danes and Norwegians ; its extinction was now a political necessity, if Northumberland was not to become part and parcel of Scotland.

CHAPTER VI.

TYNDALE.

NO sooner had Henry of Anjou resumed possession of Northumberland, than he began to fortify it against Scotland. By a rare exercise of the royal prerogative, he erected two castles on ground belonging to private subjects; with the aid of the whole county of Northumberland and the bishopric of Durham he built the castle of Harbottle at the head of Coquetdale, while William de Vesci, now Sheriff of Northumberland, began by his orders to restore in 1158 the castle of Wark-on-Tweed, which had been destroyed by David of Scotland twenty years previously. The site of Harbottle was owned by Odinel de Umfraville, that of Wark by the family of Ros. The donjons of both castles, placed on ancient mounds, were probably octagonal in outline, with open courtyards in the middle.

Intending, in 1159, to undertake an expedition against Toulouse, Henry considered it prudent to compromise matters by restoring North and South Tyndale to the dispossessed Earl William of Northumberland, to be held as a regality by homage only, an arrangement that was to be successful, on the whole, in keeping peace between England and Scotland for upwards of a century, and in ensuring the welfare of Northumberland during that long period. Ada, the widowed Countess of Northumberland, continued to hold her dower-lands in Tyndale, and granted the manor of Whitfield, which had been reclaimed from the waste there, to her chaplain Robert. Both King Malcolm and his brother William accompanied Henry to France, and in 1163 Malcolm did homage at Woodstock. The firm peace established by this act was rendered precarious by Malcolm's delicate health, and the distrust felt by the English for William, his heir-presumptive. It was at this juncture that the square keep of Bamburgh was built.

Hugh Pudsey, the Bishop of Durham, was also fully alive to the desirability of strengthening his castle of Norham on the Tweed, if Northumberland was to be retained by England. He found Norham in a weak state of defence, and employed an engineer, named Richard, to erect the massive square keep, *turris validissima*. Richard had been given a piece of St. Cuthbert's winding-sheet by a monk of Durham, and carried it and other relics about with him in a richly-embroidered silk bag. Having one day to go to Berwick, he left this bag behind him at Norham. It was found by a French clerk, who, considering it ridiculous that such a wretched rag should be kept in so beautiful a case, threw it into a fire at which a drinking party were warming themselves. To his amazement, the flames, it is said, did the rag no harm, and after it had been subjected to them for nearly two hours, he pulled it out, and restored it to Richard on his return.

The re-construction of Prudhoe Castle by Odinel de Umfraville about this time also included the erection of a square keep. All Odinel's neighbours, either through love or fear, lent him their assistance in the work, except the men of Wylam, a village which, although it was within the barony of Prudhoe, belonged to the monastery of St. Oswin at Tynemouth, freed from all contributions to castle-building by several royal charters. Neither threats nor persuasions had any effect on the Wylam peasantry. Odinel was so enraged that he sent for one of the King's officers who lived 'without fear of God in the city of Corbridge,' and bade him, on his allegiance, seize their property and bring it to the castle. According to the law of the land, a fine for neglecting to perform a customary service like that of repairing a castle was to be levied in the first instance on the private property of the serfs, and only in the case of this proving insufficient was recourse to be had to the lord's demesne. The Corbridge official, however, in proceeding towards Wylam, announced his intention of laying hands on whatever first came in his way. In vain did his companions, Richard and Nicholas, caution him not to interfere with the herd of St. Oswin. He went straight to the pasture where the demesne oxen were grazing, but, by the miraculous interposition of the saint, these, together with the ruddy youth herding them, and his barking dog, were made invisible and inaudible to him, though Richard and Nicholas had actually to drive the oxen out of his road.

On the death of King Malcolm the Maiden in 1165, it seems to have been a question whether his Earldom of Huntingdon should not pass to his successor, William the Lion, and William's Franchise of Tyndale to their younger brother, David. As a matter of fact, William retained Tyndale, and held Huntingdon also, until it was finally settled that the latter was to be given up to David. Henry appears to have attempted to infringe the privileges of Tyndale during this state of uncertainty. Adam of Nunwick, Kiochher of Wall, and a certain Turchil Cadiol, men of the King of Scotland, were summoned before the English justices at Newcastle. They refused to appear, and the consequent fines were afterwards remitted.

William's claim to Northumberland was met by specious promises on the part of Henry, whom he attended on an expedition to Brittany. There was little idea of any outbreak of hostilities between the two kingdoms. A colony of Norbertian canons from the abbey of Blanchland, in Normandy, established themselves, by favour of Walter de Bolbec, in the green valley of the upper Derwent, and gave the name of their parent house to the spot previously known as Wulwardshope. Northumberland, it is said, was then so renowned that right down to the Pyrenees there was no country so well provided with the necessaries of life nor inhabited by a race more universally respected.

In an evil hour, William received overtures from Henry's rebellious eldest son, promising, in return for his support, to restore him the Borderland that his ancestors had held. With great moderation, the Scottish King sent the friar William Dolapene to Henry, in Normandy, and offered to remain true to him if he received Northumberland, which formed only a portion of his rightful inheritance. Dolapene demanded to have William's claim there and then submitted to ordeal of battle, or he would renounce the homage William had done; but Henry was not to be frightened. Waltheof, Earl of Dunbar, tried in vain to exercise the good offices of peacemaker between England and Scotland, as he was bound to do by his curious tenure of the barony of Beanley.

William collected a great host at Caldenlea, in Selkirkshire, containing a large element of naked savages from Galloway, who were armed with small knives, dreaded by knights in close combat, and with javelins which they could hurl to a great distance. In August, 1173, he summoned Wark to surrender. Roger de Stuteville, Sheriff of Northumberland, who was in command, entreated the King to spare him the disgrace of capitulating, and to grant him a truce of forty days, that he might cross the Channel to receive Henry's instructions, or effect the same purpose by sealed letters. William agreed to these terms. Two days later a messenger arrived from Bishop Pudsey to say that he wished to be at peace with the Scots, and would not attack them. Leaving, therefore, Norham unchallenged, the host passed on to Alnwick, where William de Vesci, the brave natural son of the lord of the castle, obtained for it the same terms as had been accorded to Wark, subject to the additional proviso that he was not to increase the garrison nor strengthen the defences. Warkworth, which Henry had given to Roger-fitz-Richard, the younger son of Eustace-fitz-John, and ancestor of the Clavering family, was singled out by William as a special object for destruction. The castle was weak, both in walls and earthworks; no attempt was made to defend it, nor did the Scots think it worth while to fix their headquarters there.

Roger-fitz-Richard himself was in charge of Newcastle, assisted by the barons who owed it castle-ward. The Scots, they knew, would not leave them an ox for the plough in all their lands; still, they scorned to parley, and although the process of re-modelling the castle had not been completed, the square keep founded the previous year being still in the hands of the masons, William saw that it was useless to attempt its reduction by fair means.

The conduct of Odinel de Umfraville, who had been brought up at his father's court, and had been one of the members of his own Northumbrian household to the last, in now declaring against him, was regarded by William as the basest ingratitude. ' May I,' he cried, ' be cursed and excommunicated, if I grant term or respite to the castle of Odinel!' Accordingly, marching up the Tyne, he bade his earls and barons pitch their pavilions before the slopes of Prudhoe. ' As long as Prudhoe stands,' he declared, ' never shall there be peace.'

His camp, however, fell a prey to divided counsels. The Flemish mercenaries swore they would destroy the castle, or forego all claim to pay or rations; the Scottish lords refused to hear of the delay incident to a formal siege, and successfully urged the King to push on to the conquest of Cumberland. The advance of Richard de Lucy caused William to abandon the siege of Carlisle and retreat to Roxburgh. Lucy and his levies laid Berwick in ashes, and wasted Lothian; but, on hearing of the landing of a Flemish force in Suffolk, they were glad to accept the truce till the Feast of St. Hilary, which the barons of Northumberland purchased for three hundred marks of silver. Before the expiry of this truce on January 13, 1174, Bishop Pudsey came himself to Ridingburn on the

Border, and obtained a prolongation of it till Easter. As soon as that festival was past, William, remembering Stuteville's defiance, resolved to carry Wark by storm. His Flemings rushed bravely to the moats, and tried to force their way through the portcullis. They were beaten back, many of them being rendered incapable of ever again raising their war-cry of 'Arras! Arras!' Stuteville cautioned his men not to waste their arrows, but to reserve their strength for real emergencies.

'Bring up the *perière !'* roared the Lion-king, seeing his men falling on all sides ; ' unless our engineer is a liar, the stones hurled from it will soon break through the gate, and we shall gain the bailey without more delay.'

The machine was moved into action, but the first stone, instead of shattering the castle gate, brought one of the Scottish knights to the ground, and would have finished him had it not been for his shield and armour. William in a frenzy swore that he would rather have been taken alive before Toulouse than witness such a discomfiture. He gave orders to try and set the castle on fire, but the wind suddenly shifting prevented the execution of this design. Thoroughly disheartened, he broke up his camp the next day, and again retreated to Roxburgh. Stuteville, like a true knight, ordered the men in his garrison not to rail at the discomfited Scots, but to give expression to their joy, each in his own fashion. Wark soon resounded with trumpet and horn, but there was no abuse nor rough language, only songs and ballads wishing the Scots farewell. The irritation of the Lion-king can easily be imagined. He swore by St. Andrew and St. James that he would never end the war in such disgrace ; no, not if it should cost him his kingdom.

Having arranged a truce with the governor of Carlisle, William made a sudden dash for Prudhoe, in the hope of surprising the castle. Reaching it on the evening of Monday, July 8, his disappointment was great at finding that Odinel had put it into an excellent state of defence. The garrison knew that if it were taken scant mercy would be shown to Odinel, so they persuaded him to mount his rough-haired, dapple-bay steed, and spur night and day to the Archbishop of York. Enraged at his escape, the whole host of Scotland attacked the castle with a great shout. The garrison defended themselves manfully against the Flemings, and received no injuries, while many of the assailants were mortally wounded. Not content with destroying the corn-fields and wasting the gardens, the Scots, in a spirit of petty spite, stripped the bark off the apple-trees. Finding it impossible to reduce Prudhoe with his spears and arrows, and hearing from Roger de Mowbray that the whole force of Yorkshire was advancing against him, the Lion-king raised the siege on the Friday morning.

Duncan of Fife, with the Scots, was now ordered to ravage the sea-coast, and not to leave a house or church standing; while the men of Galloway were to kill Odinel's vassals in Redesdale. The King himself, with a small company of Frenchmen and Flemings, rode off to Alnwick, where the others were to rejoin him. That same evening, Odinel, with other northern barons, and sixty of the Archbishop of York's knights, accompanied by the garrisons of Prudhoe and Newcastle, set out on a night-march from Newcastle to Alnwick. They concealed themselves in a coppice, and sent a spy to report on William's movements.

The King of Scots was in full armour that Saturday morning. His five hundred knights bade him be of good courage, as Northumberland was his. As the July sun rose high, the heat became intense, and the King laid aside his helmet in order to dine in front of the castle. Suddenly cries of ' Glanvile, chevaliers ! ' and ' Baliol ! ' broke from the coppice, and Odinel and his companions were bearing down on the disarmed monarch. William quickly mounted his gray charger, and unhorsed the first knight he encountered. Indeed, the English were on the point of being repulsed, when a foot-soldier stabbed the King's horse with his lance, and brought it and the rider to the ground. Lying helplessly, with his horse on top

9

of him, while the battle was fiercely raging, the King was at once rescued and captured by Ralph de Glanvile. Roger de Mowbray and Adam de Port, two of William's English confederates, were glad to escape early from the field. Alan de Lascelles, an old Scottish knight, who had not jousted for thirty years, made nevertheless a good fight of it on his gray war-horse. William de Mortimer, raging like a wild boar, was laid low by Bernard de Baliol; Raoul le Rus could not withstand the hundred who set upon him at once, and Richard Maluvel, after a glorious struggle, was reluctantly forced to surrender. Besides the prisoners taken away by Odinel and his companions, nearly a hundred Scottish knights were left to settle their ransoms with William de Vesci. The Lion-king himself was mounted on a palfrey, and led to Newcastle by Ralph de Glanvile.

At the very time of this conflict before Alnwick, Duncan of Fife, literally carrying out the orders he had received, was burning the town of Warkworth and putting the inhabitants to the sword, not sparing even those who had taken refuge in the ' minster ' of St. Lawrence. The men of Galloway, after wasting Redesdale, appear to have captured the castle of Harbottle, but the booty they collected before it fell into the hands of Ralph de Glanvile. Two Northumbrians, Edgar Unnithing of Edlingham, the uncle of Waltheof, Earl of Dunbar, and Thomas de Muschamps, had openly joined the Scots. The former lost his lands in consequence, while Richard Cumin was heavily mulcted for not appearing before the English justices, and Walter Corbet judged it prudent to avoid being put on his trial by compounding. Bishop Pudsey, too, made his peace for a large sum, giving Norham, among other castles, into the King's custody.

By a convention and fine made between the captive King of Scots and his lord, Henry of England, at Falaise in Normandy, the bishops, clergy, earls and barons of Scotland became the liegemen of Henry, and the three castles of Roxburgh, Edinburgh, and Berwick were delivered up to him. William was then allowed to return to Scotland, where he founded the abbey of Arbroath, in honour of St. Thomas of Canterbury, who had been his personal friend, and at whose shrine Henry was kneeling in penitence at the very time of the fight at Alnwick. On Arbroath, William bestowed the church of Halt-whistle, in Tyndale.

In order to raise money for the Crusades, Richard Lion-heart, for the consideration of ten thousand marks, freed William from all bargains that had been extorted from him during his captivity in Normandy, and gave up also the castles of Roxburgh and Berwick. William, how-ever, was completely to perform whatever his brother Malcolm had done, or ought to have done, in the way of homage.

Richard, moreover, sold the earldom of Northumber-land to Hugh Pudsey, Bishop of Durham, for £11,000. ' See what a clever craftsman I am,' he remarked, 'to make a young earl out of an old bishop!' One of the few documents left relating to the rule of Hugh, Earl of North-umberland is an agreement made before his justiciary, Henry Pudsey, in the court of Eustace de Baliol at Wood-horn, between Gilbert Delaval and Edwulf, son of Robert. For half the township of Halliwell, Edwulf, besides other feudal services, was to pay ten shillings a year rent. He was to find Gilbert twenty-six men for reaping two days in autumn, and to do one day's ploughing with his men. Gilbert was to feed them once a day. Edwulf's men were also to do a quarter of the work of maintaining the mill of Halliwell, and to give every thirteenth bowl as multure, besides feeding the miller the days they ground there. If in summer there was not water enough to turn the mill of Halliwell, then they were to take their corn to the mill of Seaton Delaval.

On Richard's return from his captivity, William of Scotland bore the sword of state at the coronation at Winchester which was to efface that disgrace. On the occasion of this journey the Scottish King received a confirmation of the curious rights that had been attached to the homage for Lothian. He was to be paid five pounds a day on his road to and from the English Court. While there he was to receive every day thirty shillings, a dozen of the King's own wafers and cracknels, a liberal supply of wine, forty candles of the King's own sort, eighty of the sort used by the royal household, two pounds of pepper and four of cinnamon. The Bishop of Durham and the sheriff and barons of Northumberland were to receive him on the Marches and conduct him to the Tees.

Pudsey, having good reason to dread Richard's resentment, voluntarily surrendered the Earldom of Northumberland with the castles of Newcastle and Bamburgh into the King's hands. The King of Scots made Richard an offer of fifteen thousand marks for it. To this Richard consented, provided the castles were reserved. On this point the negotiations broke off. Pudsey, anxious to outbid William, sent a messenger after Richard to Normandy, offering twenty thousand marks for the county and castles, and put off the restitution of them to Hugh Bardolf, the King's Sheriff, until the messenger should return. Richard directed Bardolf to re-deliver them on receiving sufficient surety for the twenty thousand marks. Bardolf insisted that he must have possession of them before he could re-deliver them. Pudsey contended that, if he was to receive them back, there was no need to give them up. Richard took Bardolf's part, and ordered him to resume possession of the county and castles, which he did on July 1, 1194. The final incorporation of Northumberland in the realm of England was thus the consequence of the most paltry hair-splitting.

At the beginning of King John's reign a great flood carried away the bridge of Berwick. Philip of Poictou, then Bishop of Durham, objected to the Scots rebuilding the south abutment on his land. He went so far as to build a *Malvoisin* at Tweedmouth, to protect that port against the castle of Berwick. On Philip's death, John kept the bishopric vacant for eight years. In 1208 he met William of Scotland at Bolton, near Alnwick, and concluded a convention at Norham, whereby the Scots were empowered to destroy the Malvoisin at Tweedmouth, and the monopoly of the Tweed was secured to Berwick. A dispute between the Prior of Kirkham and the Abbot of Kelso respecting the church of Kirknewton was destined to find an echo, ages after, in the extraordinary plea set up by the churchwardens against the Archdeacon of Northumberland, that their parish was in Scotland. In 1211 another conference of the Kings took place at Norham, a galley with fifty boatmen being kept for their use on the Tweed. The soft words of Queen Ermengarde of Scotland ensured the maintenance of peace.

During his visits to Northumberland, John had stayed at Alnwick at his own cost. Its inhospitable lord, Eustace de Vesci, now refused to give his son as a hostage for his loyalty, and John ordered his property to be confiscated and his castle destroyed. William of Scotland had never forgotten the rough lesson he received at the siege of Alnwick, but his young son and successor, Alexander II., claiming Northumberland in its fullest extent in 1215, received the homage of the barons of Northumberland at Felton, and that of those of Yorkshire at Melrose. His forty days' siege of Norham proved, however, a fiasco. Having made his peace with Rome, King John resolved to chastise his rebellious baronage. In ungovernable rage he burnt the castles that the barons had deserted, and the villages and crops that had not already been fired to retard his advance, so that all Northumberland was one conflagration. Mitford and Morpeth, Alnwick and Wark, were all in flames. Taking the town and castle of Berwick, John handed over the inhabitants to his German mercenaries, who strung them up by their hands and feet, being assisted in this by the Jews. After ravaging Lothian, he returned to Berwick, and commenced the destruction of the town by himself setting on fire the house in which he had been entertained. On the death of this royal incendiary, King Alexander besieged

Mitford for a week in vain. Peace was soon afterwards established by the Papal Legate.

Richard de Umfraville complained in 1218 that Philip de Ulcotes, who had been a powerful favourite of King John, was building a castle at Nafferton, where no castle had previously existed, to the detriment of his castle and lands of Prudhoe. A writ, in the name of Henry III., commanded Ulcotes to stay the work. Thereupon he revenged himself by obtaining royal letters ordering the destruction of Umfraville's castle at Harbottle. It needed the protection of Hubert de Burgh to prove that Harbottle was not an adulterine stronghold. The great *bretesche,* or projecting wooden story on top of the tower at Nafferton, was cast down by the Sheriff of Northumberland, and taken with the rest of the building timber to Newcastle. The extensive earthworks and ruined walls of Ulcotes' intended castle on the tangled bank of Whittledene still remind us of this neighbourly episode.

The marriage of Alexander II. to the sister of Henry III. in 1221 tended to cement the good relations subsisting between the two kingdoms. On the occasion of this ceremony the privilege of holding a market on Thursdays at Thornton in Tyndale was granted to William Cumin, the Scottish justiciary. The next year, Robert de Ros and the Prior of Kirkham complained that the Scots had made an encroachment at Whitelaw, near Carham, and the Sheriff of Northumberland was instructed to proceed there, with the Bishop of Durham or his officials, and settle the boundary as it had been in the time of King John. So profound, however, was the tranquillity of the Border, that an entail of the barony of Wark, made with the consent of Henry III., stipulated that it was to be held by the annual delivery of a soar-hawk at Roxburgh Fair.

Alexander II. granted Tyndale to his youngest sister, Margery, reserving only the feudal services of William Cumin at Tarset, and of William de Ros at Haltwhistle, together with the patronage of the church of Simundburn. Margery gave Chirden, on North Tyne, to David de

Lindsay. If she married any but a Scotsman, she was to receive other lands in Scotland in lieu of Tyndale, and in 1235 she did marry the Earl of Pembroke.

An appeal made to the Pope by the Archbishop of York against the coronation of Alexander II. as an infringement of the rights of his metropolitan see and of the royal dignity of England, was ratified by Henry III. This nettled the Scottish King into demanding, under threat of war, the restitution of the three Northern counties as his rightful inheritance. There was a real war scare in 1237. Hugh de Bolbec, the Keeper of Northumberland, wrote in all haste to Henry to say that David de Lindsay was building a tower in Tyndale with remarkably thick walls. It was already finished up to the lines of the battlements, and Lindsay intended to crenellate it and surround it with a moat, all with the approbation of the King of Scotland. If the fortifications were completed and stores laid in, Bolbec considered that the tower—Dally Castle, no doubt—would become an admirable trysting-place for the King's enemies. On the English side, Bolbec received orders to execute repairs at Newcastle and Bamburgh, where the curtain-wall was to be raised in places, a new turret to be built, and a half-finished one completed. The Legate Ottobuoni contrived to arrange a definite pacification, by the terms of which Alexander eventually received certain manors in Cumberland. Bolbec was then instructed to spend as little as possible on the castles in his charge. It was during this lull that the Carmelite priory of Hulne was founded, in a romantic situation near Alnwick, by one of the Vescis. He had returned from the Holy Land with a Freburn of Cartington, who became the first Prior. In journeying through the royal forest in Northumberland, the Scottish barons were at this time allowed to take an occasional deer. If any knight was ill, or any lady in a state of expectancy, and had a longing for venison, it was customary for the Chief Justice of the Forest to present it.

In 1242, Walter Bisset, having been foiled by the young

Earl of Athol in a tournament at Haddington, was accused of roasting him alive with his companions in the barn where they slept. Under the circumstances, a regular trial was impossible in Scotland, and Bisset, escaping to England, appealed to Henry as suzerain. Alexander retorted by declaring that he neither did nor would hold even the smallest part of his kingdom of the King of England. There were other differences, such as the erection of a castle on the East March and another on the West by Walter Cumin and other Scottish nobles, in violation of old-standing agreements, and Henry, worked on by the wiles of Bisset, resolved to invade Scotland. The King of Tyrconnel and other Irish chiefs were summoned to assist him. Cross-bow bolts and other munitions of war were to be sent to Newcastle. Henry assembled there 5,000 horsemen, in fine armour. Alexander advanced as far as Ponteland with only 1,000 horsemen (mounted on good enough chargers, 'though not Spanish, Italian, or others of great price,' and sufficiently well provided with armour of iron or chain-work), but, then, he had 100,000 foot. Richard of Cornwall, Henry's brother, took upon him the character of mediator; and a 'Parliament' was held in the standing corn of the nuns of Newcastle. Alexander bound himself to keep the peace towards his liege-lord, and not to enter into any treaty of war against England or Ireland, except in requital of injuries. As a minor point, Henry restored to Nicholas de Soules and Annora his wife their lands at Stamfordham and Stocksfield, which had been taken into the King's hands as possessions of Normans. The building of the Black Gate as the main entrance to the castle of Newcastle shows that too much confidence was not placed in the peace thus concluded.

An attempt was made the next year to settle the old-standing boundary dispute between the canons of Carham and Bernard de Hawden. Hugh Bolbec, the sheriff, accompanied by the knights of Northumberland, met David de Lindsay, justiciary of Lothian, Patrick, Earl of

Dunbar, and other knights sent by the King of Scots, at Ridingburn (Revedeneburne). Six knights were chosen from Scotland and six from England to make a true perambulation at this debatable point. Like a modern Conciliation Board, the six English knights, with one consent, proceeded by what they declared to be the right and ancient marches, the six Scottish knights wholly dissenting. Bolbec and the justiciary and the earl then agreed to add six more knights on each side, but the result was the same. Choosing to consider that the Scottish knights stood in the way of business, Bolbec, as directed by his King, caused twenty-four knights of Northumberland to be sworn. These declared the true and ancient marches to be from the Tweed by Ridingburn southwards to the Three Carrs, thence in a straight line to Hoperiglaw, and so to Whitelaw. They were prevented from making a perambulation by the threats of the justiciary and the earl, so they signed, sealed, and delivered a document containing their verdict. At the end of the following year, the perambulation was effected by twelve English knights, in the presence of four English justices and of the Scottish justiciary, Nicholas de Soules, then sheriff of Roxburgh, and others, with the slight variation that the line, instead of crossing the Three Carrs themselves, made for a certain spring on the south side of them.

A little later, Nicholas de Soules was impleaded before the King of England for transgressions his men of Scotland, dwelling in Scotland, had committed in England. The King of Scots complained; and this time a panel of six English and six Scottish knights, convened at the march on the Tweed, did agree authoritatively to lay down that, according to march law and custom, no one of either kingdom, although holding land in both, was liable to be impleaded anywhere but at the march for any deed done in one kingdom by men dwelling in the other.

The principles of Border jurisprudence were still more clearly enunciated in the code drawn up by twelve knights

of each country at Ridingburn, on the feast of SS.
Tiburtius and Valerian, April 14, 1249. As a general
rule, those living on the East March were to answer at
Ridingburn, those on the West March at Lamyford, the
division between the Marches at the time being at 'Dedy,'
probably Deadwater, at the head of North Tyne ; but the
men of Redesdale and Coquetdale were to answer at
Gamelspeth, and those of the shires of Carlisle and Dum-
fries at the Solway. This mention of the shire of Carlisle
instead of Cumberland, and that, too, in a rider, points
to this code being only a digest of much more ancient
ones. Bondsmen escaping across the Border might be
seized and brought back within forty days by their lord
or his bailiff. After that time it became necessary for the
lord to obtain a brief from the sovereign of the country
in which they had taken refuge and to substantiate his
own oath by that of six others before he could recover
them. A similar *septima manus* on the Marches was required to defend a debt alleged to be owing to an in-
habitant of the other country. If the debt was admitted,
and bankruptcy pleaded, then the debtor had to swear
that he did not possess goods worth more than five
shillings and fourpence, and, further, that he would pay
as soon as possible, reserving only his own sustenance.
Stolen goods were to be sued for by means of a *septima
manus* in the court of the lord on whose land they were
found, but if the possessor claimed them, then the
question had to be decided by a combat on the Marches.
A malefactor fleeing across the Border might obtain peace
at the first church by ringing the bells, and was then not
liable to be brought back. A combat respecting a horse,
ox, cow, or hog, might be avoided by the possessor informing the claimant that upon inquiry he found the claim
just, and then driving the animal in question safely through
the mid-stream of the Tweed or the Esk.

At his marriage with Margaret, daughter of Henry III.,
at York, in 1251, Alexander III., a boy of eleven, did
homage for Lothian and the other lands he held of the King

of England in the kingdom of England. Through the influence of Henry, Alan Durward, the chief minister of the
young King, was replaced by Walter Cumin. Durward,
however, regained Henry's favour by the courage he displayed when with him in Guienne, and the young Queen
of Scots complained bitterly of the treatment she received
at the hands of Cumin. Henry was especially enraged
against Robert de Ros and John Baliol, whom he had
particularly favoured in Northumberland. In 1255 Durward arranged to surprise Edinburgh. He obtained
possession of the young couple, and conveyed them to
Roxburgh. Henry resolved to take up his residence with
his Queen at Wark. There had been a long dispute over
the actual ownership of the castle, and the King promised
Robert de Ros that his occupation of it should be without
prejudice. From Chillingham Henry granted a safe conduct to Alexander and his Queen to come to him at Wark.
They were to return when they liked, and were not to
tarry in England, except at the will of the magnates
of Scotland. Alexander returned to Roxburgh the evening of his visit, but Margaret remained at Wark in consequence of her mother's illness. The Scots viewed this
with suspicion, so Henry gave a solemn bond that she
should be restored when Queen Eleanor was sufficiently
recovered to leave. The Durward party were restored
to power in Scotland, and Henry imposed heavy fines
on Baliol and Ros for their alleged transgressions against
his daughter. Ros, indeed, who was the most powerful
baron in the North, was absolutely ruined, and Robert de
Cargou, his servant, sustained the greatest damages by
the work-oxen and other cattle being distrained. Cumin
contrived to possess himself of Alexander's person in
1257, and drove the Durward party from Scotland. Wark
and Norham were entrusted by Henry to Robert de
Neville, with orders to prepare an expedition intended
to rescue the young King. Neville was to receive
William de Moray, one of Henry's partizans, into Wark,
but was to prudently keep the inner bailey and the

donjon in his own hands. An agreement, however, was brought about between the two Scottish factions, and in the general peace that ensued the charges against Ros were withdrawn, his huge fine remitted, and all claim on Wark renounced by the Crown.

This change of policy with regard to Scotland was largely caused by the dissensions which had arisen between Henry and his barons with Simon de Montfort at their head. In the civil war that broke out, William Cumin, Robert de Ros, William de Vesci, Roger Bertram, and Robert de Hilton took Montfort's side. At the Battle of Lewes, where Henry, his eldest son Edward, and his brother Richard were taken prisoners, John Baliol, Robert Bruce, and John Cumin also fell into Montfort's hands. One of the results of this was the issue of a writ against Henry Spring, the constable of Bamburgh, to answer the complaint of the men of Bamburgh and Shorston, that he exacted certain unwonted services from them. It would almost seem that Spring thought it better to declare against Montfort in consequence. Two months later, the men of Bamburgh complained of the losses they suffered from certain rebels in the castle, and the Sheriff was ordered to proceed there with the *posse comitatus* and prevent any further sallies of these ultra-royalists. From Evesham, where the fortunes of war were reversed, John de Vesci escaped to the North, carrying with him the foot of Simon de Montfort, which, encased in a silver shoe, was treasured as a relic in Alnwick Abbey till the Reformation. Vesci re-seized the castle of Alnwick, but the Lord Edward coming against him, he was obliged to surrender. The cost of defending Bamburgh for a year during this revival of the rebellion in the North amounted to over twelve hundred pounds.

At the siege of Alnwick, Gilbert de Umfraville (who had already obtained the grant of a weekly market and a fair at Whelpington for his services), denounced William de Douglas to the Lord Edward as having been concerned in the rebellion, and obtained a grant of the manor of Fawdon conditionally on the charge being true. On inquiry, it proved to be false, and Douglas was reinstated. Thereupon Gilbert sent a hundred of the King's army, some of them outlaws from Redesdale, to Fawdon, July 19, 1267, and set Douglas's house on fire in three places. They wounded his son William, who was to become so famous in Scottish history, very severely in the neck, nearly cutting off his head. Douglas himself and others they led prisoners to Harbottle, and carried off silver spoons, cups, mazers, clothing, arms, and jewels, such as gold rings and gold 'fermails,' to the value of £100. Our sympathy with Douglas is somewhat abated on learning that, having bought some property at Fawdon in 1264, he had summarily ejected Gilemin de Wooler, who had just taken a six years' lease of it, and it was not till five years later that Gilemin obtained tardy and scanty compensation.

In the wild state the country was in, a license to crenellate must have had an especial value. John Cumyn was allowed to fortify his 'camera' in the manor of Tarset with a ditch and wall of stone and lime, and to embattle it, without let or hindrance from the King and his heirs, provided it were enclosed and embattled like the 'camera' of Adam de Gesemuth at Heaton. The latter was, no doubt, the ruin in Heaton Park, at the east end of Newcastle, popularly called King John's Palace.

The assize-rolls of the English justices at Newcastle, and of those of the King of Scotland at Wark, in Tyndale, are full of incidents that throw strong side-lights on Northumbrian life in the latter half of the thirteenth century. It is a pity that we have no similar rolls for Redesdale, the lord of which held his own court, though a knight of the Northumbrian *comitatus* was appointed by the justices at Newcastle to see that right was done. Fugitive serfs were constantly being claimed by their lords, but sometimes the verdict was in their favour. Ralph le Lorimer, who had run away from Roger

Mauduit in 1262, was able to prove that his grandfather was a freeman from Normandy. Adam Wyther and his brother, whom it was attempted to keep in bondage at Mousen, established the fact of their father having come with their grandfather from Flanders. Others were not so fortunate; William of Killingworth was delivered, with all his goods and offspring, to his master at Weteslade. Others again, like Ralph of Fishwick at Lucker, purchased their liberty.

The manorial lords had begun to enclose the common lands, but did not always have their own way. Roger-fitz-Roger shut the free sokemen out of a portion of the wood of Rothbury, where they had been accustomed to graze their stock, and bought off the parson's opposition by presenting him with six acres of the common pasture. The tenants of the Lees in Langley barony complained that Nicholas de Boltby had imparked the wood by which they went to Haydon church and Corbridge market. He replied that he had left them a road on either side of it. The importance of Corbridge as a market-town appears also from the presentments that the road to it from Newcastle had been rendered dangerous by pitfalls, and that the bailiffs of Bywell and Newbrough had begun to levy unjust tolls on the market-folk. The King's officers at Corbridge fair tried to put down cattle-lifting. They asked Uctred of Butterby for a surety that he had honestly acquired two oxen and a cow he was trying to sell. Thereupon, as he had stolen them, he fled to the church for sanctuary. The churches of St. John, St. Nicholas and St. Mary Magdalen at Newcastle were the habitual refuges of the numerous prisoners who escaped from the county gaol. Ralph 'le Messir de Pleden' is recorded to have jumped over the castle wall and gained the church of Gateshead. Two notorious highwaymen lay loaded with fetters and secured with double doors and great bolts in the strong prison in the basement of the keep. They made, it is said, a practice of fasting on bread and water every Saturday, and saying three hundred 'Ave

Marias' every day. On the night of the Assumption, A.D. 1265, Our Lady appeared to them, asking, 'Why lie ye idle? Wherefore go ye not forth?' Immediately their fetters became as wax, the doors flew back on their hinges, and the great dogs in the courtyard were struck dumb. Making a rope of their clothes, they let themselves down over the curtain-wall. Notwithstanding this legend, the keeper of the gaol was found guilty of connivance at their escape. At Alnwick, a Scot named Simon, who had been confined in the castle for stealing a mare, broke out of the prison. Killing the porter and another man, he took the keys, opened the gate, and escaped to the church. There he abjured the country before the coroner.

The difficulty of keeping malefactors in prison was, perhaps, one reason for executing summary justice upon them. William Yrrumpers was beheaded at Wooler for stealing seven skins. Stephen Slingsby, a Lincolnshire man, who had stolen a horse from a dyer there, was overtaken and beheaded at Mitford. Two sailors from Dunwich were hanged at Tynemouth for stealing clothes. Malcolm of Thirlwall, an outlaw, who came with a band of thieves to Redpeth and killed Robert, son of Thurkil of Blenkinsop, with a sword, had his head cut off on the spot. As in the case of Emma of Wauchope, near Kielder, who was decapitated for theft at Bellingham, time was not always allowed for the arrival of the coroner, who, it must be remembered, acted as a sort of *juge d'instruction* in prosecutions of all sorts. The most extraordinary case of all was certainly that of Gilbert of Nithsdale, a Scot who had associated himself with a hermit named Seman from Bottisham. In consequence of a dispute in going over the moors, Gilbert beat the poor hermit and left him half dead, after robbing him of his clothes and one penny. He had not gone far before he met Ralph of Belford, a King's officer, who arrested him as a rogue and took him to Alnwick. Thither also came Seman. The bailiff and men of the town heard the case, and according to the custom of the country, that the injured person was to himself act as executioner, the hermit beheaded Gilbert and received his clothes for so doing. A stranger who stole four geese at Newbrough must have considered himself fortunate in only having one ear cut off. On the miller of Bellingham being found guilty of appropriating a boll of his lord's meal, the justices of Tyndale thought it wrong to mulct him in life or limb for so small an offence, and so fined him a mark.

Few criminals were left for the judges of assize to dispose of. William Coleman was drawn and hanged by their sentence for the murder of Henry de Ilderton; William Fisher of Kestern was hanged for killing Gilbert of Farnley, and Stephen of Coniscliff for a murder at Stanton.

Suicides were of comparatively rare occurrence. There were so many opportunities of losing your life that it was not worth while to take it yourself. Richard de Newton, Master of the hospital of St. Margaret in the Westgate of Newcastle, and Beatrice de Roddam, who hanged herself in a small tower at Newton-on-the-Moor, were the most noted cases of *felo de se.*

The instrument that was the immediate cause of death was forfeited as a deodand. The parson's man at Rothbury was returning with a cask of wine in a waggon, when, having imbibed too freely, he fell under the wheel and was killed. Oxen, waggon and wine all escheated to the Church, and had to be redeemed. Adam Aydrunken—there were at least two persons with that festive surname at the time—was drowned in a boat on the Tyne at Newbrough, in the franchise of Tyndale. The question of the seizure of the boat as a deodand was complicated by the fact of its having first touched the shore within the county of Northumberland.

Fishing regulations were sufficiently stringent. Those who had *gurgites* or salmon-traps on the Tyne might remove them to mid-stream, that is to say, as far as their land went, if they got filled up with sand; but when John de Ridel removed his in A.D. 1252, Robert de Nevill, the

Sheriff and Constable of Newcastle, came with men armed with bows and arrows and hatchets, and destroyed it. At the assizes of A.D. 1269 it was unanimously agreed by the twelve jurors taken both from the north and the south of the Coquet, with the consent of the whole *comitatus* (as well of the knights as of the other freemen), that during October and November there was to be no fishing in the Tyne, Wansbeck, Coquet, Blyth, Aln, Till, and Glen, while during May and June no net was to be placed in the pools or mill-sluices unless the mesh were sufficiently large to let the small salmon pass. In Tyndale the millers of Wark and Edingham got into trouble for fishing in close time, while the *terrarius* of Hexham was charged with sending men to fish in Grindon Lough without leave.

The fishing rights of the Constable of Newcastle gave rise to constant disputes, and his arbitrary conduct was freely denounced. A sailor of Norway swore that he would never come to Newcastle again nor advise anyone else to do so during William Heron's tenure of office. This protest was supported by a merchant named Punce, whose wine Heron had seized at a fixed price and then resold at a profit.

The abduction of Denise de Bechefield from Milburn Moor, on Monday, August 22, 1271, probably had little romance about it. The daughter of John de Witton, Denise, had married Gilbert de Ba, a farmer of four bovates at Bechefield near Belsay, which she purchased after his death, and so acquired the local surname. She was thus a well-to-do widow when Walter de Swetehope carried her off to Roxburgh, as she was returning from Newcastle in the company of her uncle, and in vain endeavoured to force her to marry his son. After this escapade, Walter had little right to complain when, a few years later, Gilbert de Umfraville pulled down his house at Doctrees and carried off the timber, taking at the same time two of Swetehope's heifers and their calves to his forest of Redesdale, where he marked them with his own iron brand.

The Bishop of Durham continued to complain of Scottish encroachments at Tweedmouth, but the three carucates of land at Carham which had been such a fruitful subject of international arbitration would, it seems, have been recovered by the canons of Kirkham, under an award of twelve English and twelve Scottish knights made in Lent, A.D. 1286, had it not been for the untimely death of Alexander III. This, followed as it was by that of the King's only grandchild, ' The Maid of Norway,' entirely altered the relations between the two kingdoms.

The last days of Scottish rule in Tyndale were disgraced by a serious outrage. The Rector of Whitfield was seized by the servants of Sir Simon Fraser, and hurried off to Scotland with his feet tied under a sumpter-horse. At the end of a week he was left for dead in the forest of Selkirk at midnight. Imagining that they had got rid of him, Sir Simon's cousins, Beatrice de Whitfield and her son, took possession of his property. As William Fraser, another cousin, was the Scottish Chancellor, the Rector declared that there was no hope of his obtaining justice in Tyndale.

CHAPTER VII.

THE GREAT WARS.

EDWARD LONGSHANKS betrayed no undue haste to interfere in the affairs of Scotland. It was not until May, 1290, that, in the solemn Norman nave of the church of Norham, he explicitly declared that he was come in' the character of supreme and direct lord, to maintain the tranquillity of that kingdom, and to mete impartial justice to the numerous claimants of its crown. In a conference held on the greensward of Holywell Haugh, immediately opposite the castle of Norham, these claimants unanimously recognised Edward's suzerainty, and agreed to abide by his decision. Judgment was solemnly pronounced at Berwick in favour of John Baliol, who, among other great estates in England, owned the barony of Bywell. The new King swore fealty to Edward at Norham, and, having dined with him at Newcastle on Christmas Day, did homage on the morrow in the Moot Hall.

The franchise of Tyndale was also delivered to Baliol as the heir of Alexander III., but in order to settle the appeal of Anthony Bek, Bishop of Durham, to Edward, claiming the towns of Berwick and Haddington, he granted it to that rapacious prelate, to be held in free alms by himself and his successors—a grant afterwards repudiated by the English kings, on the ground that Baliol was in covert rebellion at the time. Acting as

Rufus did to Malcolm at Gloucester, Edward refused to allow the disputed boundary between England and Scotland at Carham and Brigham to be settled on the spot according to the practices of march law, reserving it for his own supreme court. Other instances soon occurred to prove to the Scots that the Lord Paramount they had spontaneously given themselves was no King Log, and they entered into a secret treaty with France in order to rid themselves of him.

Still, there were no certain signs of the coming storm. So late as the Michaelmas of 1295, Ellen de Prenderlath, a Scottish lady who had been for eight years a damsel of the late Queen of Norway, and had on that account received a considerable legacy under the will of Alexander III., did not hesitate to invest the whole of it in a mortgage secured by a lease of Moneylaws in Northumberland.

Matters were precipitated by the Scottish garrison of Berwick all at once burning some English ships that had entered that harbour, and slaughtering the crews. Baliol, summoned to Newcastle, refused to appear. Edward collected there an army of 4,000 heavy-armed horse and 30,000 foot, and receiving word from William de Ros that his brother Robert, lord of the great Border castle of Wark-on-Tweed, and also of that of Sanquhar in Scotland, had elected to side with the Scots, owing to his love for the unworthy Christiane de Mowbray, he despatched a thousand men to occupy Wark. These were suddenly roused in their night-quarters at Pressen by the cry, 'Death to the English!' Robert de Ros and the Scots had surrounded the village, and anyone who did not answer the password, 'Tabard,' with 'Over the tunic,' was immediately butchered. The English leader barely escaped with the loss of his horse and arms. Edward thanked God that up to that time his hands were innocent of blood, and that his enemies, by invading England, had taken the responsibility of the war on their own heads.

He marched to Wark himself, and immediately after

Easter invested Berwick from the Scottish side. Three of his ships going aground in the river distracted the attention of the garrison, and the young English knights, putting their horses at the low fortifications then surrounding the town, effected a victorious entry. Seven thousand citizens of this Alexandria of the North are said to have been put to the sword before Edward, noticing a woman slain with a child at her side, gave orders for the massacre to cease. Thirty Flemish merchants held out in their tower, called the Red Hall, till the evening, when they perished in its flames. The castle was forced to surrender, but the soldiers in it were released on parole. The King did not disdain to follow the advice,

> 'Waune thou havest Berwick, pike thee ;
> Waune thou havest geten, dike thee,'

which the Scots defiantly cast in his teeth. He himself set to work with a shovel and barrow in making the great ditch which was to defend the town from the north.

Robert de Ros and the Earls of Athol and Menteith, who, with a horde of 40,000, were afraid to attack Edward at Berwick, plundered the monastery of Carham, and besieged the castle of Harbottle for two days in vain, killing the deer in the park. They then ravaged Redesdale and Coquetdale, and reduced Tyndale to cinders and charcoal. They burnt the town of Corbridge, roasting alive 200 boys in the school. On Wednesday, April 11, accompanied by Adam de Swinburn, they reached Hexham, from which the canons had fled. The next morning, having sacked the priory, they set fire to it as well as to the church and the whole town, outdoing the horrors of Berwick in the atrocities they committed on women and children. The great church, with whatever was left of Wilfrid's work, was soon in a blaze, and the relics of the local saints were pitched from their shrines into the flames. So far from St. Andrew, the national saint of Scotland, proving this time any protection for his house, the ribald Scots cut off the head of his image, saying that it was a lesson for him not to leave his own country. Popular sentiment was especially shocked at not even the sacred rood being spared :

> 'Voillez penser des arsons
>   Du temple Deu omnipotent
> A Hexelesham, où cel host
> De la croice faisaint rost
>   Figure de humayn salvement.'

Proceeding up South Tyne, the horde burnt all the small nunnery of Lambley, except the church, and then made off home with their booty.

The victory of Dunbar, followed by the resignation of Baliol, established the rule of Edward in Scotland. On his return to Northumberland he delivered at the abbey of Newminster a great seal of his own to the Earl of Warren, whom he had appointed guardian of Scotland, declaring at the same time, in the coarse language of the day, that necessity alone led him to do so dirty an action. The security of the Border seemed assured; the park of Harbottle was restocked with bucks and does from Tyndale, and forty oak-trees from Baliol's forfeited woods of Bywell were given to the burgesses of Corbridge to aid in the rebuilding of their town.

The appearance of William Wallace completely changed the aspect of affairs. Warren fled from his defeat at Stirling Bridge in such hot haste to Berwick that his horse, when put into the stable of the Franciscans, refused to touch food again. In the panic that ensued there, Roger Heron, Rector of Ford, who kept the custom-house, sent a large sum of money in leathern bags and pouches to Warkworth Castle, in the charge of Hugh of Rothbury. The Constable of Warkworth remarked their great weight as his son carried them from the great chamber to an adjacent closet. Part of the money was returned to Heron at Durham, and properly accounted for, but a considerable balance was missing. This, whatever it was, Rothbury declared he had secreted in a sack of wool at Warkworth, with some jewels of his own, but never saw anything more of it, since Robert-fitz-Roger, the lord of the castle, arriving there, sold the wool and took possession of the valuables.

Robert-fitz-Roger was certainly not the man to be over-scrupulous in dealing with aught he found in his own castle. The hermit Martin, on Coquet Island, had the strange fancy to build a windmill out at sea there. Robert-fitz-Roger waxed furious, thinking the trade of his own mills would suffer. Accustomed to act as if he were prince of the whole country, he sent thirty men with mattocks and axes to destroy the objectionable mill. Martin was too frightened to say anything; the protests of his Gehazi nearly cost him his life. After all, the chronicler adds, many people thought that it was not quite the right thing for a professed hermit to speculate in a windmill, as mills, like shows, were apt to harbour promiscuous society.

On Wallace's approach, the garrison of Berwick retired into the castle, the town being unable to stand a siege, through the avarice of the English officials having delayed the completion of the fortifications. The terrified Northumbrians sent their wives and children with their cattle and goods to Newcastle; but when, after a certain time, they found the Scots did not cross the Tweed, they brought them all home again. This was just what the Scots were waiting for. Choosing the forest of Rothbury as a centre, they issued from it to gather in their plunder all around, meeting with little or no interference. The Prior of Alnwick, in jingling Latin couplets, rightly likened Northumberland to a widow bereft of her sons, the great families of Vescy, Merlay, Somerville, and Bertram being extinct or ruined. Alnwick itself was burnt by 'William Wallace that Robin Hood,' as the Prior calls him. The Cistercians of Newminster promised the Scots a goodly sum if they would spare their abbey, but they did not pay in time, so the Prior, being caught there, was carried away captive.

For fear of the Scots, divine service ceased in every church and monastery between Newcastle and Carlisle. The canons of Hexham, however, opened negotiations with the enemy, and obtained letters of protection from Andrew Murray and William Wallace, 'leaders of the army of the kingdom of Scotland.' On the faith of these, three canons returned soon after the departure of the horde for Carlisle. Having laid Cumberland waste as far as Cockermouth, the Scots unexpectedly came back to Hexham. The three canons, seeing them approaching, took refuge in the oratory which they had rebuilt, with the intention of celebrating Mass. Presently some of the soldiery entered, brandishing their spears, and shouting, ' Show us the treasures of your church, or ye shall die.' One of the canons replied that it was not long ago that they or their countrymen had carried everything off to Scotland, so they ought to know best where the treasures were. At this moment Wallace himself entered, and, ordering the ruffians to leave, requested a canon to proceed with the holy office. After the elevation Wallace retired to put off his armour. As the priest was about to communicate, the Scots closed in round him to snatch away the chalice, and on his returning to the altar from washing his hands, not only was the chalice gone, but all the other ornaments; even the missal itself was missing. Wallace ordered the thieves to be caught and their heads cut off, but there was only a pretence made of apprehending them.

The Scots swept on towards Newcastle, following the north bank of the Tyne. The men of Ryton jeered at them across the river, which was then in flood; but their confidence in its protection was misplaced, for Wallace's followers crossed and burnt the village. The castle of Newcastle had been put in a good state of defence by John de Kirkby, the Sheriff of Northumberland. In consequence, though the small garrison dared not advance far beyond the walls to meet the Scots, Wallace was afraid to enter the town. The same applied to Tyne-

mouth, where the Prior and convent had obtained a royal
license for the fortification of their monastery.

At last a large English army, mustered at Newcastle,
succeeded in relieving the castle of Berwick, and occupying the town which the Scots evacuated. Peter of
Kirkoswald—one of the soldiers in the castle—swam to
Norham and back with letters in his hair, in order to
open communications with the relieving force. Further
operations were deferred until Edward's return from
Flanders. Wallace was then completely routed at Falkirk, though, on the rumour of fresh trouble in Scotland,
the King prudently lingered at Tynemouth during the
autumn. His marriage with Margaret of France delayed
his return to Northumberland for nearly a year. On St.
Nicholas' Day, 1299, he witnessed the revel of the Boy
Bishop in the chapel of Heaton, near Newcastle. The
fractious conduct of his nobles compelled him to turn
back from Berwick, leaving Stirling Castle to its fate.

His subsequent expeditions to Scotland were restrained
by the influence of the Pope and the French Court, so
that it was not until May, 1303, that, having massed his
troops at Berwick, he reduced almost the whole country
to his obedience. Among the vessels employed in conveying stores for the recovery of Stirling was the *Saint-
mari-ship* of Alnmouth ; the Mayor and bailiffs of
Newcastle fitted out a large barge for the same purpose.
During her husband's absence, Queen Margaret spent
several months at Tynemouth. The erection of the two
fortified manor-houses of Aydon Hall and Shortflat Tower
by Robert de Raymes at this time cannot have been
necessitated by the requirements of national defence.
Aydon, with its fine hall and quaintly-carved fireplaces,
might seem architecturally to belong to an earlier period,
if many of its features were not duplicated at Shortflat.

The insurrection of Robert Bruce in 1306 was followed
by summary executions of Scottish prisoners at Newcastle. One of these, John de Somerville, owned certain
property at Hedgeley. Edward himself was journeying

by slow stages from Lanchester and Stocksfield towards
Lanercost and Carlisle, when he was taken ill at Newbrough.　He proceeded, however, along the line of the
Wall, halting at Bradley.　From Blenkinsop he directed
Sir John Swinburn to take twelve stags in Tyndale
Chace, and to send the venison in all haste for his table.
His health improved, and when at Thirlwall, a few days
later, he seemed strong and hearty enough, considering
his age.　He spent the winter at Lanercost, and, as
some compensation for the expenses his long illness
entailed on that house, he bestowed upon it the church
of Mitford.

Edward II. set his father's dying counsels at naught.
Bruce soon said that he feared a dead king's bones more
than a live king.　Bamburgh was granted to Isabel de
Beaumont, the widow of John de Vesci of Alnwick;
Anthony Bek, the Bishop of Durham, was restored to
all his temporalities.　This greedy prelate made the
'warm words' addressed to him by William of Kildare,
the natural son of William de Vesci, an excuse for selling the great barony of Alnwick, which he held in trust
for him, to Henry de Percy.　The Scots soon began to
carry the war over the Border.　The oats and barley
grown on the lands belonging to the suppressed Order
of Templars, at Temple Thornton, were hastily sold in
the autumn of 1308, lest they should fall into their
hands.

Edward's expedition to Scotland in 1310 produced no
permanent results.　His residence at Berwick during the
following spring is chiefly remarkable for the length of
his fish-bill.　As the result of much negotiation, he
received the homage of his ambitious cousin, Thomas
of Lancaster, for the earldom of Lincoln, at Haggerston;
Lancaster refused to kiss Piers Gaveston, which bitterly
mortified that favourite.　Scarcely had Edward gone
south, than Bruce burnt Haltwhistle, and harried the
Valley of South Tyne.　A month later he came down
on Corbridge by Harbottle and Holystone, and made a

clean sweep of everything still left in Tyndale, including Robert Pykewell, the Vicar of Haltwhistle.

Edward returned to the North to protect the country from similar depredations. He and Gaveston had only just sufficient time to escape from Newcastle to Tyne-mouth, when the town was betrayed to Lancaster, who seized the treasury and ninety-seven war-horses, keep-ing the royal household under arrest for three days. In order to save Gaveston's life and satisfy his rebellious barons, Edward consigned him to pretended captivity in Bamburgh Castle. Under such circumstances any organized defence against the Scots was out of the question. Aymer de Valence, the English guardian of Scotland, was chased by Bruce as far as Corbridge, which was burnt, together with Hexham. Bruce quietly established himself at Corbridge, like another King Reginald, while his men fired the city of Durham, and exacted tribute from the four northern counties. His attempt to surprise the castle of Berwick by an escalade with well-contrived rope-ladders was frustrated by the barking of a dog.

Thomas of Lancaster, who had treacherously decapit-ated Gaveston, was in almost open rebellion, when by his orders the first stones of Dunstanburgh Castle were quarried on May 7, 1313. For the lord of Kenilworth and Pontefract to raise illegally a vast stronghold on the wild coast of Northumberland was not calculated to allay suspicion as to his ultimate intentions. The colossal pro-portions of the Great Gatehouse conjure up a vision of what the rest of the castle would have been, if Lancaster, whose foible it was to assume the character of King Arthur in the pageants of the Court, had completed the construction of this new Tintagel.

After the fatal rout of Bannockburn, Edward was glad to escape from Dunbar to Bamburgh with seventeen men in a boat. On his arrival, on account of the imminence of the danger, he appointed Roger Horsley constable of the castle by word of mouth. The consternation at Berwick can readily be imagined. Three little boys had gone out to play in the Magdalen fields, and were returning to the town-gate, when one of them found he had lost his song-book, and went back to look for it. They were at once arrested on the charge of trafficking with the Scots, but were acquitted. Three Northumbrians, however, who really attempted to sell the town to the enemy were tried before Colle of Derby, and two other justices in eyre, and executed forthwith. As Colle was returning through Aln-wick, he was set upon by Sir John Lilburn, the brothers Roddam, and other friends of the traitors, and only rescued by the exertions of Sir John Felton, the Constable of the castle. Sir John Wischard of Moneylaws, and others, openly rejoined the Scots, who extended their raids right into Richmondshire.

The condition of Northumberland was terrible in the extreme. For fifteen years after 1316 the whole country remained waste, no one daring to live in it except under the shadow of a castle or walled town. The poor people of Bamburgh Ward were not allowed by the Constable of the castle to purchase a truce from the Scots unless they paid him a similar amount of blackmail. He also mulcted them severely for the privilege of storing their goods and chattels in the castle, while the porters would neither let them in nor out without heavy fees. In addition, John the Irishman and his fellows in the garrison robbed them of provisions, with no pretence of payment. The Twelve Towns of Tyndale (Kirkhaugh, Knaresdale, Thirlwall, Walltown, Haltwhistle, Thorngrafton, Elrington, Melk-ridge, Ridley, Whitfield, Ulmston (Ouston), and Plen-mellor), found themselves equally between the upper and nether millstone. They had given the sum of £35 to William de Soules, to whom Bruce had granted the manor of Wark, in order, as they declared, to defer acknowledging him as their lord; but the people of Cumberland and Westmorland regarded them as traitors, and not only refused to allow them to take refuge in those counties, but came by night and plundered their homesteads.

The national defence had completely broken down. Aymer de Valence, in engaging Sir John Eure to keep his castle of Mitford, was obliged to pay him in that 'time of war' twice as much as in the 'time of peace,' when the King was on the Border with his army. Sir Maurice Berkeley and the garrison of Berwick found themselves left to their fate. The soldiers sallied out in quest of provisions against his orders, declaring it was better to die fighting than to starve. If a horse died in the town, the men-at-arms carried it off to boil, and would not let the foot-soldiers touch it till they had appeased their own hunger. Even if a brave Northumbrian did occasionally get the better of the Scots, he was more often than not defrauded of the fruits of his valour. Roger Mauduit attacked a great multitude of them pillaging and burning at Redpeth, near Haltwhistle; but when he had made Richard Middleton and four others prisoners, Thomas Fishburn and his crew took them from him, sold Middleton to the King for £100, and let the others go their way. So, too, when Mauduit had seized Simon Locard and two more Scots at Mitford, and lodged them in the castle, Sir John Lilburn let them out and pocketed their ransom.

Mitford Castle was soon afterwards stealthily seized by Gilbert de Middleton, a warden of the marches, said to have been driven into rebellion by the conduct of Edward in arresting his kinsman, Adam de Swinburn, for speaking rudely to him on the desperate state of Northumberland. In company with Walter de Selby and a party of Scots, Middleton waylaid and robbed, near Durham, Gaucelin d'Euse, Cardinal of SS. Marcelin and Peter, and Ludovico Fieschi, Cardinal of S. Maria in Via Lata, who were on their way to negotiate a truce with Scotland. At the same time he carried off prisoner Louis de Beaumont, Bishop-elect of Durham, to the castle of Morpeth, and his brother Henry to that of Mitford.

Middleton, no doubt, was in secret understanding with Lancaster, with whom he had a meeting in Durham

Cathedral, much to the horror of the despoiled cardinals. His ravages extended from Newham, near Bamburgh, where he wasted the lands of Edmund Cumin's widow, as far south as Cleveland, the priory of Tynemouth being an especial sufferer. Bamburgh, Alnwick, and Norham were the only castles that stood out against him in Northumberland. Bamburgh gave hostages for its surrender, and Alnwick was about to be delivered to him by his kinsmen. The dungeons of Mitford were filled with his neighbours, whom he kept in durance for the purpose of extorting heavy ransoms.

At last, William de Felton, Thomas de Heton, and Robert de Horncliff, pitying the captives, and fearing their own turn might come next, came under a safe-conduct to Middleton. After much bargaining, they settled the terms on which some prisoners were to be set at liberty at once, and others detained as hostages till the whole of the stipulated sum was paid. The Prior and convent of Durham ransomed Bishop Beaumont, at whose abduction they were suspected of conniving, while Peter de Salso Marisco was accepted as a hostage for Henry de Beaumont.

On the day appointed for the final payment, while Middleton's band of outlaws were absent on their work of rapine, Felton and his friends returned to Mitford, and, telling Middleton that they had left the money in the village, they obtained his leave to pass and repass the gates to fetch it. Then of a sudden they cut the throats of the porters, and let in a number of armed men they had lurking outside. Middleton, never expecting anything of the sort, was speedily overpowered and put in irons. His men, returning too late with the prisoners and cattle taken in their raid, betook themselves to the pele of Horton-next-the-Sea. Here Walter de Selby appears to have successfully held out, notwithstanding the considerable debt incurred by Richard de Emeldon, of Newcastle, in supplying provisions for the siege of the little fortress.

Middleton, with his brother, was led bound to Newcastle, where the inhabitants gave him an ignominious reception. He was detained several days on board ship in the Tyne, waiting for a north wind to carry him to Grimsby, and when it came, it blew such a gale that his life was almost lost on the voyage. From Grimsby he was taken on horseback, with his feet tied together under the girth, to be hung, drawn and quartered at London. His execution and that of his brothers put an end to the claim which they had preferred to the Earldom of North-umberland, and which was supported by actual possession. The rebellion had been widespread: Roger Purvis and others were taken resisting the King in the peles of Bolton and Whittingham; John Maitland of Howick, John Wid-drington of Denton, John Hazelrig of Akeld, and Walter Corbet of Lanton, were among those whose estates were forfeited.

In consequence of the alleged malversations of his officials at Berwick, the King had entrusted the keeping of the town to the Mayor, bailiffs, and community. Through their carelessness, Peter Spalding, one of the burgesses, was enabled to treacherously admit the Scots under Murray and Douglas on March 28, 1318. They came at midnight to the town-wall at the Cow Gate, and, climbing over it unperceived, lay concealed within the town until daybreak, when they issued from their hiding-place and drove any of the English who opposed them into the castle. This made a brave defence for eleven weeks longer, Roger Horsley, the Constable, losing an eye, and Robert de Blakeburn crossing the Tweed at great risk to himself with twenty-one horses and letters for the King. It only capitulated for want of provisions. The whole of Scotland,

'Fra the Red Swyre unto Orkney,'

now acknowledged the sovereignty of Robert Bruce.

Soon after the capture of the town of Berwick, the castles of Wark and Harbottle, not being relieved within a certain fixed time, were forced to surrender. The Scots even surprised the castle of Mitford, and intrusted it to their old ally, Walter de Selby. He, however, on promise of a full pardon from Edward, delivered it up to Robert Umfraville, Earl of Angus. Notwithstanding this, his manor of Seghill, held by the service of acting as steward in the hall of Tynemouth on St. Oswin's Day, continued to be confiscated.

During the whole of this troublous time, Sir Thomas Gray and his friends were holding out in Norham Castle. At a great feast of lords and ladies made in Lincolnshire, a 'damsel faye' brought to Sir William Marmion a helm of war with a golden crest, accompanied by a letter from her lady bidding him go into the most perilous place in Great Britain, and there make this helm famous. The knights present decided accordingly that he should go to Norham. Within four days of his arrival, Alexander, brother of Philip de Mowbray, the Scotch Warden of Berwick, came before the castle at noon with more than eight-score men-at-arms, the boldest horsemen of the Scottish march. Rising from dinner, Sir Thomas Gray brought his garrison in front of the barriers; then seeing that Marmion, richly arrayed and glittering in gold and silver, the helm on his head, was following them on foot, he shouted: 'Sir knight, ye be come hither as a knight-errant to fame your helm, and since deeds of chivalry should rather be done on horseback than on foot, mount up on your horse and spur him into the midst of your enemies yonder. I forswear God if I rescue not thy body dead or alive, or I myself will die for it.' Marmion, thus put to the test, could do no otherwise. The Scots slashed his face and dragged him from the saddle. Thereupon Gray, with the whole garrison, their lances couched, charged in among the Scots, and so pricked their horses that many threw their riders, while the rest galloped away. Marmion was rescued and set on his horse again. The enemy were pursued, the first-comers of them slain, and fifty 'horses of price' taken. The women of the castle led these horses to their husbands, who mounted and followed the chase, laying low the Scots they overtook.

A Fleming named Cryn, who was a pirate admiral in the good graces of Robert Bruce, was slain by Gray's orders at the Yarrowford; the pursuit of the other Scots was continued to the nunnery of Halidon, just outside Berwick.

Another day Adam de Gordon, a Scottish baron, came before Norham with 160 men-at-arms, thinking to surprise the cattle grazing outside the castle. The young men ran out to the other end of the village, then all in ruins, and began skirmishing. Surrounded there by the Scots, they took refuge behind some old walls, and made a bold defence. Then Sir Thomas Gray, issuing from the castle with his garrison, and perceiving the jeopardy they were in, said to his under-constable: ' I pledge thee this castle, which I ought to guard for the King's use, that I will drink out of the same cup as my men there.' He advanced so rapidly that, although he had no more than sixty men with him, including common soldiers, the Scots, seeing him coming in this bold fashion, left the skirmishers and took to the open. The young men who had been surrounded then sprang out of the ditches and, charging the enemy, forced them to turn their horses round so suddenly that many stumbled and their riders were killed by the footmen. The whole English force, now being united under Sir Thomas Gray, drove the Scots over the Tweed, taking and killing many. If they had only been better horsed, scarcely a Scotsman would have escaped.

In September, 1319, Edward made a great attempt to recover Berwick. Although the walls were still very low, the Scots offered a stubborn resistance. A general attack was made with scaling-ladders, while a ship with a boatful of soldiers half-mast high was towed close to the walls on the river-side. Unable, however, to approach sufficiently near these to let fall a drawbridge from the boat, owing to the hailstorm of stones discharged from the battlements, the vessel eventually ran aground at the ebb of the tide, and was burnt in a sortie of the garrison. A week later, a great machine called a Sow,

sheltering a number of sappers and miners, was moved up
to the walls. With the enforced assistance of an English
engineer, who had been seized on the grounded ship, the
Scots hurled a huge stone high in the air. This
descended with such force on the Sow as to split it in
two, causing the men in it to rush out amid jeers to the
effect

'That thair sow ferryit was thair.'

A crane on wheels, constructed by the Flemish engineer,
Sir John Crab, completed the destruction of the Sow by
lowering on to it a bale of flaming faggots. The Mary
Gate, however, was almost burnt by the English, when a
descent of Sir Walter Stuart from the castle forced them
to retire. A renewed attack from the Tweed was not
more successful; the ships had their top-castles filled with
armed men and boats hauled high up the masts, but a
stone from the walls hit one of these boats with such fatal
consequences that the crews lost what little courage they
had left.

The Earl of Lancaster had now withdrawn from
Edward's camp with his friends and their forces, and
Douglas and Murray had defeated the Archbishop of York
at Mitton-on-the-Swale, so the King found himself obliged
to abandon the siege. He waited at Newminster expecting to intercept the plunder of Yorkshire, but Douglas and
Murray marched home by Stainmoor and Gilsland. Disheartened by so much ill-success and treachery, Edward
consented to a two years' truce. One of the conditions
was that Harbottle Castle, then held by the Scots, should
be delivered to Edward's commissioners in their private
capacity. If a final peace were not concluded, it was either
to be restored to Bruce, or to be completely dismantled
before the expiration of the truce. When the time came,
all hope of peace being at an end, John de Penrith, the
Constable, was ordered to demolish it with as little ado as
possible. Sir Thomas Gray had taken advantage of the
truce to go to the south of England. It had still a month

or so to run when, on St. Catherine's Eve (November 24), one of the garrison of Norham killed the porter, and let in a mixed band of miscreants who lay in ambush in a house before the gate. These made themselves masters of the outer ward, and, after failing to mine the inner ward and donjon, burnt it for fear of Gray's return.

Thomas of Lancaster had all this time maintained very questionable relations with the Scots. They were said to have intentionally spared his estates in the course of their ravages; even after Bannockburn they contented themselves with only lifting one horse from the 'garniture' of Dunstanburgh. Messengers bearing 'secret news' and 'rumours from northern parts' were sent by the bailiff of Embleton to the Earl at Donnington and Pontefract. The address on some of Lancaster's Scottish correspondence, which fell into Edward's hands, referred to him as 'King Arthur.' The air was full of popular ballads on the subject of Merlin's prophecies, like that beginning

> 'As I went on a Monday
>   Between Whittington and Wall,
> Me alone on the broad way,
>   A little man I met withal,
> The least saw ever I, sooth to say,
>   Either in bower, either in hall.
> His robe was neither green nor gray,
>   But all it was of rich pall.'

The little man, the minstrel went on to say, had come, he knew, from the parkside at Lanchester, and he exhibited his marvellous strength in taking up a great stone and casting it strides three. He then conducted him to his mysterious habitation close by, where he beheld lords feasting and ladies singing. Then follow the prophecies, with dark allusions to T and L, and promises of a good time in store, when wrong works should cease and husbandmen have rest. This rigmarole may have been the production of William de Hexham, a canon whom Lancaster interested himself in having preferred from the priory of Hexham to that of Leicester. The canons of Hexham were not above composing ballads in derision of the mendicant orders. The traditions of Arthur's Court entranced in the basalt caverns of Dunstanburgh and Sewinshields are evidently referred to in the political literature of Lancaster's conspiracy. Refusing to follow the advice of his friends and place himself in safety at Dunstanburgh, the Earl was defeated at Boroughbridge, and shortly afterwards beheaded at Pontefract.

Relieved of the opposition of his barons, Edward determined to march on Edinburgh. In passing through Newcastle, his common soldiers were in such high spirits that they fell upon the commonalty of the town, and in endeavouring to quell the riot, Sir John de Penrith and certain esquires of the Marshal and Constable lost their lives on Tyne Bridge. The King was compelled to recross the Border, owing to the scarcity of stores and a consequent outbreak of the plague. The Scots followed close upon his heels. Henry de Beaumont, brother of the Bishop of Durham, and the Constable of Norham refused to allow him to victual the castle and increase the garrison at his own cost. Edward addressed a sharp remonstrance to the Bishop from Newbiggen. The matter was arranged by Sir Thomas Gray, the Constable, undertaking to find twenty knights and fifty light horsemen, in addition to the episcopal garrison. His dame received a month's pay for these in advance at Newcastle, but before she could return to Norham it was already invested. The King expressed his confidence in Gray's great loyalty for the defence of this Castle Dangerous, and begged him to send daily reports of the Scots' movements, accompanied by his counsels how to act.

It turned out that the Scots, entrenched probably at Upsetlington, did not muster more than a hundred knights and a hundred light-horse, while in Berwick there were only forty Scottish knights in addition to the burgesses. Edward was naturally enraged that the Constables of Bamburgh, Warkworth, Dunstanburgh, and Alnwick, who had much superior forces, did nothing to secure the safety of the March, which he had spent so much in strengthening. The unfortunate inhabitants rightly represented that it was useless for him to pay away large sums to the Wardens, and that nothing but his return with the whole power of England could save them from annihilation. He was exerting himself to raise a fresh army, when he was nearly captured at Byland in the heart of Yorkshire by a band of Scots, whom the treachery of Andrew de Harcla had allowed to slip past Carlisle. This new proof of perfidy, where it might least have been expected, led the unfortunate King to consent to the Truce of Bishopsthorpe in 1323. This was to be prolonged for thirteen years. One article stipulated that the English were not to build or repair any fortress north of the line of the Tyne and South Tyne, except those already existing or in course of construction. A final peace failed to be concluded in consequence of the extraordinary claim advanced by the Scots to all the country up to the gates of York. This seems to have been based rather on the right of conquest than on any remembrance of the heritage of Waltheof. The poor people who had taken refuge in Bamburgh were now emboldened to remove their wooden shanties and goods and chattels from the castle and the ditch and moat. Some of them obtained leave to send coals from New-castle to Scotland as their sons' ransoms. All trouble, however, was not at an end ; by the King's order a pele-yard was constructed outside the gates of Prudhoe Castle for the protection of the peasants and their property.

On the night of the coronation of Edward III. a large band of Scots, expecting to profit by the festivities of the garrison of Norham, attempted to surprise the castle. Sixteen of them had already mounted the battlements, when Robert de Maners, the Constable, who had been forewarned by a Scotsman in his service, fell upon them. One only escaped, and the incident was considered a good omen for the Scottish wars of the opening reign. Negotiations for a final peace were nevertheless carried on until the Scots entered England in the middle of June, destroying everything with fire and sword to within four miles of Newcastle, the garrison of which remained inactive, though it included 1,000 men-at-arms. A month later, 4,000 Scottish knights and squires, under Douglas and Murray, crossed the South Tyne by a ford near Haydon Bridge, and commenced ravaging the west part of the bishopric of Durham. They were followed by 20,000 bold and hardy men on little cobs that were never tied up nor groomed after their day's march, but were immediately turned out to graze at will. No baggage-waggons accompanied the Scots, on account of the mountains they had to pass in Northumberland. The river-water served them for wine, and they required neither pots nor pans, since they dressed the flesh of the cattle they caught in kettles made of the hides. Bread they had none ; each man carried a small iron 'girdle' under the flaps of his saddle, on which to bake a 'bannock' from the small bag of oatmeal at his back.

With a great army of over 60,000 men the young King Edward set out from Durham to attack these marauders, who were encamped at Stanhope. He had not gone far before the spies of his vanguard brought word that the Scots had broken up their camp at his approach, and by the advice of the Borderers he accomplished a forced march of twenty-six miles through Allendale that hot summer's day, thinking to cut the Scots off from their own country. He crossed the Tyne near Bardon Mill, and drew up his host at Haydon Bridge, expecting the Scots to return by the same route as they had advanced. Rain fell day after day; the very leather of the Englishmen's accoutrements rotted. They were reduced to starvation for want of supplies, though they scoured all the country round, especially the estates of Hexham Priory. Still, they comforted themselves with the conviction that they had foreclosed the Scots. At last, after a week of mire and misery, the poor young King went in despair to Haltwhistle. Then, after much reconnoitring, Sir Thomas Rokeby discovered that the Scots had never left Stanhope at all. The main body of them gave the English the slip, and got safely back to Scotland by a roundabout road.

Soon after this extraordinary affair, Robert Bruce laid siege to Norham. The Constable, Robert de Maners, by a successful sortie discomfited the watch the enemy set before the gates. Sir William de Monthaut, a Scottish banneret, and others, were slain through their own negligence; the captain of the watch, a miserable coward, would not allow anyone from the village to attempt their rescue. Murray and Douglas, meanwhile, appeared before the castle of Alnwick, where there were 'great jousts of war by covenant taille.' Henry Percy, however, maintained so resolute a defence for a fortnight or more that the Scots left for Warkworth. Foiled here again, they returned to Bruce at Norham. Percy thereupon started on a raid into Teviotdale, but had scarcely gone five miles before Douglas, apprised of this, got between him and Alnwick. The English had at that time so little courage in the open that Percy was glad to escape to Newcastle by night.

The desultory nature of these campaigns brought both sides to yearn for a definite peace, and the First Great Scottish War, after having lasted more than thirty years, was brought to a conclusion by the Treaty of Northampton in April, 1328. The King of England renounced all claim to sovereignty over Scotland, the boundaries of which were to be restored as they had existed in the reign of Alexander III.

The general restitution of confiscated lands in both kingdoms, which was provided for by this treaty, was on the whole loyally carried out. A difficulty arose at West Upsetlington, near Norham, which, although on the north side of the Tweed, had been from time immemorial the property of the Bishops of Durham and parcel of

England; at least, no Bishop of Durham had ever done homage or service for it to a King of Scots. Bruce now insolently summoned Bishop Beaumont to attend his Parliament at Scone. The ferry between Tweedmouth and Berwick was also another bone of contention; the Scots claimed the whole of the Tweed as parcel of Scotland, and would allow no English boat to touch the north bank. To clear up these and other doubtful questions of frontier, a new perambulation of the Border was ordered to be made by the English justices.

It proved in the end impossible to reinstate all the English lords in their hereditary estates in Scotland. Consequently Henry de Beaumont and others fitted out a private expedition which, invading Scotland by sea, proved so unexpectedly successful as to place Edward Baliol on the throne. The excitement on the Border, where Edward III. had endeavoured to keep faith with David Bruce, naturally became intense. Thomas Gray the Younger and his men pounced down like true banditti on John de Reynton, a rich burgess of Berwick, at Holburn, and carried him off to unknown places till he had paid a considerable part of the ransom demanded, and had left his sons prisoners at Norham as hostages for the rest. The English, however, felt equally insecure; the burgesses of Bamburgh obtained a royal license for the fortification of their town. Reprisal followed reprisal, and the two countries drifted into a regular war.

Berwick was invested by sea and land by Sir William Montagu at the end of February, 1333. The King, having at Newcastle on St. George's Day besought the prayers of the nation for his success, arrived before Berwick in the second week of May. His first assault failed, but the Scots gave their sons as hostages that they would surrender the town by a certain day if not previously relieved. Before that day came the whole power of Scotland crossed the Tweed by the Yarrowford at dawn, and 'showed themselves at the Sayning-side,' in full view of Edward and his army. Having passed Sir William Keith with a supply of men and victuals into the town across the Tweed, Archibald Douglas proceeded to attack Bamburgh. Queen Philippa of Hainault was in the castle at the time, and her presence no doubt encouraged its gallant defenders; the Scots were effectually repulsed.

Meanwhile the day stipulated for the surrender of Berwick had arrived, and Edward called on the garrison to carry out the arrangement. They, on the other hand, declared it was no longer binding, since they had been relieved; and in proof of this they appointed Sir William Keith Governor of the town. The English thereupon hanged Alexander Seton, the son of the former Governor, and one of the hostages, in the sight of his father and mother. The parents of the other hostages were of softer mould, and, fearing for the lives of their sons, they brought about a fresh and more explicit capitulation. Fifteen days were allowed within which the Scots were either to pass 200 men-at-arms into the town by dry land between the English camp and the sea, or to give battle in the open; if they did neither, then the town was to yield. Three fresh hostages were given to ensure the fulfilment of these conditions. Sir William Keith and other knights set out under a safe-conduct to bring back the Scottish army, which they overtook at Witton Underwood.

In their over-confidence, engendered by the successes of

' Mitton, Bannockburn, and Byland,'

the Scots made light of the strong position taken up by the English on Halidon Hill, to the west of Berwick. They descended into a great sike, and began climbing the steep brae on the other side, fighting bravely all on foot. They were, however, completely blinded by showers of English arrows, and on the advance of the English spearmen and men-at-arms, followed by the death of their leader Douglas, were routed with immense slaughter. Edward at the commencement of the battle made a vow that, in case of victory, he would found a Benedictine house for a prior and twelve monks. He afterwards granted the

rich church of Simundburn, in dispute between himself
and the Bishop of Durham (in consequence of John
Baliol's grant of Tyndale to Anthony Bek, and the royal
contention that Baliol was a rebel at the time), for the
purpose of endowing such a house at Oxford in honour
of St. Margaret, on whose vigil the battle was won. It
was, however, the chapel of St. George at Windsor that
eventually obtained the benefaction.

In gratitude for the English King's assistance, Edward
Baliol ceded to him Berwick and all Lothian, to be annexed for ever to the southern crown. But the tide of
war ebbed rapidly. Already in 1336, 200 Scottish horse,
led by Thomas Pringle, entered Redesdale. They were,
however, cut off at a ford on their way home by the Earl
of Cornwall and the Lords Percy and Neville. The next
year Coquetdale and Redesdale were again harried; but
the inhabitants, having received timely warning, had removed their cattle. In 1338 Sir Alexander Ramsay,
raiding at Pressen, was nearly surrounded by the English
marchers. He feigned flight; the Northumbrians, quarrel-
ling among themselves, became scattered in the pursuit,
and were easily vanquished. Sir Robert Maners was
taken prisoner. The scar received by the builder of
Ford Castle was scornfully recorded in the distich:

> ' Schyr Willame Heron wyth a strake
> In to the cheke his way can take.'

In 1342 the young King David Bruce, having returned
to Scotland from France, rode over the Border with the
new knights he had made — a right sturdy company.
They fell in with Sir Robert Ogle, who retreated across
a morass. Only fifty Scots succeeded in crossing after
him; then Ogle turned, and easily captured five knights
and others. At the end of August David Bruce was
encamped on Heddon Law. A vision of St. Cuthbert
dissuaded him from entering the Bishopric at Ryton.
Two months later, after an ineffectual attack on Roxburgh, he marched past Berwick into Northumberland.

The town of Alnwick was given to the flames; the castle offered a successful resistance. Discomfited before Newcastle by a sudden sortie, in which the Earl of Murray, who had just been exchanged for the Earl of Salisbury at the siege of Tournay, was again taken prisoner, the Scots crossed the Tyne higher up, and extended their ravages to Auckland.

The news of this invasion reached King Edward at Stamford. In four days he was at Newcastle. The army of David Bruce, in full retreat, passed under the battlements of Wark, where the fair Catherine de Grandison, Countess of Salisbury, was living in retirement during her husband's absence. The sight of the rich booty being carried off to Scotland proved too much for Salisbury's nephew. Falling on the Scottish rear-guard, he drove off more than a hundred pack-horses to the castle. Bruce and his whole force turned back, and commenced a formal siege. Encouraged by the beautiful Countess, the garrison repelled their assaults for two days. Hearing from some Scottish prisoners that Edward had reached Alnwick, Salisbury's nephew profited by the heavy rain to steal out of the castle before daybreak and to ride away to implore the King's immediate assistance.

Edward reached Wark at noon, to find the enemy decamped. He at once disarmed, and, accompanied by Sir Reginald Cobham, Sir Richard Stafford, and a few other knights, proceeded towards the castle to inquire for the safety of the fair châtelaine. The gates were thrown open, and the Countess of Salisbury, in her richest attire, advanced to meet him. With a low reverence she tendered her thanks for the relief of her castle, and then, hand-in-hand, the two passed up the hall into the chamber. The King was so struck by Catherine's beauty that he never took his eyes off her until she retired to give directions for dinner; then, leaning on a window-sill, he fell into a long day-dream. From this he was aroused by the return of the Countess, who, however, cut short the declaration of his passion with the very practical rebuff:

'Come, sir, to the hall; your knights are waiting for you, to wash their hands, for they, as well as you, have fasted too long.'

After dinner, when the trestle-tables were removed, Edward ordered his main force to follow the Scots, promising to rejoin them in the evening. He then called for a chess-board, and, persuading the Countess to play with him, staked the very beautiful ruby ring he wore on his finger against a little gold ring of hers. The Countess was so confused by the King's marked attentions that, do all she could, she played very badly; he, however, played worse intentionally, and in the end was checkmated. Spices and wines were brought in; the King would partake of nothing before the Countess, nor the Countess before the King, so in the end they helped themselves simultaneously. It being now time for the King to leave, his palfrey was led into the hall. He refused to mount in the Countess's presence, so she retired to her bower. As his foot was in the stirrup, a damsel fell on her knees before him and tendered the ruby ring, which Catherine had been forced to accept through politeness, though she thought it a breach of hospitality to have won it from a guest, especially a guest who had just effected her deliverance. Edward determined that his ring should remain as a souvenir at Wark, and what the Countess would not keep he presented to her damsel.

The romantic relief of Wark became a favourite topic of Court gossip. Though the character of the Countess of Salisbury was never called in question by writers most hostile to that of the King, it seems that in adopting the device HONI SOIT QUI MAL Y PENSE in the tournaments he subsequently gave in Catherine's honour, and to which the origin of the Order of the Garter is referred, it was this adventure that Edward had in mind.

Edward's wars in France caused the knights and squires of Northumberland to rely more on their own resources for protection. A great impulse was given to the building of castles and towers. On the very eve of sailing for Antwerp, in 1338, the King at Ipswich had granted Sir William Heron a license for the crenellation of Ford. Bothal Castle, licensed in 1343, still retains among the carved shields that adorn the battlements of its massive gate-house the rare blazon of Edward on first adopting the style of King of France, with the quarter of leopards before the quarter of lilies, and that of the Black Prince with a *bordure bezanty* of Cornwall, which seems absolutely unique. Ford and Etal and Chillingham, which also date from this period, were all castles enclosed by a curtain-wall with towers at the four corners. At Etal one of these corner towers is a fine donjon, with small traceried windows; and another a gate-house, with the barred shield and peacock-crest of Maners over the entry. Blenkinsop (1340) and Crawley (1343) belonged, probably, to the type of solitary tower, which was splendidly developed in Widdrington, with its lofty battlements and corner bartizans, built in 1341, and ruthlessly levelled in 1777, and in Belsay and Chipchase, which still survive. The Lucy stronghold of Langley, with its profusion of window-tracery and massive corner towers and the less elaborate home of the Widdringtons at Haughton on North Tyne, are fourteenth-century tower-houses on a larger scale, which ranked as castles from the very first.

In 1346, David Bruce, confident that, all the English, except 'sutlers, skinners, and merchants,' being engaged in France, he could march unimpeded on London, entered Northumberland at Redpeth, and ravaged the lands of the barony of Langley. No more than 2,000 men-at-arms answered his roll-call in the abbey of Hexham, which he burnt, but he had probably 30,000 irregular troops besides. The towns of Hexham and Corbridge were arrogantly spared for winter-quarters. The fortalice of Aydon Hall surrendered on conditions. Having destroyed the town of Slaley, the Scots wasted the lands of Sir Robert de Herle and his tenants at Styford, Broomhaugh, Riding, Merchenley, Shildford, Newbiggen-by-Blanchland, and Shotley, 'riding over them with a great host,' and then crossed the Derwent into the Bishopric at Ebchester. The havoc wrought in St. Cuthbert's patrimony was fully avenged by the battle of Neville's Cross. David Bruce, taken prisoner by Sir John Coupland, was conducted first to Prudhoe Castle, and then to Bamburgh, where two barber-surgeons from York extracted the arrow from his wound. Malcolm Fleming, Earl of Wigton, another prisoner, was deemed so important a prize that strict injunctions were given Robert Bertram, Sheriff of Northumberland, to guard him in the castle of Newcastle, and not admit him to ransom. As, however, Fleming was too ill to be sent to London with the King and others, Bertram transferred him to his own castle of Bothal, in the custody of Robert Delaval of Newsham. Prisoner and keeper escaped to Scotland together, and Bertram, though one of the twelve knights who received the royal thanks for their bravery at Neville's Cross, was arrested and sent to the Tower for contempt.

A truce of eight years brought some tranquillity to the Borders. Trollope in the Cheviots was restored to the monks of Melrose. Permission was given to go into Scotland to buy cattle and horses; but the great plague of 1348 added to the general desolation, and no truce could stem the disorders in Northumberland itself. William Heron and Roger Widdrington, with William Swinburn and two Silvertops, carried off the goods of Gilbert Umfraville from Birtley. Thomas Hatfield, the Bishop of Durham, was seized at Morpeth by Robert Usher and others, and his servants so wounded that the lives of many were despaired of.

On the expiry of the truce in 1355, Sir William Ramsay of Dalhousie plundered the town of Norham, and drew Sir Thomas Gray and his son out of the castle into an ambush laid for them at Nesbit in the Merse. The young Sir Thomas Gray employed his comparatively short captivity in Edinburgh Castle in writing the

'Scalacronica,' a valuable French chronicle, named after the *scala*, stair-ladder or *gré*, a canting badge of his house. In the quaint allegorical preface he says that one night, after he had been thinking on the subject, he dreamt that a Sibyl led him into an orchard, where placed against a wall was a ladder of five rounds. This was supported by Thomas de Otterburn, a gray friar, and a master of divinity, on whose works he was generally to rely. Ascending the ladder, Gray and the Sibyl found at each round the historian who treated of the period typified. At the fourth, in a chamber in a village before a strong castle, a chaplain was writing on a lectern. This was John de Tynmouth, Vicar of Tilmouth, who wrote the 'Historia Aurea,' from the Conquest downwards. The fifth round they did not mount; that was not History, but Prophecy.

Soon after the capture of the Grays at Nesbit, the Scots, aided by Sir Eugene de Garencières and other French knights, came on a dark night in ships up the Tweed, and disembarked unperceived beneath the walls of Berwick. In the early dawn, scaling the Cow Gate, they soon made themselves masters of the town, Sir Robert Ogle, the Captain, being slain. The burgesses escaped from their beds through the other gates or over the walls. Some of them got into the castle through the Douglas Tower. Edward marched north and entered the castle, intending to let down the drawbridge and sally into the town, while his army and navy, assisted by miners from the forest of Dean, assaulted the walls. The Scots, alarmed at these formidable preparations, abandoned the town. Baliol, tired of the long contest, and having no heirs, confirmed a formal surrender of his rights in Scotland and his English estates, including Bywell, to Edward at Bamburgh. The truce between England and France after the battle of Poictiers included Scotland, and Edward renouncing his demand of homage, and receiving guarantees for the payment of David Bruce's ransom, the King of Scots was set at liberty, and a ten years' truce concluded at Berwick in 1357; nor was there any more open war between the two kingdoms for the remaining twenty years of Edward's reign. Roxburgh and a considerable territory remained English. In 1363, Sir John Coupland, then Warden of the Marches and Keeper of Roxburgh, was murdered on Bolton Moor by John de Clifford and others. His widow, who courageously took a lease of Wark Castle, granted her pasture of Colpenhope in Lanton to the Abbot and convent of Kelso to found a chantry for the souls of her husband and herself, so thoroughly did Kelso seem to have become incorporated in England.

CHAPTER VIII.

THE PERCIES.

HENRY PERCY, as Marshal of England, led the coronation procession of Richard II. He was made a belted earl after the ceremony, by the title of the county in which his great Border castles of Alnwick and Warkworth were situated. The name of Percy, derived from a village in the west of Normandy—perhaps originally built in a *percée*, or forest glade—became thus indelibly associated with that of Northumberland.

The year after Hastings William de Percy had crossed over to England with his neighbour Hugh d'Avranches, the Conqueror's nephew. Through this connection he received grants of large estates in Yorkshire, where the castles of Spofforth and Topcliffe remained the chief seats of the male line of his descendants. The heiress of this line (which had next to nothing to do with anything north of the Tees), married Jocelin, half-brother of Henry Beauclerc's second Queen, and younger son of Godfrey, Count of Louvain, who had risen to be Duke of Brabant. The Counts of Louvain sprang from Ragnar Long-neck, who, in the ninth century, had established himself on the Hayne at Mons, and who, after attempting to dislodge the celebrated Rollo from the island of Walcheren, was made prisoner by the Norman, and only ransomed through the exertions of his brave wife Alberade. By his marriage with a daughter of the house of Charles the Great,

Lambert, the first Count of Louvain, acquired Brussels and other towns ; he gained an unenviable notoriety by hanging his enemies with the bellropes of the churches in which they had taken refuge. Henry, son of Jocelin of Louvain and Agnes de Percy, assumed his mother's surname. His descendants continued to bear the five golden spindles of Percy on an azure shield until Henry Percy III.—the name of Henry, borne by three Counts of Louvain, became so constant in the Percy family that a royal notation had to be adopted—preferred to assume, towards the close of the thirteenth century, an azure lion on a golden shield.

The traditions of the city of Louvain itself—Lovan or Luvanium—are concerned with wolves, and not with lions, as its German name of Loewen might lead one to suppose. The lion of Brabant is a golden one on a black shield. Whether Henry Percy III. assumed his lion-coat in remembrance of his ancestry in Brabant, or of his own alliance with the Earls of Arundel (who bore a similar lion in their arms), he remained true to the azure and gold of the ancient Percy coat, which was itself still emblazoned on the *lambrequin* that flowed from his knightly helm.

As has been said, Henry Percy III. purchased the barony of Alnwick from Bishop Bek. His son, Henry Percy IV., rebuilt Alnwick castle, and increased his possession in Northumberland by acquiring the Clavering baronies of Warkworth, Rothbury, Newburn, and Corbridge. The Yorkshire property of the direct male descendants of Jocelin of Louvain continued, however, to be always of rather more value than the Northumberland. It might have been supposed that the titular Earldom of Henry Percy VI. had reference to the whole country between the Humber and the Tweed, instead of the modern county, had not its dignity been supported by an annuity of £20 from the revenues of the latter. By a special clause, however, all the Earl's territorial possessions, present and future, were to be parcels of his

Earldom. Not only his Yorkshire estates, but places like Petworth in Sussex and Cockermouth in Cumberland found themselves in this honorary county of Northumberland.

In the autumn of 1378, during the progress of negotiations with Scotland for a final peace, seven Scottish Borderers surprised the castle of Berwick. The Governor was killed in jumping out of a window. A faithful soldier named Thomelin Friane rode in hot haste to Alnwick to acquaint the new Earl of Northumberland with the disaster, and 7,000 archers and 3,000 horse were soon collected round the castle. This the Scots, forty-seven in all (their exploit being disavowed by their own Government), had the effrontery to hold for the King of France. It is during this eight days' siege, one of the most extraordinary episodes of medieval warfare, that the Earl's son, Henry Percy VII., makes his first appearance in history, thundering at the great gate with that ardour and impetuosity that gained for him the name of Hotspur, while other successful assaults were delivered by Sir Alan de Heton, Sir Thomas Ilderton, and the whole Heron clan.

Much to the chagrin of the Percies, no doubt, the young King's uncle, John of Gaunt, Duke of Lancaster, and titular King of Castille, proceeded to the North with a great army in 1380, for the purpose of establishing a lasting peace. Dissatisfied with the state of his castle of Dunstanburgh, he engaged John Lewyn, of Durham, the master-mason who built Bolton Castle, in Wensleydale, to raise a lofty stone mantlet round the Great Tower. Receiving private tidings of a great insurrection in the eastern counties, he hastily concluded a long truce with the Scots, and, when the Earl of Northumberland treated him with disrespect, made his escape to Edinburgh, where he was most hospitably received.

On his return journey the gates of Berwick were closed in his face by the Constable, Sir Matthew Redman, acting under the orders of the Earl. Northumberland subsequently declared that this was nothing more than strict compliance with the King's injunctions against admitting anyone into the cities, towns, and castles of the county, who had no property in them; but Lancaster threw down his gauntlet to challenge him in the King's presence, and Richard had difficulty in patching up the quarrel. In virtue of the strange settlement made by Gilbert Umfraville, third Earl of Angus, on his marriage with Maud de Lucy, heiress of the honour of Cockermouth and the barony of Langley, Northumberland, on the death of Angus in 1381, succeeded to the castle and barony of Prudhoe. Soon afterwards, by marrying the widow, he acquired Cockermouth and Langley, on condition that he and his descendants by his first wife should always quarter the three pikes of Lucy with the Percy lion.

Lancaster resumed his negotiations with Scotland, and even obtained an indemnity for the damages done to Wark Castle during the truce. His faith in the ultimate success of his mission cannot have been great. On visiting Dunstanburgh he set out a further work of masonry, and ordered the erection of a new gatehouse on the west side of the fortress, measures of defence that were justified by the raids made by the Scots as far as Embleton in 1384. The English were soon afterwards driven out of Teviotdale. Berwick, Roxburgh, and Jedburgh alone remained of all their conquests. Even Berwick itself was betrayed to the Scots during a truce by the Earl of Northumberland's deputy. Accused in consequence of treason, by Lancaster, and condemned by the Parliament, the Earl hastened to the Border, and, assembling a large force, persuaded the Scots to restore Berwick for 2,000 marks. Upon this he received the King's pardon.

On the truce expiring, the Scots, with a French contingent under John de Vienne, are said to have destroyed the castles of Wark, Ford, and Cornhill. Another truce was concluded at Billymire in 1386. Undeterred by this, a band of Scotch freebooters lifted the cattle of William Heron of Ford, killing some of his men in the process.

Heron retorted by a raid across the Tweed, but North-umberland ordered him to restore the cattle and money taken, promising compensation for his previous losses. On his proving refractory, the Earl sent Henry Lilburn and Thomas Roddam to seize Ford, and lodge him in Newcastle gaol.

The Truce of Billymire having run out, a large Scottish force mustered at Southdean, in the forest of Jed-burgh, in the beginning of August, 1388. The main body proceeded to ravage Cumberland, while 300 chosen spears and 2,000 footmen and archers, led by the Earls of Douglas, March, and Moray, diverted the attention of the English by invading the eastern Border. This latter expedition, the details of which are given with great accuracy in Froissart's contemporary chronicle, has become especially famous in English literature from its connection with the ballads of ' The Battle of Otterburn ' and ' Chevy Chase.' These are really fragments of a great cycle of Percy traditions tacked ignorantly together, without regard to their chronological sequence, by some degenerate south-country minstrel in the sixteenth century.

Rapidly and stealthily the three Scottish earls made their way through the heart of Northumberland. They plundered no house, assaulted no tower, and, traversing the Percy barony of Prudhoe, crossed the Tyne near Bywell. As soon, however, as they had got into the richer parts of the county of Durham, they began slaying the inhabitants and burning the villages. It was the fire and smoke of these conflagrations that gave the first alarm at Durham and Newcastle. To the latter town the Earl of Northumberland despatched his sons Henry and Ralph, while he himself remained at Alnwick, in the hope of cutting off the Scots' retreat. On Saturday, August 15, the marauders appeared before Newcastle. In the skirmishes that took place at the barriers of the town, the two young Percies were always among the foremost, and at last Hotspur met Douglas in single combat. The encounter ended in Douglas winning the gauntlets—each embroidered in pearls with a lion of England and two Percy lions—which Hotspur bore as a favour at the end of his lance.

'Henry, Henry,' cried the Earl, 'this much of your finery I will carry back with me to Scotland, and set it on the highest point of my castle of Dalkeith, that it may be seen the further.' Hotspur, all rage, replied : '*Par Dieu*, Earl of Douglas, never shall you carry it out of Northumberland. Be sure of that !'

To the Scots' surprise, Hotspur for once allowed his impetuosity to be restrained by his knights, who fancied that Douglas was only the van-guard of a large army, and represented that it were better to lose a pennon than two or three hundred knights and squires, and so put the whole country in jeopardy. The Scots were allowed to quietly break up their camp. On their way home they took the castle of Ponteland, with Sir Aymer de Athol in it. This good knight's arms are still in a window of Ponteland Church, and the great slab which contained his memorial brass—one foot of which has alone been saved—has been recently rediscovered in the chantry he founded in St. Andrew's Church at Newcastle.

From Ponteland the Scots proceeded to Otterburn in Redesdale, about thirty miles from Newcastle. There they wasted a whole day in attempting to reduce the castle. Worn out by the unsuccessful attack, most of them were for leaving on the morrow for Carlisle. Douglas, however, remembered Hotspur's threat, and resolved to give him a chance of realizing it by tarrying two or three days longer at Otterburn; so his men made them bowers of trees and leaves in a strong position, surrounded by great marshes. The entrance to these, on the Newcastle road, was occupied by the 'varlets and foragers,' and the cattle which had been lifted were left to graze between the two camps.

Some good men of Northumberland, who had followed on the heels of the Scots, now brought word to Newcastle that Douglas would for a certainty rest that night at Otterburn without being joined by the main body of the host; as for the morrow, they could not answer. 'Then, to horse, to horse!' cried Hotspur; 'my duty to God and my father bids me seek my pennon and dislodge the Scots this night.' This time he met with little opposition. Walter de Skirlawe, Bishop of Durham, was to have arrived at Newcastle that evening, but Hotspur considered his own force of 600 lances and 800 foot sufficient for his purpose. In his immediate following were Ralph Lord Lumley, Sir Matthew Redman, Sir Robert Ogle, Sir Thomas Gray of Heton, Sir Thomas Gray of Horton, Sir John Felton, Sir John Lilburn, Sir William Wessington, Sir Thomas Abreton (probably a Gascon knight), the Baron of Hilton, Sir John Copeldyke, John Saville Sheriff of Yorkshire, and two young Gascons: John, brother to the Seigneur of Castelnau-de-Tursan, and John de Cantierain. The roll of Otterburn has been as much tampered with by minstrels anxious to flatter their patrons as was that of Hastings by the monks of Battle.

The Scots were sitting at supper that St. Oswin's Eve, August 19, 1388, when suddenly the cry of 'Percy! Percy!' rang from the camp of their 'varlets,' which the English had mistaken for the camp of the knights. The Scottish lords at once despatched their 'varlets' and foot-soldiers to take part in the skirmish, while they themselves armed and formed into three companies, led by the respective earls. Night was falling fast, but the moon was up, and the air clear and calm. The Scots had carefully thought out the tactics they were to follow in case of a night attack. Falling silently into line, instead of advancing straight against the English, they skirted the marshes and, making round a hill, fell on the rear of their assailants, who, having sent flying the first batch of 'varlets,' kept meeting fresh relays as they forced their way further into the camp. Taken between two fires, the English kept their ground manfully, and

were on the point of routing the Scots, when Earl
James ordered his great silken banner (blazoned with
St. Andrew's cross, a white lion, the hearts and stars
of Douglas, and the proud motto '*Jamais arryere*') to
be advanced, to the cry of ' Douglas ! Douglas !' The
brothers Percy now directed their whole attack on this
standard. Sir Patrick Hepburn and his sons were
struck down in defending it. Douglas, seeing his men
swerve, seized a battle-axe, and cut his way into the
midst of the throng. He was armed neither with breastplate nor bascinet, and in the uncertain light of the after-
glow and the moon was recognised neither by friend
nor foe. Three lance-thrusts bore him down. His
standard-bearer and the faithful Sir Robert Hart fell
beside him. His chaplain, William of North Berwick,
more warrior than priest, staved back the enemy until
Sir James Lindsay came up with Sir John and Sir Walter
Sinclair, and vainly endeavoured to raise the wounded
Earl. ' Cousin, how fare you ?' asked Sir John. ' Poorly,
praised be God,' was the reply ; ' for few of my ancestors
died in bed or chamber. I count myself dead, for my
heart beats slow. Think to avenge me. Raise my
banner, and shout " Douglas !" and let neither friend nor
foe learn the pass to which I have come.'

On hearing this new cry of ' Douglas!' the Earls of March
and Moray threw themselves on the Percies. The battle
became a regular hand-to-hand fight ; every knight and
squire stood his ground. Sir Ralph Percy allowed his
valour to carry him into the midst of the Scots. Hemmed
in on all sides, the blood gushing from his hose and grieves,
he was compelled to surrender, ' rescue or no rescue,'
to John Maxwell, a new-dubbed knight of Moray's household. Hotspur was engaged in mortal combat with Sir
Hugh Montgomery. There is nothing unlikely in the
poetical tradition that makes him yield to the ' bracken
bush' in which the dead Douglas lay. More than a
hundred English knights shared Hotspur's fate. The
ferocity of the Scots and English in the fight was, how-

ever, only equalled by their chivalrous conduct to each other when once it was over.

Seeing that by himself he could not retrieve the fortunes of the day, Sir Matthew Redman reluctantly mounted his horse, and rode off in the direction of Newcastle. This was noticed by Sir James Lindsay, who gave chase, crying, 'Sir knight, turn ye! It is base and shameful to flee. I am James Lindsay, and if ye turn not, I will run you through with my lance from behind.' But Redman only galloped on the faster. At last, when the pursuit had lasted some twelve miles, his horse stumbled near Shafto, and, rising on foot, he prepared to defend himself with his sword. Parrying Lindsay's lance, which stuck in the ground, he cleft it in two. Thereupon Lindsay also dismounted, and attacked Redman with his axe so fiercely that he yielded, and was allowed to proceed to Newcastle, after promising to present himself as a prisoner in Scotland in a fortnight's time.

The moon had now gone down. Lindsay, having ridden two or three miles towards Otterburn, as he supposed, found himself face to face with a company of horsemen. Thinking they were Scots, he rode in among them. 'Who goes there?' demanded the leader. 'I am James Lindsay.' 'You are right welcome, sir knight; and I take you my prisoner. I am Walter de Skirlawe, priest and Bishop of Durham.' The Bishop had reached Newcastle in the evening with the levies of Yorkshire and Durham, and had sat down to supper, when it struck him that it was not quite right to leave the Percies unsupported. Accordingly, at eight o'clock at night the trumpets sounded 'To horse!' and, issuing at the Berwick gate at the head of a thousand followers, the Bishop finally took the Redesdale road. The fugitives from Otterburn whom he met told anything but reassuring tales. His own ranks thinned so rapidly in consequence that he had only 500 men left when he encountered Lindsay near Belsay. There was nothing for it but to turn back. At three in the morning the Bishop re-entered Newcastle, and, fearing a night attack, remained himself at the gate until sunrise.

On coming to Skirlawe's lodgings that morning, what was Redman's surprise to see Lindsay leaning out of a window. The two prisoners naturally concluded they would now be exchanged, and, in the best of spirits, Redman took Lindsay to dine with him. Skirlawe was much put out by the ill-success of his night-march, and, taking with him all the available troops, got within four miles of Otterburn, when a furious blowing of horns and beating of drums by the Scots in their fortified camp caused his craven following to retreat.

A succession of truces secured the peace of the Border for the remainder of the reign of Richard II. At a march-meeting at Hawden-stank in 1397, Hotspur appeared in complete armour, whereupon Sir David Lindsay demanded:

> ' " Sir Henry, what makes you to be
> Sae warlike as you now we see?"
> To him then answered the Percy:
> " I will that you wit, Sir Davy,
> Of Scottish men I dread nae force,
> But this I do for English horse."
> Then said the Lindsay Sir Davy:
> " Thou kens right well yet, Sir Henry,
> That oft have Scotsmen with their force
> Thee sarer grieved than English horse " '

—a bitter allusion to Otterburn.

While Sir Thomas Gray of Heton, who had recently acquired the barony of Wark-on-Tweed, was attending the first Parliament of Henry IV., the Scots seized Wark Castle, carrying off his children and many of the tenants. Sir Thomas thought it necessary to obtain the King's pardon for the inefficiency of his garrison. Further ravages of the Scots were checked at Fulhopelaw, in Coquetdale, by Sir Robert Umfraville. Among his many prisoners were Sir William Stewart, John Turnbull (known as 'Out-with-the-Sword') and Sir Richard

Rutherford and his five sons. All these, by King Henry's orders, were forbidden to be ransomed. In August, 1400, the King himself led an expedition as far as Edinburgh. The Scots slipped in behind him, and ravaged Bamburghshire. It was probably on this occasion that

> ' Over Ottercap hill they came in,
>   And so down by Rothley crag ;
> Upon Greenleighton they lighted down,
>   Stirring many a stag.
>
> ' And boldly burnt Northumberland
>   And harried many a town ;
> They did our Englishmen great hurt
>   To battle that were not bound.
>
> ' Then spake a bairn upon the bent
>   Of comfort that was not cold,
> And said : " We have burnt Northumberland,
>   We have all wealth in hold.
>
> ' " Now we have harried all Bamboroughshire,
>   All the wealth in the world have we " '

—an opinion as to the richness of Bamburghshire that was endorsed by its inhabitants, who were wont to describe it as ' the finest coonty in a' England.'

Two years later, in 1402, whether or not in connection with hunting in Cheviot, Archibald Douglas appears to have accepted a challenge from the Percies to meet them in battle about August 15, the Feast of the Assumption. At any rate, King Henry gave orders for raising levies to assist them by that day. The Scottish raid seems to have extended nearly to Newcastle. The Percies resolved to cut off their retreat. Hotspur was at this time Constable of Bamburgh, and the ballad tells us :

> ' Then the Percy out of Bamburgh
>   With him a mighty many,
> With fifteen hundred archers bold ;
>   They were chosen out of shires three.'

Unfortunately for Northern pride, the retinue-lists and muster-rolls of the period show that these archers, instead of being raised from Bamburghshire, Islandshire, and Norhamshire, must have been mainly Welshmen.

Riding all night, the Percies posted themselves on the right bank of the Glen at Homildon, a little beyond Wooler, between the river and the Cheviots. The next morning —it was probably Monday, August 14, the vigil of the Assumption, for writers who, in the case of Otterburn, mistook St. Oswald's Eve for St. Oswin's, may easily have got confused between the Assumption and the Exaltation —they despatched 500 archers in quest of food :

> ' The drivers thorowe the woodes went
>   For to reas the deer ;
> Bomen bickarte upon the bent
>   With their broad arrows clear.
>
>   *   *   *   *
>
> The begane in Chyviat the hyls above
>   Yerly on a monnynday ;
> Be that it drewe to the oware off none
>   A hondrith fat hartes ded ther lay.'

It was about noon when the Scots, hurrying homewards and imagining they were pursued by the Earl of North-umberland, suddenly found themselves confronted by the Percy forces. Instead of giving battle, they took up a defensive position on Homildon Hill. Hereupon the English ascended the opposite slope of Harehope. Just then the Percy archers, returning with their quarry, entered the Monday Clough (as it is now called), between the two hills. Catching sight of the resplendent armour of the Scottish knights, which had been two years in making, they let fly their arrows among them :

> ' The Yngglishe men hade their bowys yebent,
>   Ther hartes were good yenoughe ;
> The first of arros that the shote off
>   Seven skore spear men the sloughe.'

Notwithstanding this, the Earl of Douglas decided 'to bide upon the bent.' Sir John Swinton denounced in vain the folly of stopping to be shot at like fawns in a park. Adam de Gordon, who had been Swinton's mortal enemy, was so pleased with his courageous bearing that he begged to be knighted by him, and then the two charged down the hillside together, followed by a hundred others. It was all the Earl of March, now on the English side, could do to restrain Hotspur from assailing the Scottish position, instead of leaving the entire battle to his archers. The showers of arrows at last forced the Scots to come down on to the plain towards the river; but the marksmen successfully followed them up. The traditions of the splendid archery at Homildon, transferred by the ballad-mongers to Otterburn, should be restored to their rightful place:

> 'Ther came an arrow hastily
>   Forth of a mighty wane.
> It hath stricken the earl Douglas
>   In at the breast-bane.

> 'An archer of Northumberland
>   *   *   *   *
> He bar a bend bow in his hand
>   Was made of a trusty tree,

> 'An arrow that a cloth yard was long
>   To th' hard stele halyde he ;
> A dint that was both sad and soar
>   He set on Sir Hugh the Montgomery.'

The revenge for Otterburn was complete, but it had been fourteen years in coming. Douglas, pierced with five arrow-wounds, and blinded in an eye, was taken prisoner together with Montgomery, Murdack of Fife, the eldest son of the Duke of Albany, and eighty other persons of note. Among these were Sir Walter Stewart of Forest and Thomas Ker, 'another good squire,' who, after being acquitted by a jury of the charge of treason, on account of their having been born English subjects in Teviotdale, were summarily executed by Hotspur. The exposure of Stewart's limbs over the gates of York is said to have shocked even the English, and to have given rise to the prophetic reflection that Hotspur's might soon take their place.

Carrying out the policy initiated in the case of Lindsay after Otterburn, and again adopted after Fulhopelaw, Henry IV. forbade the acceptance of ransoms by private persons for the prisoners they had taken at Homildon, and ordered Douglas and the rest to be sent up to London. It was not intended that the captors should lose their reward, but the Government's possession of the prisoners was felt to be a powerful lever in negotiating a lasting peace. Hotspur, however, refused to give up Douglas, and Northumberland reproached the King that they had spent their all in his service without receiving payment for the custody of the marches. Henry, with his treasury bare, could only reply, 'Gold I have none; gold thou canst not have.' Hotspur, too, required that his brother-in-law, Edmund Mortimer, should be ransomed; but the King, with good reason, declared that Mortimer's captivity in Wales was a mere feint to cover his treason. 'And thou, too, art a traitor,' he continued, charging Hotspur with letting Glendower slip out of his hands. Hotspur replied that his honour forbade him to violate the safe-conduct he had given Glendower, and when Henry actually drew his dagger on him, muttered the challenge, 'Not here, but in the field.'

Although Edmund Mortimer now wedded the daughter of Owen Glendower, and openly renounced his allegiance to Henry, the King, anxious to conciliate the Percies as far as was in his power, bestowed on them the greater part of the South of Scotland. This he declared to have been conquered and annexed to England. Hotspur was not content with the fertile tract already subdued, and proceeded to overrun the whole country up to the Forth. On his summoning the little tower of Cocklaw in Upper Teviotdale (just to the north-east of Ormiston, near Hawick), which belonged to James Gledystanes, the captain, John Greenlaw, refused to surrender. After some show of a siege, an armistice was agreed to on condition that the garrison should capitulate on August 1, 1403, if not previously relieved by the Scottish

Government. Hotspur declared that his intention was to provoke the Scots to a pitched battle, more disastrous to them than even that of Homildon. He and his father urged the King to send the large sums they claimed in order that they might prepare for the engagement. Henry had no such sums to send, but announced his intention of coming himself to their assistance. This was not what the Percies wanted. If Hotspur's squire, John Hardyng, is to be believed, they had, under the cloak of the exploit of Ormiston, formed a league with all the English lords, except the Earl of Stafford, for asserting their privileges and removing the King's evil counsellors. Hardyng even says that Hotspur intrusted the sealed bonds given by these lords to his keeping at Warkworth, but his own subsequent forgery of Scottish documents throws some doubt on the matter. At any rate, by the time Henry IV. had reached the Trent, Hotspur, with only eightscore horsemen, had ridden off to Chester, and was openly raising the country against the King. His defeat and death at the battle of Shrewsbury, fought on Saturday, July 21, was largely due to that uncurbed spirit of adventure—*effrænata temeritas*—which had given him his name.

On the Monday following, the Earl of Northumberland, cautiously advancing to Hotspur's assistance, was forced back towards Newcastle by the levies of the Earl of Westmorland. The townsmen closed their gates, and, after attempting to storm the place, Northumberland had to be content with permission to enter himself for a night's rest, leaving his armed followers without. The next day, while he was at breakfast, his troops again tried an escalade. At this juncture the tidings of Hotspur's death arrived, and, excusing himself as best he could, the Earl disbanded his army, and withdrew with his household to Warkworth.

Although the architectural details of the marvellous donjon of Warkworth, with its maze of chambers and passages, may appear to many of slightly later character, it is extremely improbable that Northumberland, pos-

sessed of such power and ambition, did nothing to render
his favourite home more habitable and magnificent, or
better calculated for a refuge in the time of need. Until,
then, we are vouchsafed direct documentary evidence on
the subject, we may well regard this 'worm-eaten hold of
ragged stone' as the work of the first and greatest, but
by no means the best, of the eleven Earls of the princely
House of Louvain. The neighbouring rock-hewn hermitage of the Trinity, so beautifully placed on the brink of
the Wansbeck, was probably founded some thirty years
earlier as a chantry for the soul of his first wife, Margaret
Neville.

At Warkworth, Northumberland received a letter from
Henry IV., promising to receive him into favour if he
would repair peaceably to his presence. On doing so
he was, however, arrested, and though he agreed to surrender his castles of Alnwick, Warkworth, Prudhoe, and
Langley into the King's hands, was cast into prison at
Baginton, near Coventry. William Heron, Lord Say,
proceeded to Warkworth to take possession of the castle
for the King. Sir Henry Percy of Athol, the Earl's
grandson, who could not have been more than eighteen,
refused to evacuate it and betake himself to Court,
unless he were provided 'with horses, armour, vessels of
silver, and beds suited to his rank. These the chaplain
and 'wardrober' of Alnwick Castle refused to let Say
have without a warrant from the Earl their master. For
the moment Say had to be content with the oaths of Sir
Henry Percy and the Constable of Warkworth, that they
would keep the castle loyally for both King and Earl.
He proceeded, however, to Baginton, and there extorted
a promise from Northumberland, in the highly suggestive
presence of his seven gaolers, that he would affix the
great seal he had left in London 'to everything that was
pleasing to his Sovereign Lord.' The letters and orders
authenticated by this seal proved, however, of little use.
Berwick, Alnwick, and Warkworth continued to defy the
royal authority, and Sir Henry Percy of Athol and his

brother, advised by Sir William Clifford, began distributing the 'livery of the crescent,' the badge of their house, to the large forces they had collected. In February, 1404, the Earl of Northumberland, having been acquitted of treason by his peers, was, with diplomatic generosity, restored to his estates by the King.

Writing from Warkworth in January, 1405, Northumberland excused himself from attending the King's Council in winter-time, on account of the long and bad road, and his great age and feebleness—he was really only sixty-three. The following May, tearing off the mask, he put Robert Waterton, the King's messenger, in durance vile at Warkworth, and promised his support to Archbishop Scrope. As in the case of Hotspur, however, the insurgents were defeated before he appeared in the field.

At the head of 37,000 men, Henry Bolingbroke now marched in person into Northumberland, taking with him every conceivable engine of war. The Earl fled into Scotland with his grandson, Henry-fitz-Hotspur. After the fall of Prudhoe, most of the Percy retainers submitted to the King at Widdrington. John de Middleham, Captain of Warkworth, however, determined to hold it for the Earl. The royal cannon, brought into position on July 1, wrought such havoc on the walls that, after the seventh discharge, Middleham and his company cried ' Mercy!' and were allowed to depart with the honours of war. The small towers of Alnham and Newstead likewise capitulated. Alnwick held out until the King returned in triumph from Berwick, which suffered greatly from the bombardment, and where stern justice was meted out to the principal rebels. Henry now bestowed the forfeited baronies of Alnwick, Prudhoe, and Langley on his third son, John, a boy of sixteen, whom he had already made Warden of the East March.

John of Lancaster resided principally at Warkworth. Though he had undertaken the custody of the March for considerably less than was allowed to Hotspur, he received payment with no greater regularity, and was forced to pawn his plate and jewels to provide for the defence of Berwick. The Earl of Northumberland continued to stir up mischief in the North from his retreat in Scotland. John de Middleham was condemned to death for receiving a letter from him in 1407. The letter had been communicated to William de Alnewyk, a canon of Alnwick and Vicar of Chatton. He fled across the Border to the Earl, but was soon pardoned, and became afterwards Bishop, first of Norwich, and then of Lincoln. Henry Percy VI., now more than sixty-five, had the imprudence to appear in hostile array as far south as Bramham Moor, and was there defeated and slain.

Just as he was setting sail for Harfleur and Agincourt in 1415, King Henry V. determined on the politic restoration of Henry Percy VIII., the son of Hotspur (who counts as Henry Percy VII.), to the Earldom of Northumberland and his settled estates. He accordingly granted an annuity of 3,000 marks as compensation to his own brother John, now Duke of Bedford, who retained the barony of Prudhoe and manor of Shilbottle. About the same time a valuable list of the castles and towers of Northumberland and their owners was drawn up in order to show in whose hands the defence of the Border would be left during the King's absence. The names of thirty-seven castles and seventy-eight towers are given, including the castle of Roxburgh and the tower of Denton-in-Gilsland. Sir Thomas Gray, who appears as the owner of the castles of Heton and Wark-on-Tweed, and the towers of Wark-on-Tyne and Nesbit-in-Glendale, was arrested at Southampton on August 1, for conspiring against the King with the Earl of Cambridge, and was executed a week later.

The negotiations for exchanging Murdack of Fife, who had remained a prisoner in England since Homildon, for the heir of the Percies fell through, and it was not till the spring of 1416 that Henry Percy VIII. was given up by the Scots at Berwick. He married almost immediately

Eleanor Neville, daughter of the Earl of Westmorland, with whom he lived long and happily at their favourite castle of Warkworth.

In 1453, after a marriage feast at Tattershall in Lincolnshire, some followers of their son, Thomas Percy, Lord Egremont, came to blows with the retinue of Richard Neville, Earl of Salisbury, and the old feud between Percy and Neville blazed forth anew. The Duke of York, then Protector of England, exerted himself to put down this private war, and the Percies ever after bore him a grudge. The second Earl of Northumberland fell the following year fighting for the Red Rose at St. Albans. York's victory there was due in a great measure to the vigour of his faithful henchman, Sir Robert Ogle. The third Earl, Henry Percy IX., was cut off in his fortieth year, on the disastrous field of Towton, on the ' Evil Palm Sunday' of 1461.

From Towton Margaret of Anjou fled with her husband and their adherents towards Scotland. They were supposed to have halted at Newcastle, and Edward IV. sent 20,000 men to besiege the town. It was necessary for the fugitives to obtain a safe-conduct before crossing the Border. The delay appears to have led to their being overtaken and besieged by Sir Robert Ogle and Sir John Conyers in the castle of Wark near Carham. Certain esquires of the Earl of Northumberland gathered together 5,000 or 6,000 Lancastrians, and effected their rescue after 3,000 north-country men had fallen in the ' bicker.'

In consideration of their promised assistance, Henry VI. made over Berwick to the Scots. A little later, accompanied by Sir John Fortescue and others, ' with standards and gyturons unrolled,' he rode through Ryton as far south as Branspeth. The timely arrival of Lord Montagu saved Carlisle from sharing the fate of Berwick. Before Michaelmas Dunstanburgh, with its constable, Sir Ralph Percy, uncle of the young Earl Henry Percy X., declared for the White Rose.

Sailing from Kirkcudbright in the spring of 1462, the

intrepid Margaret engaged the services of Pierre de Brezé, Seigneur of Varennes and Count Maulevrier, a brave French knight, with a contingent of 800 men. Henry VI. did not remain inactive. He appears to have attempted to recover Dunstanburgh, the cornfields around which were trampled down by his horses. In July, however, Alnwick, which was held for him by William Tailbois, was forced to capitulate to Lord Hastings, and was committed to the custody of Sir Ralph Grey. A month later, the castle and manor of Warkworth were granted by Edward IV. to his brother George of Clarence. Bamburgh, too, became Yorkist in the hands of Sir William Tunstal. But when Queen Margaret landed near it with her French auxiliaries on October 25, the garrison, influenced by Sir Richard Tunstal, the Governor's brother, threw open the gates to receive her. Still there was no general rising in her favour ; indeed, the peasantry of Rock and Beadnell proved particularly vigilant in the Yorkist interest. Sir Ralph Percy, however, went over to Margaret with the garrison of Dunstanburgh, and Alnwick was obliged to surrender for want of provisions.

The great Earl of Warwick hastened to the North. He fixed his headquarters at Warkworth, and rode round every day to direct the sieges of Alnwick, Dunstanburgh, and Bamburgh, which were all invested on December 10. The operations at Dunstanburgh, which was defended by Sir Richard Tunstal, Dr. Morton (afterwards Archbishop of Canterbury), Sir Philip Wentworth, and 600 or 700 men, were carried on under the more immediate command of the Earl of Worcester and Sir Ralph Grey. Worcester subsequently proceeded to the siege of Bamburgh. His place in the camp before Dunstanburgh was occupied by the lords Fitzhugh, Scrope, Greystoke, and Powys. In their turn Greystoke and Powys marched off to Alnwick, leaving Scrope and Fitzhugh in the company of Wentworth and Hastings, who had come up from the South.

In Bamburgh the Duke of Somerset and Sir Ralph Percy had with them no more than 300 Lancastrians. Margaret herself had taken advantage of the presence of a French fleet, to effect her escape from the beleaguered fortress on board a ' carvyle.' A violent storm arose; some of the French ships went ashore. The blockade of Bamburgh was so close that the 400 soldiers who were saved considered their best chance lay in occupying Holy Island. Margaret, forced to abandon the ' carvyle,' which had foundered with all her treasure, was now with them. A force of 200 Yorkists who happened to be on Holy Island allowed themselves to be surprised. No sooner, however, did the news of this exploit reach the Earl of Warwick, than he determined to dislodge the Frenchmen. It was in vain that they tried to bar his passage across the sands at low water. Margaret fled to Berwick in a fishing-boat. The French took refuge in the priory, where 200 of them were killed or made prisoners. Among the latter were Louis Malet, Seigneur de Graville, and Raoul d'Ally, Seigneur d'Araines.

Bamburgh capitulated on Christmas Eve ; three days later Dunstanburgh did the same. The garrisons, reduced to eating most of their horses, were glad to have their lives spared, and to be allowed to make for Scotland with white staves in their hands. With the assistance of the Earl of Angus, Brezé was enabled to bring off the greater part of the garrison of Alnwick on January 6, 1463 ; but the Scots were afraid to assume the offensive, and the castle fell at the end of the month.

Edward IV. sent £100 to the Abbot and convent of Alnwick to compensate them for the losses they sustained during the siege of the castle. He evidently never thought of fresh trouble in Northumberland. Suddenly, during Lent, the Scots and French once more seized Bamburgh and Dunstanburgh, with the passive connivance of Sir Ralph Percy, who, on turning Yorkist for the second time, had been appointed Governor of both fortresses. Margaret, indeed, appears to have pushed forward into the neighbourhood of Hexham, and to have been advancing on April 3, 1463, to attack the strong position occupied by the Yorkists at ' Rel,' or Ryal, on the right bank of the Devilswater, when a panic seizing her Scottish allies, they deserted the braver Frenchmen, and a hopeless rout ensued. The Queen herself was overtaken by a party of the enemy, who made free with her royal jewels. They were quite capable of cutting her throat, but began fighting among themselves over the booty. While their attention was thus engrossed, Margaret prevailed on an esquire to let her mount behind him, with her little son Edward in front, and all three rode off into the recesses of Dipton Wood. They had not gone far before up came one of the cut-throat robbers who infested it. Margaret boldly bade him approach. ' Man,' she cried, ' thou wast born under a lucky star. After all the wrong thou hast done, a chance is now given thee of doing a good deed that never shall be forgotten. It is to turn thee from thine old way of life that I, the wretched Queen of England, am fallen into thy clutches. If thou hast any knowledge of God and of His Passion, take pity on my misery. Save, at any rate, this youth, thy King's only son. By this deed of mercy, all thy past cruelty shall be forgotten. Hide him in thy woods and thickets; let him eat roots and acorns with the swine, and pass his nights on the cold ground. On such a royal bed, and in such baronial company, his life will be safer than if he tasted the fitful fortunes of a throne. Save my son; keep him for me; and if God grant his restoration, be sure that he will well reward a service such as never yet hath fallen to the lot of a man like thee to perform.'

The astonished robber threw himself at the Queen's feet, and, swearing to die a thousand deaths rather than abandon the Prince, besought her pardon for his misdeeds, as though she still bore the sceptre in London. The Prince was intrusted to him, and he honourably performed his promises. Margaret, consoled with the thought that her son was in safety, got up again behind the esquire, and found her way, without the aid of a guide, to King Henry, near the Border.

Towards the end of May, Sir Ralph Grey, disgusted at having been made only Captain of Alnwick, delivered Sir John Astley, who had been placed over him as Constable, into the hands of Sir Ralph Percy, and admitted Lord Hungerford and the French into the castle. On hearing of this, Henry and Margaret came to Bamburgh with Brezé and 2,000 men. On the other side, Lord Montagu immediately marched North from London, followed on June 4 by his brother Warwick.

Montagu reached Newcastle just in time to defend it from a sudden attack from Sir Ralph Grey. Several Lancastrians fell in a skirmish under the walls, and the men of Newcastle captured four French vessels. Grey and Brezé then engaged on the siege of a castle near Alnwick, probably Warkworth, but they were compelled to abandon this on the advance of Montagu, who had been relieved at Newcastle by the arrival of Warwick's army.

About Midsummer, Henry and Margaret, with the young James III. of Scotland, laid formal siege to Norham. Warwick and Montagu 'put them in devoir' to relieve the castle. This they effectually did ; the Scots were put to flight, and Henry and Margaret forced to conceal themselves and the young Prince of Wales, till they could make good their escape to Bamburgh. For five days the royal fugitives had only a single herring among them ; one day they were actually left without bread. On July 20, the festival of her patron St. Margaret, the unfortunate Queen found she had not even a black penny to offer in alms at the Mass. She therefore begged a Scots archer to lend her something. With scant civility, the man ruefully took a Scots groat out of his purse—a touch of national character that brings the scene vividly before us.

On Warwick and Montagu approaching Bamburgh,
Margaret determined to embark while opportunity offered,
and place her son in safety. Leaving Henry, with her
horses and arms, in the castle, which she knew was
capable of resisting any immediate attack, she set sail
with the Prince of Wales for Flanders on July 30, accompanied by Brezé and his Frenchmen. One valiant French
drummer declined to go on board, and remained ' tabour-
ing and piping,' on a hill—possibly the sand-hill near the
postern—till Warwick came up. He was taken into the
Earl's service.

Having no large force at his disposal, and possibly not
altogether desirous of entirely crushing the Lancastrian
party, Warwick retired to the South of England. For
the next nine months Henry VI., in the lone solitude of
the old Northumbrian capital, continued to reign over
Alnwick and Bamburghshire. His little Court received
the envoys of Charles the Bold and Louis XI. About
Christmas, 1463, the Duke of Somerset, who had been
in high favour with Edward IV., secretly left Wales for
Newcastle, which was garrisoned by his retainers, with
the intention of betraying it to the Lancastrians. The
plot was, however, discovered, and the town placed in
the trusty keeping of Lord Scrope of Bolton. Somerset
reported to Henry that Wales and the West of England
were prepared to support his cause. The Privy Council
at Bamburgh thereupon requested Pierre Cousinot, the
envoy of Louis XI., to return to France, and arrange
with Queen Margaret that Charles the Bold should send
artillery and provisions to Bamburgh, and that her father,
René of Anjou, the titular King of Sicily, should supply it
with cannon and culverins.

The active measures concerted by Warwick induced
Kennedy, the Scottish Regent, to sue for peace. But
before the commissioners of both nations could meet, the
Lancastrians made themselves masters of the castles of
Norham and Skipton. Edward's Parliament was sum-
moned to assemble at York on May 5, 1464. As the

Scottish mission expected at it required a strong escort to pass through Northumberland in safety, Lord Montagu set out towards Norham with all the troops at his disposal. On April 25, St. Mark's Day, he found his progress barred on Hedgeley Moor by the Duke of Somerset and 5,000 men, drawn chiefly from Alnwick and Dunstanburgh. Sir Ralph Percy fell, crying, 'I have saved the bird in my bosom,' meaning, it is said, that, after so many tergiversations, he died true to his original liege. The other Lancastrian lords took to flight. The Scottish commissioners were now able to reach York and conclude peace with Edward. 'An the Scots be true, the treaty may continue fifteen years,' says the chronicle; 'but it is hard to trust Scots: they be ever full of guile and deceit.'

Somerset and the other lords followed in the wake of the convoy, and took up their quarters at Hexham, in the neighbourhood of which they held the castles of Langley and Bywell. Instead of proceeding to York, Montagu marched up the Tyne from Newcastle, with Greystoke and Willoughby and 4,000 men. The Lancastrians attempted to dispute the passage of the Devilswater at the Linnels, but Sir Ralph Grey ran away before the battle began, and his cowardice proved contagious. Somerset, with 500 others, made a last stand on a hill a mile out of Hexham.

Pursued and taken by the servants of Sir John Middleton, the Duke was beheaded the next day at Hexham, together with Sir Edmund Fitzhugh and Black Jack, a Border thief, who may have been the faithful protector of Prince Edward after the first battle of Hexham. The lords Ros and Hungerford were discovered hiding in a neighbouring wood, and immediately executed at Newcastle. The prompt severity with which this rising was put down contrasted strongly with the mild measures that had accompanied previous successes of the White Rose.

Langley and Bywell offered no resistance to the

victorious Montagu. In the latter castle were found King Henry's helmet with his 'bycocket,' or cap of state, his sword, and the trappings of his horse. 'How and whither the King himself escaped,' adds the contemporary chronicler, 'God only knows, in whose hands are the hearts of kings.' Events proved that, like Sir Ralph Grey and many others, Henry of Windsor had galloped back to Bamburgh. Warwick, who had now come North, assisted Montagu at the storm of Dunstanburgh. John Gosse, the captain of the castle, who had been carver in Somerset's household, was taken by them in triumph to Edward IV. at York, and there beheaded with a hatchet. As a reward for these signal services, Montagu was created Earl of Northumberland, and received a grant of most of the Percy estates in the county.

Alarmed at the fall of Dunstanburgh, Henry VI., with the assistance of Sir Henry Bellingham and others, cut his way through the Yorkist levies that were already closing in round Bamburgh. It was not, however, till June 23 that Warwick 'came with his puissance' before Alnwick, which at once surrendered. The Feast of St. John Baptist he kept at Dunstanburgh, and began next day the formal siege of Bamburgh. Two heralds, Chester and Warwick, were sent to Sir Ralph Grey and 'other that kept his rebellious opinion,' commanding them to deliver up the fortress, when all the garrison, except Sir Humphrey Neville and Sir Ralph Grey, who were 'out of the King's grace without any redemption,' would receive the royal pardon.

Fired with the courage of despair, Sir Ralph replied that he had 'clearly determined within himself to live or die in the castle.' Thereupon the heralds laid all guilt of bloodshed to his charge, and one of them delivered the parting defiance: 'My Lords ensure you upon their honour to sustain siege before you these seven years or else to win you. If ye deliver not this jewel the which the King our most dread Sovereign Lord hath so greatly in favour, seeing it marcheth so nigh his ancient enemies of Scotland, and specially desireth to have whole, unbroken with ordnance ; if ye suffer one great gun to be laid unto the wall and be shot, to prejudice the wall, it shall cost you the chieftain's head ; and so proceeding for every gun shot, to the last head of any person within the place.'

Notwithstanding this terrible warning, Sir Ralph Grey 'put him in devoir to make defence,' while Warwick ordered all his great guns to be charged and 'shoot unto the castle.' ' Newcastle,' the King's great gun of iron, and ' London,' his lesser gun, so 'betide ' the place, that the stones flew into the sea. The brass gun ' Dijon ' ' smote through Sir Ralph Grey's chamber oftentimes,' and the cannonade was kept up by the bombardels ' Edward ' and ' Richard.' A breach having been effected, Warwick won the castle with his archers and men-at-arms. Grey was led prisoner to Edward IV. at Doncaster, where he was executed. One of the chief articles in his indictment was that he had ' withstood and made fences against the King's majesty and his Lieutenant, the worthy Lord of Warwick, as appeareth by the strokes of the great guns in the King's walls of his castle of Bamburgh.'

In 1469, after the rising led by Robin of Redesdale, and the capture of his own person by Warwick, King Edward released Henry Percy X., the eldest son of the third Earl of Northumberland, from the Tower. On the open treason of Clarence and Warwick in the following year, he intrusted him with the custody of their Percy estates as well as with the wardenries of the East and Middle March. The more faithful John Neville surrendered the Earldom of Northumberland, and received in exchange the purely honorary Marquisate of Montagu—' with a pye's nest to maintain it,' as he said. Soon afterwards Henry VI. was restored to the throne for six months. During these Sir Henry Percy naturally bore his father's title. The complications of his position with respect to the Marquis of Montagu, who, having now turned Lan-

castrian, was made Warden of the East March, led **Percy**
to acquiesce in the restoration of Edward, by whom he
was, however, not finally restored in blood to his father's
earldom and estates till the autumn of 1472.

The Percy whose desertion of Richard III. decided
the fortunes of Bosworth Field appears to have been Sir
Henry Percy, son of Sir Ralph, and heir of his father's
craft and courage.   The fourth Earl of Northumberland,
far from betraying the White Rose, did not accept
Henry VII. till he had been imprisoned and further
resistance was out of the question.   His loyalty to his
new Sovereign cost him his life.   The murder of

> 'The famous Erle of Northumberlande,
>   Of knyghtly prowes the sword, pomel and hylt,
>   The myghty lyon doutted by se and lande,'

while enforcing the fiscal exactions of Henry Tudor,
marks the rise of a strong central monarchy on the ruins
of the old provincial nobility.   The Earl just before his
death had built the strong tower at Hulne Priory, and
had ordered a large stone with a lion rampant to be
carved there, and placed over the outer gate of Alnwick
Castle.   The stone has been replaced, but the original
cornice and ledge, with the motto

> '*Esperance Ma Comfort*'

and the initials and badges of the Earl and his Countess,
are still preserved in the castle.

CHAPTER IX.

THE EAST AND MIDDLE MARCHES.

THANKS to the virtuous diplomacy of Richard Fox, Bishop successively of St. Asaph, Bath and Wells and Durham, peace with Scotland was preserved during the reign of Henry VII., by a succession of truces, until, in 1496, James IV. actively espoused the cause of Perkin Warbeck. The Scots at first demanded from this most chivalrous of pretenders the eventual cession of the seven sheriffdoms north of the Humber as the price of their assistance. Warbeck ultimately agreed with them for Berwick and £50,000. The Border was laid waste, neither sex nor age being spared; the towers of Twizel, Tilmouth, Duddo, Shoreswood, Brankston, Howtell, and Lanton were destroyed. Warbeck, disgusted at the brutal conduct of the war, withdrew from the siege of Heton. Encouraged by 'drinksilver,' the masons mined all night at the walls of that fortress, which was taken and razed to the ground. An attack on Norham during the following summer, though prefaced by a triumphal procession of 'Mons Meg' down the Canongate, was less successful. Thomas Howard, Earl of Surrey, carried the war into Scotland, but prudently declined James's challenge to stake the retention of Berwick on the issue of a single combat between them. Peace was restored in the last year of the century by the Treaty of Stirling. Its maintenance was imperilled by the Captain of Norham

falling upon some young Scotsmen whose idle curiosity
led them to inspect too closely the defences of his castle.
Bishop Fox not only prevented a rupture in the relations
of the two kingdoms, but placed them on a surer footing,
by the marriage of James with Henry's eldest daughter.

The murder of Sir Robert Ker, the Scottish Warden, by
John Heron the Bastard of Ford, and others, engendered
a feeling hostile to England, which in 1513 found expression in a declaration of war.   Lord Hume headed a
formidable raid across the Border, but suffered a serious
defeat from the archers posted by Sir William Bulmer in
the tall broom of Milfield Plain.   To avenge this, and to
assist the French by causing a diversion of the English
from the siege of Terouenne, James IV. passed the
Tweed with an army of 80,000.   Norham was the
only stronghold capable of real resistance, and it fell
after a five days' siege.   Etal, Ford, and even Chillingham, were captured in quick succession.   James
established a fortified camp on the heights of Flodden,
and then quietly awaited Surrey's advance at Ford.
There is no reason to attribute this inactivity, largely
due to the desertion of 20,000 of his followers, to the
charms of Dame Elizabeth Heron, who vainly pleaded
for the preservation of her castle.

The Earl of Surrey had been joined by 14,000
tenants of the Stanleys, who brought with them the
banner of St. Audrey, Queen of Northumberland and
foundress of Ely, where James Stanley was Bishop.   On
reaching Alnwick, Surrey was further reinforced by
the arrival of his son, the Lord Admiral, with 1,000
' merry mariners.'   The Scottish lords, desirous of re-
treating, were overruled by La Motte, the French envoy.
James concluded that if Surrey attempted to carry the
camp on Flodden, it must be by forcing a passage over
Ford Bridge, but he indignantly scouted the proposal of
Robert Borthwick, his master-gunner, to blow this up
when only half the English host should have crossed.
Dismantling, most ungallantly, the castle of Ford, and

planting a battery to openly command the bridge, he removed his headquarters to Flodden.

Surrey pledged himself to give battle by Friday, September 9, at the latest. A formal challenge from his camp on Wooler Haugh, bidding James ' of his noble courage' descend into Milfield Plain or some other equal ground, was, coming from an earl, regarded by the King as a piece of impudence, and he taunted Surrey with relying on sorcery in wishing to choose their battle-field. For days there had been scarcely an hour of fine weather; the English, ' clemmed' with the cold and wet, threatened to return home, unless at once led into action. Surrey crossed the Till; but although his whole army descended the right bank in sight of James all that Thursday, the King was not to be tempted down to attack them. After an evening reconnaissance, the Lord Admiral suggested to his father the advisability of recrossing the river further to the north, and sweeping round at the back of the Scots, so as to compel them to fight or suffer their communications to be cut—tactics the elaboration of which may be traced to the local knowledge of the Bastard Heron, who, in spite of outlawry and feigned death, had rallied to Surrey's standard. The English encamped that night at Barmoor Woodside. By noon the next day, while James thought they were in full retreat on Berwick, their vanguard and artillery had accomplished the passage of the Till by Twizel Bridge, the reanguard following through the Mill Ford, a little further up the stream.

Once safe on the left bank, Surrey continued to ascend it, as if marching straight for Flodden, until he was confronted by the great swamp that then stretched for nearly a mile and a half from just north of the village of Brankston to the hamlet of Sandyford, where a little brook connected it with the Till. It was about four o'clock in the afternoon when King James saw the English vanguard moving westwards along the northern margin of this morass. Suddenly the right wing, 3,000 strong, and led by Surrey's younger son, Edmund Howard, commenced

wading through the middle of the swamp that the Scots
had deemed impassable. It was followed by the main
body under the Lord Admiral, consisting, with the left
wing, old Sir Marmaduke Constable's, of from 12,000
to 14,000 men. James at once rightly conjectured that
the English were making for Brankston Hill, their occupation of which, rising as it does almost to the same level
as Flodden, would have completely severed him from
Scotland. He at once ordered the camp refuse on
Flodden to be set on fire, and, taking advantage of the
clouds of smoke with which a south-easterly wind en-
veloped the whole range, transferred his forces and
artillery to the summit of Brankston. When the smoke
rolled away, the Lord Admiral, who had arrived at
its foot, was terrified to find the four battalions of the
Scottish vanguard bearing down on him at only a quarter
of a mile's distance. In all haste he sent the *Agnus Dei* at
his breast as a signal for his father to instantly advance
the English rearguard.

Surrey had been permitted to pass unchallenged over the

'brook of breadth a tailor's yard'

at Sandyford with the ordnance that the Lord Admiral had
been obliged to leave behind in plunging through Brankston
Moss. His right wing, under Lord Dacre, pushed forward
at full gallop to support Edmund Howard, whose division,
having begun to climb Brankston Hill, at the extreme
west of the field, received the full shock of Hume's Border
Horse and Huntley's Highlanders. The first boom of
the Scottish cannon was followed by a stampede of the
men of Tynemouth and Bamburghshire, in Dacre's wing,
and Edmund Howard's Cheshire contingent, already half
mutinous at not being led by a Stanley, immediately
profited by their example. Thrice brought to the ground,
Edmund himself was rescued by the timely arrival of the
Bastard Heron. Even then, in escaping towards the
Admiral, he was nearly cut off by Sir David Hume.
At this critical moment a successful charge was delivered
by Dacre with the levies of Gilsland and Alston Moor

and the light horse from the Esk and Line. The Admiral and Sir Marmaduke Constable having now routed the Earls of Crawford and Errol, turned to Dacre's assistance, and the victorious Earl of Hume was likewise driven from the field.

On seeing the discomfiture of Edmund Howard's division, King James could restrain himself no longer. Without waiting for his rearguard, he charged madly down the hillside with the Scottish centre on the very inferior force being brought up by Surrey. The English artillery had, however, now been got into position, and mercilessly raked the royal columns, killing Lord Sinclair, Master of the Scottish Ordnance, and silencing its misdirected fire. James's lance broke, but, undeterred by the entreaties of old Earl Douglas, drawing his sword, the King made on foot towards Surrey's standard, supported by his natural son the Archbishop of St. Andrew's, and the lords Herries and Maxwell. A hand-to-hand fight with Surrey, Latimer, and Conyers followed. The King himself slew Guischard Harbottle, and then, learning of the defeat of his entire left, gave orders for the advance of Bothwell and the rearguard. Dacre, drawing in from the west, had only just time to form and receive them. The fortunes of the day were anything but decided, when Sir Edward Stanley and the strong left wing of the English rearguard, composed largely of the 'lads of Lancashire,' climbing on their hands and feet the steep hillside on the east of the field, turned the position of the last Scottish battalions (those of Lennox and Argyle), and after sending them flying, in spite of the stubborn resistance of the Seigneur d'Aussi's reserve, charged down on the rear of the royal division, while Dacre and the Admiral closed in from the west. The death of King James on Pipard's Hill under the banner of St. Audrey sealed the fate of the battle.

Lord Dacre found it easier to deal with the Scots in the open field than to stem the turbulence of Tyndale and Redesdale. He received Margaret of Scotland and her husband Angus at Harbottle in 1515, where their daughter, the mother of Darnley, was born soon afterwards. He also took an active interest in Wolsey's restoration of Wark Castle. In 1521 the garrison there rescued some cattle from a Scottish foray, but that same night 500 masked men from Teviotdale burnt Learmouth. Seton, the Captain of Wark, avenged this in a sally two years later, putting Davy Hume to flight 'with a broken spear in his coat or body.'

The fifth Earl of Northumberland, Henry Percy XI., accepted and then resigned the office of Warden-General of the Marches—conduct possibly explained by the havoc wrought in his finances by a love of display that gained him the title of 'the Magnificent.' The Lion Tower of Warkworth (with the *bascule* of the Herberts, his mother's family, carved on the cornice), and the foundations of the cruciform chapel, are melancholy memorials of the College he began to found, but lacked the funds to finish.

In October, 1523, the long-expected army of the Duke of Albany appeared before Wark. For two days the Scots bombarded the castle over the Tweed; then, as the river was in flood, a storming party of 2,000 French crossed in boats. They occupied the undefended base-court, and some of them forced a passage into the inner ward. Sir William Lisle and the small garrison gave these a too warm reception. The French leader and nine others were cut down; the rest were so hotly chased out by Lisle that the 1,000 French and 500 Scots in the base-court also took fright and fled pell-mell towards the Tweed, where many of them were drowned in the panic.

More pillage, however, continued to be done by the thieves of Tyndale than by all the Scots of Scotland. They came down on Ingo and Kirkheaton, and extended their ravages to within eight miles of Newcastle. Wolsey, following Fox's precedent, placed the 'Evil Country' under an interdict. At Easter, 1524, Hector Charlton, of the Bower, took the Sacrament out of the sepulchre in Bellingham Church, and carried it with a firkin of wine and 800 'breads' to Tarset Hall. A Scottish friar gave the thieves their communion 'after his fashion,' and Hector served them all with wine and received the parson's dues. Joining with the Scots in 1525, the Tyndale men burnt Tarset Hall, where Sir Ralph Fenwick then lay in garrison.

Better order was kept on the appointment of Henry Percy XII., the sixth Earl of Northumberland, as Warden-General of the Marches in 1528. William Charlton, of Shitlington Hall, 'rode' into the Bishopric with Harry Noble and seven others, and carried off the parson of Muggleswick. The Bailiff of Hexham led a foray after them, and as Haydon Bridge had been barred and chained by Northumberland's directions, they were obliged to leave their horses and try to escape on foot. Thomas Errington, the Constable of Langley, pursued them with a sleuth-hound. To everyone's surprise, they were captured by the assistance of another William Charlton and his friends in Tyndale.

The gibbeting of these marauders inspired such terror that 500 of their comrades submitted. Sir William Lisle, the gallant defender of Wark, who had been committed to ward in Newcastle on charges of murder, and outlawed for escaping, accompanied by his son Humphrey and fifteen other rebels, in their shirts, with halters round their necks, met Northumberland coming from Mass, and placed themselves at the King's mercy. The mercy of Henry VIII., interpreted by Wolsey, whom Sir William had threatened to 'pluck by the nose,' sent them all to execution except the boy of thirteen.

The official reception of the banished Earl of Angus by all the gentlemen of Northumberland at Newcastle did not tend to the peace of the Border. Nicholas Ridley of Willimoteswyke, in attempting to rescue some cattle from the thieves of Liddesdale, was himself carried off prisoner. Negotiations conducted in 1531 for the release of captives in Scotland failed to effect more than the return of Beaumont of Charlton with a velvet coat as compensation. The Kers especially refused all redress, and 'ran an open-day foray' to Felkington. An attack made by them on Haltwhistle, in company with the Rutherfords and Davidsons, cost them sixscore slain outright and a dozen executed the next Sunday. Mark Ker vowed that he would burn a village of Northumberland's within three miles of Warkworth, so as to give the Earl 'light to put on his clothes at midnight.' Thirty light horsemen sent by him to Whittle on Shilbottle Moor found no fire there, and they had forgotten to bring any with them. They seized a poor woman near her travail, and shouting, ' Where we cannot give the laird light, yet we shall do this in spite of him,' dealt her three mortal wounds on the head. A month later, 3,000 Scots crossed the Border at nightfall and lay in ambush ' on the edge of Cheviot,' while ' forays ' were ' cast off ' to ' take up ' Ross on the coast, Ingram and Fawdon, and Ryle and Prendwick.

Sir Arthur Darcy, the Captain of Berwick, had disapproved of a policy of retaliation, by which ' when the Scottish thieves rode, the English thieves rode also.' Henry VIII. now gave direct orders for reprisals. Northumberland's raid to Dunglas in December, 1532, was one the like of which had not been seen in winter for two centuries. By the mediation of Francis I., a truce with Scotland was concluded at Newcastle, which ripened into a formal peace in May, 1534. The Earl of Northumberland was obliged to advance the money for paying off the Border garrisons. They were nearly all south-country men ; experience had proved that northerners were not amenable to discipline if plunder were in sight. The Marches, still nominally in Northumberland's keeping, had never been in such good state since the time of his grandfather, the fourth Earl, thanks to the vigorous administration of Sir Thomas Clifford. As usual, during such a lull, the Northumbrian gentry fell out among themselves. Although commanded in the King's name to desist, Sir John Fenwick of Wallington mustered his friends to make a forcible entry into Harterton Hall, while John Fenwick of Stanton prepared to repel him. Ralph Widdrington accused Cuthbert Shafto of pulling down a 'shield' he had built at Carry Coats, and of coming with forty others to pick a quarrel with him at Stagshawbank Fair. Northumberland had done nothing to carry out the provisions of his father's will until, on his brother Sir Thomas Percy's marriage, he gave him some lands of little value. Sir Thomas was at great labour to defend these from the Scots, and on the Earl now granting the lordship of Corbridge to Sir Reginald Carnaby at a ridiculously reduced rent, he remonstrated with his brother, who thereupon turned him out-of-doors.

In the beginning of 1536, Dr. Layton and Dr. Legh completed their hasty visitation of the Northern monasteries. No charge of laxity could be procured against Newminster, Alnwick, or Blanchland. Among the relics still venerated were the girdle of St. Robert at Newminster, the red Mass-book of Hexham, and the foot of Simon de Montfort and cup of St. Thomas of Canterbury at Alnwick. The suppression of all houses not possessing rents above £200 a year was determined on. The King had promised Northumberland the preferment of Hexham and Newminster, on paying for them at a valuation, yet the latter was granted to Sir Oswald Wilstropp, whom the Earl 'never took as his friend.' Hexham was, at the Earl's request, destined for Sir Reginald Carnaby, but its revenues proved to slightly exceed £200. The Prior hastened to London to make a suit to the King for the exemption of his house. During his journey North he met the barge of the Archbishop of York, who charged him to offer no resistance to the royal commissioners. The canons of Hexham, however, kept their gates closed against the Carnabies for a whole month, and when the commissioners arrived in September, the Master of the cell of Ovingham appeared above the gateway in armour, with a bow and arrows, saying, ' We be twenty brethren in this house, and we shall die all, ere that ye shall have the house.' The Sub-prior, in canon's dress, displayed a confirmation of the monastery under the King's great seal, and declared that it was not to his honour ' to give forth one seal contrary to another.' After this war-like reception the commissioners ' recoiled' to Corbridge.

The Earl of Cumberland had already set out from Skipton to enforce the submission of the Hexham canons, when the outbreak of the Pilgrimage of Grace, on Sunday, October 15, forced him to turn back. That same day, John Heron of Chipchase rode up to Halton Tower, and persuaded Sir Reginald Carnaby's father to use him as an intermediary in receiving the submission of Hexham Priory. He then treacherously told the canons that their only chance lay in continued resistance, and summoned the Tyndale freebooters to their aid under promise of certain annuities. In his alarm, old Carnaby was nearly allured to Chipchase, when a timely whisper caused him to put spurs to his horse and gain the security of Langley Castle.

As if all were preconcerted, Sir Ingram Percy that same Sunday summoned the gentlemen of Northumberland to a meeting in Alnwick Castle, for the nominal purpose of taking measures to stop the depredations of Tyndale and Redesdale. To complete the arrangements, Sir Ingram met at Doddington Tunstal, Bishop of Durham (who had fled from Auckland at midnight), and Sir Thomas Clifford, the Constable of Berwick. On the other hand, Lionel Grey, the porter of Berwick, his nephew Thomas Grey, of Newstead, and others who were on Coldstream Haugh, seeing Sir Reginald Carnaby safe into Scotland, formed a conspiracy to kill Clifford at Alnwick or on his way home. Clifford received a hint of his danger, and did not attend. A similar plot to kill him at Berwick, and, in case of necessity, deliver the castle to the Scots, was defeated by the ' babbling' of Odinel Selby. Meanwhile, at the county meeting, Sir Ingram Percy caused a letter to be read which John Lumley, Heron's son-in-law, had brought, in the name of 'Captain Poverty,' from the Commons of the Bishopric. Everyone present was called on to swear to the articles of the Pilgrimage of Grace; and in spite of protestations, 'being enclosed in the castle of Alnwick, will they or not, sworn they were.'

Sir Thomas Percy, who had been led to join the rising in Yorkshire, hastened back to Prudhoe after the first truce concluded at Doncaster. He was there joined by Heron and his friends, the Charltons and Robsons. His priest was sent to take possession of Halton Tower, and certain stuff and apparel the Carnabies had deposited at Capheaton was brought in triumph to Prudhoe. Sir Reginald Carnaby now came out of Scotland to Edderston. Sir Ingram Percy was about to formally besiege that house, when Thomas Forster allowed him to enter. Not finding Sir Reginald, Sir Ingram swore, nevertheless, to be revenged on him 'for being the destruction of all our blood, for by his means the King shall be my lord's heir.' He was with difficulty restrained from casting down Thomas Grey's house at Newstead. Word then came that Sir Reginald was at Chillingham. Sir Ingram sent to Berwick for great ordnance to bombard the castle; while, on the other hand, Sir Robert Ellerker, who was living there, was disappointed of any assistance from Clifford. Sir Thomas Percy assured Sir Ingram in the chapel of Alnwick Castle that the leaders of the Pilgrimage would not submit without informing him, and obtaining a general pardon for all offences, 'wherefore let us do what we think to do whilst we may, and that betimes.' The Friars Observant returned for a short time to Newcastle; otherwise the Pilgrimage in Northumberland was devoid of all religious, or even political, significance, being a mere struggle between a party thirsting for revenge on Sir Reginald Carnaby and a party plotting the assassination of Sir Thomas Clifford.

The arrangement effected by Norfolk with the Commons at Doncaster on November 30 did not clearly state whether the monks who had been reinstated in their convents by them were to remain in possession till the promised Parliament was assembled. A month later, George Shuttleworth, a servant of the Abbot of Salley, came to Prudhoe with a letter for Sir Thomas Percy. He was accompanied by William Leach, a desperate ruffian, who had been specially exempted from the general pardon, and who, after provoking a fresh rising in Westmorland, escaped into Scotland, where he assassinated Somerset Herald in 1542. The Abbot, told by Aske that he ought to surrender his house again, appealed to Percy for advice as being of his ancestors' foundation. The whole country round Salley was ready to support the monks and 'extend' the Pilgrimage. Percy is said to have counselled submission, but the Abbot did not submit, and, in passing through Durham, Leach and Shuttleworth nearly murdered Lancaster Herald, who was proclaiming the pardon. Ninian Stavely and other bravados, sent by the Abbot of Jervaux, left Prudhoe with the impression that Sir Thomas was coming into Yorkshire to take part in the new movement. The two Percies did cause a 'cry of the whole county' to be made at Morpeth; but this was met by a counter-proclamation of Lord Ogle, and the news of Hallam's failure to surprise Hull put an end to any further disturbance on their part. Orders were sent to arrest them. They voluntarily yielded themselves to Norfolk at Doncaster, and were sent up to London, encouraged by a letter to the Council to say that they would be found of better sort than represented by the Earl their brother.

Popular sentiment was appeased by the refounding of the abbeys of Alnwick and Blanchland. The Duke of Norfolk dissolved the priory of Hexham 'with very good exhortations to the inhabitants.' Sir Reginald Carnaby vouched for the good conduct of the canons, since the conclusion of the Pilgrimage of Grace, and although only their Prior received a pension, none of them suffered either death or imprisonment. The pacification of the whole county seemed nearly complete, when Roger

Fenwick, Keeper of Tyndale, was cruelly murdered near Bellingham.

Sir Thomas Percy pleaded guilty to the charge of conspiracy subsequent to the general pardon of the Pilgrims of Grace, and was executed at Tyburn. Sir Ingram, who had been more active during the Pilgrimage, but was far less implicated in subsequent matters, was set at liberty. The sixth Earl of Northumberland soon afterwards ended his miserable life at Hackney. Renouncing his power of appointing an heir of his own name, he made over his estates to the King, lest any portion should fall to his widow. Never had a finer inheritance been wasted by the folly of the owner and the untruthfulness of his servants.

The Tyndale men refused to restore even a third of the plunder they seized during the troubles of the Pilgrimage, and entered into an alliance with the thieves of Liddesdale, who had just run a foray to Haydon Bridge and captured two of the Carnabies. The gaol at Hexham was broken open and all the prisoners in it carried off to Scotland. Sir Reginald Carnaby allowed himself to be surrounded in Tyndale, and was rescued with some difficulty. It was proposed to order all the inhabitants to evacuate the district by a certain day. A change of policy supervened, and John Heron was appointed keeper of both it and Redesdale. The Liddesdale thieves, however, continued their ravages. They 'broke' Haughton Castle, scaling it with ladders, and during a greater raid slew seven Fenwicks who rallied to the rescue of their goods. Henry VIII., losing patience, ordered Sir William Eure 'to let slip as many under his rule as should do the Scots three hurts for one.'

The Border Survey, undertaken by Sir Ralph Ellerker and Sir Robert Bowes in 1541, gives a valuable account of twelve castles and more than a hundred lesser holds on the frontier. It describes the strong houses of the headsmen of Tyndale as built of great square oak-trees strongly bound together and covered with great roofs of turves and earth, very difficult to break

into or set on fire. The habitations of the Redesdale
chiefs, although these were richer, were not so strong.
The two valleys had a superabundant population, and could
put 500 men into the field. ' If a man sat on a holding of
not 6s. rent, and had ten sons, every one must have a
piece of it.' The young men were reduced to 'thieving' for
a livelihood. They were so attached to their birthplace
that a forcible transportation of them to a distance was recommended as the only effectual remedy. Watches were
set at night along the confines of both dales in order to
protect the more peaceful inhabitants of Northumberland,
among whom the men of Coquetdale were in best repute.

As Bowes and Ellerker were resting at Hexham, the
light horse of Liddesdale, who had recently burnt
William Carnaby's village of Little Whittington, had the
effrontery to return and set on fire his stacks and farm-
buildings at Halton. John Heron's connivance was so very
evident that he was shamed into solemnly renouncing his
old-standing feud with the Carnabies. At Haddon Rigg,
the following year, he could not restrain his Redesdale men
from breaking ranks and galloping after the cattle they
had taken, thus causing the rout of the English forces.
The Duke of Norfolk, appointed to the chief command
against Scotland, found Northumberland never more out
of order, the countrymen looking ' through the fingers '
at raids and robberies. The Scots carried off the horses
and carts engaged in taking the stones of Carham Church
to Wark Castle, under the very noses of the garrison. The
Earl of Hertford's chaplain was ' lifted ' from Belford ;
his master had a narrow escape, which is to be regretted,
as it might have prevented his abominable expedition to
burn the nunnery of Coldstream.

In 1543 the outlawed Charltons of Tyndale led the
Eylwhites, Nixons, and Crosiers of Liddesdale to burn
Capheaton. A widow from Tyndale, who chanced to be
living there, sent home to her kinsmen, who rescued her
goods in a tussle that left ugly marks on both sides, and was
important in destroying the good understanding between

the Scottish and English thieves. Jack Pringle, while raiding with 200 men from Teviotdale, was taken prisoner 'bloody-handed' by Henry Collingwood, Constable of Etal. Lord Parr intended to have had him summarily executed; but Cuthbert Ogle, the parson of Ford, who had been Pringle's prisoner after Haddon Rigg, interceded for him on account of the gentle treatment he had received. In May, 1544, Hertford sailed from the Tyne with a large fleet, and, after sacking Edinburgh, marched back to Berwick. Soon after this 1,000 Scots, engaged in burning Twizel, Tilmouth, and Heton, were surprised by Sir Ralph Eure, who was returning from a raid to Jedburgh. Sir Ralph's successes led him to forget that 'Fortune is not always one woman'; he was defeated and slain on Ancrum Moor.

On hearing of this victory of the Scots, Francis I. despatched about 4,000 Frenchmen to their assistance, under the command of the Seigneur de Lorges. These had taken the outworks of Wark, when a flood in the Tweed caused them to abandon the siege. Hertford mercilessly ravaged the whole Scottish Border with an army of Germans, Albanians, Spaniards, Burgundians, and Italians, recalling the heterogeneous garrisons of Roman times. Having been created Duke of Somerset and Lord Protector during the minority of his nephew, Edward VI., he led a large army to Leith.

In June, 1548, the Sieur d'Essé arrived in Scotland with a reinforcement of 6,000 French. The Border, intrusted to the care of the too-lenient Lord Grey of Wilton, was in no state to withstand them. There was no money to pay the regular garrisons. The gentlemen of Northumberland who held commands in them lay at home hawking, hunting, and going to weddings. Better order prevailed among the Tartars than in Berwick, where the sick and wounded were shut out in the streets, and left to perish from want. D'Essé took the castle of Cornhill by force of arms, and Etal appears to have prudently surrendered. The Seigneur de la Chapelle de Biron was sent to burn and plunder all the villages as far as Newcastle. During this expedition, the success of which gained him the character of 'excellent and stainless chevalier,' he regarded with curiosity Coldmartin Lough, one half frozen over, the other at summer temperature.

D'Essé burnt the greater part of Ford Castle, but left unreduced a tower defended by Thomas Carr, whose bravery seems to have won him the hand of the young heiress Elizabeth Heron. The French proceeded to set on fire the Ten Towns of Glendale, the richest and best built villages on the whole Border. They caught the savage-looking priest of one of these, who told them that they had come to see the fields where they would soon be yoked to the plough, for before three years were out the English would be masters of Scotland, and, requiring all their horses for the subjugation of France, would replace them at home with French prisoners. Bidden to turn from his visions of the future to the smoking villages and troops of captives of the present, he buried his face in the ground and died of patriotic starvation. It was not till June, 1551, that a treaty of peace was concluded in the church of Norham.

Henry Grey, Marquis of Dorset, the Warden-General, requested Sir Robert Bowes to draw up a report on the state of the frontier. His successor, John Dudley, Earl of Warwick, shortly afterwards created Duke of Northumberland, energetically inaugurated a great scheme of Border reform, which he left Lord Wharton to complete. Regular watches were to be established through the country; all cultivated land was to be hedged and ditched, and all superfluous fords were to be deepened and stopped. The Northumbrians, however, proved recalcitrant. They almost ceased to attend the musters, or, if they came, were badly armed. As usual, the enclosure of wastes, the rebuilding of houses, and the increase of small holdings at fair rents, were the remedies propounded.

The reign of Mary Tudor opened with honest endeavours on both sides to maintain justice on the Border. Her marriage with Philip of Spain was, however, regarded as a menace by the French and Scots. In 1555 the English Parliament passed an Act appointing commissioners for rebuilding castles and forts and promoting tillage within twenty miles of Scotland. The French general d'Oysel began to fortify Eyemouth, and war broke out. In July, 1557, Lord Hume attempted to win Ford and burn the Ten Towns of Glendale, but fled from Fenton on the approach of Sir Henry Percy. The main army of the Scots declined to assume the offensive; the French threatened Wark, but were sent flying across the Tweed by a sudden sally of the garrison. Sir Thomas Percy's elder son Thomas, whom Mary had created Earl of Northumberland, set out on an expedition to Scotland. He was repulsed near the Cheviots by Sir Andrew Ker, but the English successfully rallied, and took Ker prisoner. Thomas Bates of Prudhoe received a letter from the Queen thanking him for his valour. The following summer 1,000 horsemen, led by French officers, were overtaken at Grindon by Sir Henry Percy, and forced first over the Till, then over the Tweed. Soon afterwards a body of Scottish horse set Fenton in a blaze. Sir Henry chased them as far as Haltwellswire, when the Earl of Bothwell opened fire from an ambush, and utterly routed Percy's following. Northumberland was denounced to the Council for suppressing bad news. He regarded the Earl of Westmorland as the informer.

At the accession of Elizabeth the state of the county was terrible indeed. The Scots rode as far as Morpeth, driving home the cattle as from a fair in Teviotdale. They would steal horses and oxen for ploughing and harrowing, and then, by private agreement, restore them exhausted to their owners. The Northumbrian peasant roused in the night demanded who was there. 'Dost thou not know me by my tongue?' was the cool reply. 'I am Jock of the Hare Well; rise quickly, the great host of Scotland is coming; all your town shall be burnt. If thou wilt be my prisoner, I will save thy house, cattle, and corn.' The simple countryman, thinking this all true, would give his hand out of the window, and promise to pay the necessary blackmail. Did any refuse, like the Bailiff of Ross and the Laird of Buckton, two very rich men, they were spoiled and burnt, and left without a groat. Instead of attending the musters themselves, the Northumbrian landowners sent their 'plough slaves'— their Cuddie Headriggs—at a crown a head. Albany Featherstonhaugh laughed to scorn Northumberland's letter ordering him to restore a rich chain taken from Ninian Menvill. Captains of horse put pay for thirty or forty men into their purses without even having stirrups to their own saddles. The garrison of Berwick had been long unpaid; the roads were so deep that the men of Felton resisted their small oxen being taken to transport the treasure ultimately sent down. There was no bedding in Berwick; a mattress-maker was urgently demanded. The men working on the fortifications were 'sore decayed,' having been fed chiefly on herrings. To add to all this, the Scots had again stormed Cornhill, burnt Ord within cannon-shot of Berwick, and carried off many prisoners in spite of the combined attack made on them at Fenton by the two Percies. Their overtures for peace were very welcome, and the Treaty of Upsetlington ended the war.

Northumberland demanded an impartial inquiry into the charges of misgovernment brought against him. Sir Ralph Sadler was sent down. Continuing the old blood-feud of his father, the Earl sought to turn Sir Reginald Carnaby's widow out of her house of Hexham Abbey, on the plea that it was required for the official residence of the Keeper of Tyndale. Sadler reported that it was ill suited for the purpose, that it was a shame to wrest their home from Lady Carnaby and her widowed daughter, and that Northumberland was very 'unmeet' for the charge he held, especially owing to his animosity against Protestants, at a time when the Government were intriguing with John Knox. The wrecks on the coast of the *Bonaventure* and the *Mary*, ships laden with the costly wares of Scottish merchants, were destined to give rise to long diplomatic negotiations and legal proceedings.

Most of the inhabitants of Tyndale having submitted to Sir John Forster, their new keeper, at Chipchase, he entrusted the charge of their wild country to George Heron. A month later, however, the prisoners in Hexham Gaol escaped with their gaoler, leaving the doors wide open; while Liddesdale was permitted to 'take up' Sweethope. As a party of these Scots were slumbering round a fire at Cottonhope, certain thieves of Tyndale, on their way to steal in Scotland, relieved them of the cattle they had driven off.

The spring of 1560 was occupied by the 'Journey of Leith.' The English had been ignominiously repulsed by the French, when the death of the Queen-Regent, Mary of Lorraine, brought about the Treaty of Edinburgh.

Preaching, it is said, at this time was more needed at Berwick than in any other town in Europe. It was doubted whether the Vicar could say the 'Paternoster' in either English or Latin. 'The Mass,' the people declared, 'was never half so dear as the free Gospel.' Bernard Gilpin delivered a few sermons, but could not be prevailed on to remain, and the work was handed over to a Scotsman.

A fray between Robert Forster and Muschamps of Barmoor again divided the gentry of Northumberland into two camps. In church, market, and field, arms and armour were daily used as in war-time. Lord Grey of Wilton, the Warden, exerted himself to change them all into loving neighbours. At the end of the year a 'brabbling variance' between the Revelys and Swinhoes was the only thing left to disturb internal peace, while a bill for eight geese was the only Scottish claim that remained unsettled. A new survey of the Border was undertaken: the little closes and crooked lanes round the villages were to be enclosed with quick hedges from sets sold in the churches; the fords of the Tweed were to be planted up with willows, and a 'dyke of force' cut from Ridingburn to Harbottle.

Unfortunately, Lord Grey allowed himself to be involved in disputes about the fisheries on the Tweed, especially with the men of Norham. He attempted to seize Thomas Clavering, the Captain of Norham, in connection with the plunder of the *Bonaventure*. Wark, too, caused him much uneasiness; the young men of the company of the Lord of the May Games there took prisoner the Lord of the May Games of Cornhill, who was rescued by his followers. 'Undone before he came to Berwick,' Lord Grey found himself 'a very beggar, every day the longer the worse,' and resigned in despair. Many of the Berwick garrison were withdrawn to Havre de Grace, and the construction of the new fortifications was abandoned. The Earl of Bedford found Berwick a thing of such little strength that a man might soon make as much in the open. The other castles were in their chronic state of ruin. An attempt was made to repair that of Harbottle. Some Redesdale men, whom Sir John Forster had summoned there, made a sudden rush on his servants, and were with difficulty overpowered. Thirteen were tried at Morpeth; Clement Hall and five others were beheaded. To avenge his brother's death, John Hall, with the aid of Liddesdale, burnt Barrow and the Peels with Forster's corn, and drove off his sheep. The gaol at Morpeth was soon choke-full of Redesdale prisoners. If it had not been for Sir William Drury, the whole East March would have been laid waste. Cessford, the Scottish Warden, allowed Drury to be openly insulted at a Border meeting, but the latter had come 'not slenderly accompanied,' and retired in good order.

The defeat of Mary Stuart at Langside in 1568, and her flight into Cumberland, made her partisans still more anxious to provoke a quarrel with England. A foray to Hethpool was pursued by the English regulars as far as Yetholm. Eight hundred Scots collected and charged the English four times as they fell back at nightfall on Pawston, throwing stones and piercing the drum-head with an arrow. Lord Hunsdon, the cousin of Elizabeth, was appointed Governor of Berwick and Warden of the

East March. He had scarcely gone to bed for the first time in Berwick, before the town was in alarm, owing to Dan Ker of Shylstock having killed one of the sentries. On his way to church, six poor men presented themselves, saying they had come to live on him, as the Scots had gone with all their substance. At last English patience was once more exhausted; Tyndale and Redesdale were let slip over the Border, and Buccleugh overthrown.

Meanwhile, contrary to the counsels of his confessor, the Earl of Northumberland had been drawn into a dangerous conspiracy with the intention of re-establishing the ancient faith. A false alarm, alluded to in the ballad,

> ' Earl Percy into his garden is gone,
>   And after him walks his fair ladie:
>   I hear a Bird sing in mine ear
>   That I must either fight or flee,'

caused him to ride by night from Topcliff to Branspeth, on November 9, 1569. He had almost escaped to Alnwick when the Earl of Westmorland took him to Durham. There the two Earls threw down the Communion-board and tore the Bible in pieces. Their hopes of assistance from Leonard Dacre of Naworth and Captain Read of Berwick proved misplaced. Instead of Sir Cuthbert Collingwood, the Sheriff, and 600 horse, barely a hundred of the Percy tenantry, and sixty of the Neville from Bywell, came to join them. Captain Carvell organized the defence of Newcastle, while Sir John Forster affixed an energetic proclamation to the gates of Alnwick Castle. Having received the submission of it and Warkworth, Forster raised a large body of horse at Hexham, and, sallying from Newcastle with Sir Henry Percy, forced the insurgents to fall back on Durham. Deserted by all their foot, the Earls fled with their horse through the wastes to Hexham. Two days later they crossed the Tyne and marched six miles in the direction of Alnwick, but were ' so impeached by the hot pricking and skirmishing ' of Forster's scouts that they turned back. The number of their followers having increased to fifteen hundred, they set out the next morning for Naworth. The Countess of Northumberland, who was supposed to be the heart and soul of the Rising—'the gray mare, the better horse'—concealed the Percy plate near Hexham. Disappointed in the reception they met with from Leonard Dacre, the Earls made off the same night to Liddesdale. Sussex arrived the following day at Hexham from Newcastle with a force nowise superior; his horses were sore beaten with the frost and snow. He sent Forster with a strong reconnaisance to Fetherstonhaugh and posted his foot soldiers at Haydon Bridge, but preferred himself to await the course of events at Hexham. On Christmas Eve Northumberland was betrayed by Hector Armstrong to the Regent Murray. In his distress, the Earl sent a letter to his brother, which, being intercepted, compromised Leonard Dacre. Joined by Forster at Belford, Hunsdon reached Hexham with difficulty, owing to the 'deep waters and ways.' Passing Naworth after a forced night-march, they defeated Dacre, who pursued them, at Gelt's Bridge. The Earl of Westmorland adopted the state of a prince in Teviotdale, and was never merrier in his life. He appeared with 2,000 horse in the neighbourhood of Harbottle. Whole townships in Glendale were wasted by him and Buccleugh. They went the length of preparing ladders for the escalade of Wark and Newcastle. The names of Tristram Fenwick of Brinkburn, Cuthbert Armorer of Belford, George Horsley of Acklington Park, and two Robert Collingwoods (of Abberwick and Etal) were inserted in a bill of attainder for participation in the Rising. Among those indicted were Robert Carr of Ford, John Carnaby of Langley, William Welton of Welton, Thomas Errington of Walwick Grange, and Thomas Bates of Prudhoe. Most of these were eventually pardoned; none appear to have suffered more than a year or two's detention in the Tower. Hall and Humberton were charged to make a survey of the forfeited lands. It was a 'happy rebellion' for Sir John Forster, who obtained £4,000 in plunder, and an additional £500 a year in grants. No man, howsoever oppressed, dared complain of him. He gutted Hulne for his own house at Alnwick Abbey, and began dismantling the castles of Alnwick and Warkworth. In August, 1572, having none of Lord Hunsdon's high-minded scruples, he dragged the unfortunate Earl of Northumberland, who had been basely sold to Elizabeth by the Scots, to his martyrdom at York.

That same year the Fenwicks, bearing in mind how one of their clan had been murdered some thirty years before by the Crosiers, rode by night into Liddesdale and slew many of them in their beds. Carmichael, the upright Deputy-Keeper of Liddesdale, obtained the surrender of their guide from Sir George Heron, the Keeper of Redesdale. Thereupon Forster not only suspended Heron, but outraged all Border etiquette by agreeing to hold a court, himself Warden of the Middle Marches, with Carmichael, a simple keeper, on July 7, 1575. He came with an unusually large following to the Redeswire. All went well for nearly three hours, till, after he and Carmichael had 'courteously drunk together,' Forster refused to order the surrender of an Englishman condemned for non-appearance. 'You cloke justice,' cried Carmichael, 'and are not willing that it should proceed, so long as your nowt and the keepers do go quietly on the Borders.' This Forster denied, and declared he was ready to settle all causes within his office. 'I am as able to answer mine office as you are yours, and am of as good a house as yours,' replied Carmichael. 'You are not so able as I,' bragged Forster, 'for I am the Queen's Majesty's Warden of the Marches, and you are but a keeper.' Then, if the Scottish ballad is to be trusted,

> ' He raise and raxed him where he stood,
>   And bade him match him with his marrows,
>   Then Tyndale heard these reasons rude,
>   And they lute off a flight of arrows ;'

while, according to the English, shouts of ' I say ! I say !

Comparison! Comparison!' cut short this odious altercation.

Martin Crosier let fly an arrow that wounded William
Fenwick of Wallington. ' A Tyndale! a Tyndale!' cried
the North Tyne men, falling on the pedlars of Jedburgh.
These, gathering round their drum and pennons, replied
with, ' A Jedworth! a Jedworth!' The Scots were
driven back. Forster, by ' stroke and hasty proclamation,' calmed his own men, and allowed Carmichael to
leave his side to quiet his. Hardly, however, was Carmichael out of sight before the whole Scottish force
reappeared, charging down on the English Warden and
his gentlemen, who were without armour. Sir George
Heron and others were killed; Forster and others were
taken prisoners; the rest

> ' No put the bussing on thair theis,
>   And so they fled with all their main
>   Down owre the brae lyke clogged beis,'

the chase lasting three miles into England.

An outrage similar to that of the Redeswire was per-
petrated at Hexpethgatehead, in July, 1585. Sir John
Forster on dismounting found himself practically surrounded by more than 2,000 armed followers of his
Scottish colleague, Sir Thomas Ker of Fernyhurst. On
being shown a letter from King James, bidding him give
satisfaction to the complaints of Henry Collingwood,
Fernyhurst haughtily replied: ' I will answer the King.'
A disturbance presently arose owing to the alleged theft
of a pair of spurs by an English boy. Forster offered
to have him instantly hung, and he and Fernyhurst proceeded quietly with their business. Suddenly, as if by
premeditation, the Scots' drums and fifes struck up,
and their foot musketeers came charging down on the
English. Ker of Ancrum called on Forster's son-in-law,
Lord Francis Russell, to surrender, but in another moment
a volley had laid the young nobleman low. Fernyhurst
did nothing to stop the Scots as they charged past
within forty yards of him, and allowed Forster and a

hundred of his horses and men to be carried off into Scotland.

The immense number of Scots settled in Northumberland had long been a subject of complaint. The English Government seemed powerless to prevent this *Drang nach Suden.* The wife of Robert Roddam, after forcibly turning one of her English tenants at Ilderton out of his house, and imprisoning his children in the tower, planted four Scottish households there in one year. In Moneylaws there was not an Englishman left. Generally speaking, every third man along the Border was a Scot in the service of a Northumbrian master. Lord Hunsdon declared he could rid the country of nearly 3,000 Scots, and yet leave sufficient as colliers, fishers, herds, and shepherds.

Through the labours of Father Sheppard, who had said Mass at Warkworth Castle, and other Jesuits who were concealed at Cartington, Langshaws, Ryle, and Ford, the country suddenly became almost entirely Catholic. Not three Protestant gentlemen were left in the East Marches. Although some of the Catholics would conform by coming to church once a quarter, yet their wives were notorious recusants.

At the head of this large Catholic party was Sir Cuthbert Collingwood, who, by his vehement denunciations of Forster's misrule, became at last Keeper of Redesdale. The 'beggarly Border,' as Collingwood termed it, was indeed in a 'ruinous state.' On all the Percy estates there were not a hundred able men, horse or foot. Three day-forays were run by the Scots to Harbottle, Ilderton, and Clennell. Five hundred Liddesdale men wasted Ryle, Prendwick, and Revely, and tore twelve webs of lead off Ingram church. Thomas Errington's house at Haughton was broken into. Fifty houses were burnt in Redpeth, Wyden, and Bellister, and £1,000 worth of household stuff carried off. A raid of the Laird of Mangerton on Haydon Bridge and Rattenraw secured loot of equal value and twenty-four prisoners. Cattle were even 'reived' from a place so far off the Border as Ulgham Grange.

In revenge for all this Sir Cuthbert Collingwood undertook a bootless expedition to Teviotdale. On his return, Buccleugh and young Cessford came down on Eslington. Sir Cuthbert, with his son and a few servants, sallied out to the hill above his house. Attacked by a whole army of Scots, more fortunate than his sons, he got back through the orchard gate. Captain Bellasis took refuge behind the walls of an old house on the hill, and after most of his men had been massacred was carried away prisoner.

So helpless were the Northumbrians, that it was actually proposed to build an 'insconce,' in imitation of the Roman Wall, along the whole Scottish Border. Inhabited 'sconces' were to be planted on this Elizabethan Wall at about a mile apart, fortified towards Scotland to resist artillery, but next England merely with a thin wall to resist assaults made without cannon. The Queen was to assign 1,000 acres near each 'sconce' at a penny an acre, as preferment to the gentlemen appointed to defend it; the only paid men in each were to be ten gunners.

In 1595, alleging that the North Tyne men had 'long since in a war time' taken away his grandfather's sword and refused to restore it, Buccleugh burnt a widow's house at Greenhaugh, and slew four Charltons at the Bowght Hill. The previous summer some of Cessford's men had stolen a few sheep from the parson of Wooler. To recoup himself, the parson and his friends went and took 'one sheep hogg' from Cessford's shepherd. Cessford's honour was so highly touched that he vowed to kill the parson, who left his all and fled to Berwick. On this, Cessford rode with eighty horse and trumpet sounded to Wooler, and killed two of the parson's men, and also the Laird Baggott, in a village near, hacking them all in pieces. Two Storeys, Baggott's brothers-in-law, thereupon 'got to horseback,' and, going to Scotland, cut up Cessford's shepherd. Cessford lay in wait for them on their way to the Whitsun Fair near Weetwood. Though they escaped him then, he subsequently slaughtered William Storey.

Lord Hunsdon now appointed his third son, Robert Carey, his deputy in the East Marches. The young man sent to Cessford to express his hopes that they would be good friends as colleagues. Cessford put the messenger to bed drunk, and took the opportunity of going to kill an Englishman against whom he had a spite. Carey requited this breach of courtesy by summarily executing Cessford's particular favourite, a ruffian called Geordie Bourne. In 1598 Carey became Warden of the Middle Marches, in succession to Lord Eure, whose five years' tenure had been disastrous to the country, owing to his misplaced confidence in his officers. Carey obtained King James's permission to take revenge on Liddesdale for a raid on Haltwhistle. During this expedition a Ridley from that town slew Sim of the Cat Hill. This brought the whole of the thieves down on it again, when a Ridley shot one of the sons of Sim of Whitram in the street. By passing the whole summer in a fort he built at the foot of Liddesdale, Carey reduced all the thieves to submission.

Owing to Sir John Forster's imbecility, Hume and other Scottish lords had been suffered to come and hunt in Northumberland. Carey had a dozen of them brought prisoners to Widdrington. Not long afterwards he proclaimed James King of England there, during his hasty ride to carry the tidings of Elizabeth's death to Edinburgh. He had left London after nine in the morning and reached Widdrington the next night. One of the last exploits of the Scots before the Union was kidnapping William Wicliffe, the Earl of Northumberland's commissioner, in October, 1602. Wicliffe lost his apparel, three horses and their furniture, and a considerable sum of gold and silver. His enlargement was only accomplished by a heavy ransom.

CHAPTER X.

THE RADCLIFFES.

'BY ma saul, they are enough to spoil a gude King,' is said to have been the comment of James I. on the frantic demonstrations with which the people of Newcastle greeted his entry into their town as the first Sovereign of Great Britain. The weary story of Border warfare appeared to have been closed for ever by the dynastic union of the two crowns. No one could have foreseen the decadence of the monarchy and the Scottish invasions that were soon to follow.

Final articles for the pacification and disarmament of the 'Middle Shires of Britain' were agreed upon by English and Scottish commissioners in 1605. Noblemen and gentlemen unsuspected of felony were allowed to retain their arms, but the commonalty were ordered to put away all weapons and warlike accoutrements. An attempt was made to draft the young men of Tyndale and Redesdale into the army in Ireland. But, in spite of all King James's endeavours, old Border habits were not easily laid aside. So late as 1611, Robert Elliot of the Redheugh, with fifty Scottish horse and twenty foot, all furnished with 'long pieces, pistollets, or lances,' came to Leaplish in the upper valley of North Tyne, and 'cut down' Lionel Robson's dwelling-house with their axes. Lionel himself was shot through the heart with a bullet, and many other men and women were killed and wounded.

The gentry of Northumberland transferred their family feuds to the field of politics. John Clavering, the Sheriff, opened the poll only half an hour before the time fixed for the election of a Knight of the Shire in 1614. Then, finding he had not got twenty-four votes for his candidate, Sir George Selby, he had the clock put back till they came, taking no notice of any votes given for Sir Ralph Grey. As Selby, after all, was ineligible, being Sheriff of Durham, a serjeant's officer was sent down by the House of Commons to attach Clavering. Without even offering the officer a drink, Clavering rode post-haste to Westminster, and appeared at the bar of the House, by whom he was committed to custody.

The influence of the House of Percy, weakened by the long absence of the eighth and ninth Earls of Northumberland in the South, sustained a severe shock through Thomas Percy's participation in the Gunpowder Conspiracy. He had in hand at the time the rents of the Northern estates of the Earl his kinsman, with whom he actually dined at Sion on the eve of Fawkes's apprehension. Northumberland was committed to the Tower on suspicion, and Sir Henry Widdrington was instructed to take possession of the castles of Alnwick, Tynemouth, and Prudhoe. The Earl was eventually released on the payment of a heavy fine, but was forbidden to visit the North. The value of land in Northumberland had been enormously enhanced by the Union. This led to a certain disintegration of society: as long as the Scottish ravages lasted, all the peasants were much on the same level of poverty; the sudden prosperity caused by their cessation led to extravagance and excess, and gradually the richer farmers in a village ate up the smaller ones—a result favoured by the demand for wool, and the general dislike of land-agents for small holdings.

The eclipse of the Percy crescent left the first place in Northumberland to the Radcliffes, who, quitting their home on Derwentwater, had acquired Dilston and Cartington by marriage at the end of the fifteenth century.

They now purchased the manor of Alston, with its rich lead-mines, and the extensive barony of Langley. Their devoted attachment to the Stuarts in sunshine and storm gives a special interest to the history of their family.

King James spent ten days in Newcastle in 1617, staying at the house of Sir George Selby. Henry Babbington, whom he visited at Heaton Hall, 'endured knighthood' in company with Peter Riddell and John Delaval.

The thieves and outlaws of the Northumbrian Highlands proved a great terror to Newcastle during the French war of 1627. Many of them were tried and punished during the shrievalty of Sir Thomas Swinburne in the following year. Sir Thomas has left most curious details of his official expenditure: how he gave a dinner to the 200 gentlemen and their servants who rode with him to meet the judges at Sheriff Hill; how he provided blue coats for the twenty-four bailiffs, Lancelot Allgood the county clerk, the two gaolers, and the Under-Sheriff's men, as well as for ten men of his own; and how he gave the judges a pound each at their parting on Benwell Hills. Sir Robert Branding, of Alnwick Abbey, who had already once been Sheriff, was pricked again for 1629. He refused to serve, and fled to Scotland, so Swinburne had to continue in office; he had learnt by this time how to cut down the expenses. Sir Robert Brandling consented to serve the year after, but his many offences against morality and his violent vagaries at Alnwick Church—beating the minister before the sermon, laying his staff about his wife, locking the Percy servants out and the Archdeacon's official in—led to his being fined £3,000 in the Court of High Commission.

Amid the persecutions to which Catholics were constantly subjected, the widowed Dorothy Lawson enjoyed singular quietness, owing to her acknowledged piety and goodness. She built a house at St. Anthony's, below Newcastle, where a picture of the saint had formerly been 'decently placed' in a tree near the Tyne 'for the comfort of seamen.' At the end of her house towards

the river she ' caused to be made the sacred Name of
Jesus,' and each room inside was known by the name of
some particular saint. On her death, in 1632, her body
was brought on a barge to Newcastle, where in the evening the streets were illuminated with tapers, ' as light as
if it had been noon.' The magistrates and aldermen
received the coffin at the landing-stage, and, after accompanying it to the church-door, adjourned to the funeral
feast.

Charles I. visited Newcastle on his way to his Scottish
coronation in 1633. Soon afterwards three Norwich
soldiers on their travels arrived in the town, the captain
and ensign ' clad in green like young foresters.' They
found the people and the streets much alike, neither
sweet nor clean. The quay was fair and long, but there
were few ships in the river. Mr. Cole, the Mayor,
was fat and rich, vested in a sack of satin. The Nag's
Head, ' the princely inn of freestone ' on the Sand-hill,
excited their admiration more than the seven gates or
four churches. They marched away, with pretty
murmuring music, along the banks of the Tyne, which
kept them from straying on the left, as the Picts' Wall
did on the right. The road, especially in one place, was
so steep, narrow, and intricate, that they expected their
nags to fall upon them. When they thought all dangers
past, they had to cross the rough ford at Hexham, in 'the
vale of night.' Fortunately, they were rewarded in finding in the ' Heart of all England ' that rarest of rarities,
an inn ' with cheap and good fare, sweet lodging, and
kind usage, a traveller's desire.'

The Puritans were gaining ground considerably in
Newcastle and the neighbourhood. Dr. Jenison, Vicar of
All Saints', who wrote ' Newcastle's Call, to take Warning by her Sins and Sorrowes,' during the plague of 1636,
which carried off a third of the inhabitants, greatly
favoured them, while continuing to profess conformity.
Alvey, the Vicar of Newcastle, on the contrary, was, a
zealous High-Churchman, and took proceedings against a

mercer named John Blakiston, the son of a prebendary of Durham, for refusing to kneel in St. Nicholas'. John Fenwick and Bittleston, a tanner, went into Scotland to observe the manner of keeping the day of humiliation, and were believed to have subscribed to the Covenant. Many of the party gathered in Henry Dawson's house on Sunday nights, to hear unauthorized prayers and repetitions of sermons.

In consequence of the grave aspect of affairs in Scotland, energetic measures were taken for the defence of New-castle in 1638. The following spring King Charles re-solved to lead in person an army to the Border. He was magnificently entertained in Newcastle; the whole town seemed as one man against the Scots. His artillery and five regiments of foot, which on May 21 were en-camped on Bockenfield Moor, were joined next day by the Guards on Rock Moor. After encamping again near Detchant Wood, and on Goswick Moor, they marched on to the ' Grand Leaguer' on the Tweed at the Birks near Ord. Charles himself, who went straight to Berwick, sleeping on the road at Alnwick Abbey, arrived in camp on the 30th. A contemporary plan shows the position of the royal tents with

> ' The Glorious Standard of our Gratious King,
>   whence streams of peace to Loyall Subjects spring.
>   But seas of Ruine and sterne war to them
>   perturbe that Peace, moleste his Diadem.'

Charles's untrained levies were so eager to fight that ' they cast up their caps with caprioles, shouts, and signs of joy' on the first news of the Scots' approach ; but although his forces were slightly superior in number, the King did not dare to attack Leslie at Dunglas. A great want of discipline prevailed; the men fired off their guns at random in the camp. Many of them were compelled to lie all night on the ground, sheltered only by walls of turf and branches of furze. When Leslie advanced to Dunse Law, Charles was content to examine his forces through a telescope, and to calmly observe, ' Let us go to

supper; the number is not considerable.' The Pacification of Berwick was concluded on June 22, and both
armies fled homewards ' like a broken-up school.'

Disaffection became more and more rife in Newcastle.
At Michaelmas two Puritans, Robert Bewick and John
Emerson, were chosen to be Mayor and Sheriff. The
people began to give up coming to church till the singing
of the psalm before the sermon. Two leading Covenanters, Sir Walter Riddell and Sir John Buchanan, came
to Newcastle, and were accompanied on their suspicious
walks round the town walls by Mr. Middleton, at whose
private chapel at Belsay all comers were allowed to
preach to the factious spirits who flocked from Newcastle.
Pressed by Sir John Marley as to why he let these
strangers view the town, the Mayor replied it was because
Mass was suspected to be said in it.

The Pacification of the previous year failing to produce
any good effect in Scotland, Lord Conway arrived to
undertake the defence of Newcastle in the spring of 1640.
He found the walls for the most part difficult to scale, but
the cannon on them of little use. In addition to a portcullis, each of the principal gates was provided with great
bars fitting into the walls to stop horsemen, an iron gate
of broad bars, and great gates of wood. Hundreds of
Scottish families had settled in Northumberland, particularly on Lord Grey's estates; there were about 300 of them
employed in the coal-mines, and many in Newcastle, all
Covenanters, and as devoted to the Scottish party as if
they lived in Edinburgh. Conway could only persuade the
Corporation to arm all their companies with muskets and
a certain number of keelmen and colliers with pikes. Sir
John Marley considered that, as the King received £50,000
a year from the town, he ought with that money to pay
soldiers for its defence. Twopence was deducted from
each soldier on the pay-day to cover the cost of his
wretched accoutrements. A mutiny took place in consequence, and one of the malcontents, chosen by dice-
throwing, was shot. Rumours of the intended advance

of the Scots in June were discredited by Conway, and the
King refused to provide for the defence of the town by a
slight duty on coal. It was, however, an open secret that
the Scots intended to seize the Tyne and Wear, and so,
by stopping the coal trade, exact extreme terms from
England. Conway selected a site for a citadel, both to
defend and overawe the town. He refused to send for
more foot, dreading unpaid soldiers more than the Scots.
Finally, on August 20, Leslie did cross the Tweed with
about 30,000 men. A week later a drummer brought two
sealed letters to Sir Jacob Astley. One of them was addressed 'For him that commands in chief in Newcastle,'
the other 'To the Mayor of Newcastle.' Astley stopped
the Scotsman beating his drum, and, pretending he himself was the Mayor, refused to receive the letters.

The blue-bonneted host—the Highlanders still armed
with bows and arrows—pitched their camp on Heddon
Law, about three miles to the north of Newburn. The
great fires they made with coal worked on the spot made
their army appear more numerous than it was. They
had had no meat with them the whole day before crossing
the Tweed, but they assured the people of Northumberland that they would not take a chicken or a pot of ale
without paying for it. They met therefore with no
resistance, and were even entertained and feasted by
some of the country gentry.

Conway considered that Newcastle was untenable
if the Scots crossed the Tyne and attacked it from
Gateshead. Compelled to leave the greater part of
the garrison in the town to prevent its betrayal, he proceeded with 2,000 foot and 1,000 horse to Stella Haugh,
in order to guard the ford at Newburn. He threw up two
'sconces,' or breast works, one close to the river, the other
a little in the rear, placing in each 400 musketeers and four
guns. His horse he drew up in squadrons on the haugh,
some distance further east. As the soldiers were moving
into these hastily constructed earthworks, they perceived
the Scots marching down the hill into the village, where

they planted some of their guns on the church tower, and
lined the houses, lanes and hedges with musketeers. Both
parties continued watering their horses at the river all the
morning of that 28th of August. At last a Scottish officer,
well mounted, with a black feather in his hat, came out
for this purpose from one of the thatched cottages. An
English officer seeing him regarding the 'sconces,' took
aim and brought him from the saddle. The Scots immediately opened fire on their side. The duel, commenced
with musketry, was continued by artillery. Between
three and four in the afternoon, when the tide was low,
the Scots, thanks to the immense superiority of their
position, made a breach in the 'sconce' commanded by
Colonel Lunsford, 'bowling their great shot' into it.
Several officers and many of the men were killed; the
rest threw down their arms and fled from the colours.
Thereupon twenty-six of the College of Justice troop
crossed the Tyne to reconnoitre. At the same time
the English foot were driven by the guns from the other
'sconce.' At about four o'clock, Colonel Blair passed
the river with 1,000 musketeers, and Colonel Leslie's
and Sir Thomas Hope's troops of horse, but was forced
to fall back on the advance of twelve of the English
squadrons. A Scottish battery of nine guns placed on
the hill to the east of Newburn now opened fire on
the Royal horse, and threw them into disorder. The
foot brigades of Loudoun and Montgomery, each 1,800
strong, ran boldly down to the ford. The English
sounded a retreat, Lunsford drawing off his cannon.
In protecting the flight of the foot up Ryton and
Stella banks, Commissary Wilmot, Sir John Digby, and
Daniel O'Neill, were made prisoners by the Scottish
horse. The Royal standard was taken, Charles Porter
the bearer being killed. A rally made in a wood by
Sir Jacob Astley proved unsuccessful. Fugitives crying
'Fly for your lives; naked devils have destroyed us!'
caused a panic in Newcastle. Vicar Alvey jumped up
on horseback behind a countryman, 'without waiting

for a cushion.' The next day the town was abandoned by Conway. Sir William Douglas, Sheriff of Teviotdale, with a company of horse, demanded the surrender of Newcastle from the Mayor on Tyne Bridge. Leslie and his guards, entering the town on the Sunday, went in solemn state to the great church, where the 'organs, sackbuts, and cornets' were silenced. The Scots continued their 'destruction of idolatry' by defacing the 'spoons' or canopies of the church fonts. The collieries and shipping, which then employed 10,000 people, were all laid idle. It was not until August, 1641, that the invaders, having been paid £60,000, agreed to recross the Tweed. That same month King Charles passed through Northumberland on his way to Edinburgh, returning in November.

William Cavendish, Earl of Newcastle, was appointed Governor of the town by King Charles in June, 1642, and at once began to put it in better trim for resistance. At the end of the year, Colonel Goring landed with a great supply of arms and ammunition from the Low Countries. He brought with him the standard of Queen Henrietta Maria to be displayed at the head of the Earl's army. Cavendish united the four Northern counties in a league for the King and was rewarded with the Marquisate of Newcastle. Sir George Muschamps of Barmoor, his commissioner for raising a regiment of foot, was refused permission to have his drum beat by the Berwick Corporation. Soon afterwards he received instructions to arrest Thomas Armorer of Belford, Richard Forster of Newham, and Robert Carr of Howick, all suspected of treasonable practices. Cavendish, however, lacked the chief sinew of war; 'a little barrel of ducatoons' from Henrietta Maria had not done much to replenish his military chest. Robert Rugg, the bottlenosed Governor of Holy Island, an extraordinary character who had dubbed Tom Coryat 'first English Knight of Troy' on the banks of the Simois, was left without pay for more than sixteen months. Finding all prose remonstrances unavailing, he sought inspiration in a cup of canary, and addressed the paymasters in verses headed:

> 'The Great Commander of the Gormorants,
> The Geese and Ganders of these Hallowed Lands,
> Where Lindisfarne and Holy Island stands,
> These worthless lines sends to your worthie hands.'

The Parliament, which at first had forbidden all ships to trade with Newcastle, now found that London and the greater part of the kingdom were likely to suffer very deeply for want of coal, 'that commodity so absolutely necessary to the maintenance and support of life.' Accordingly it hit on the more practical expedient of levying on each chaldron an import duty, to be applied in raising forces to reduce the town. For the same end it entered into a close alliance with the Scottish Covenanters. On January 19, 1644, three regiments of Scottish foot and thirteen troops of horse crossed Berwick bridge and advanced to Haggerston; while Colonel Welden's regiment took up its quarters at Pressen, Learmouth, Wark, and Mindrum. The Royalist Colonel, Francis Anderson, drew back his men to Wooler. The Marquis of Argyle sent his trumpeter to Sir Thomas Glenham and Colonel Grey at Alnwick, but received a loyal answer of defiance. On the 23rd, Lieutenant-General Bayly marched from Kelso to Wooler, over the two nights' ice of the Tweed, and General Leslie removed his headquarters to Edderston. On the 25th, though the thaw had so swelled the waters that their infantry were often up to their waists, sometimes to their armpits, Leslie and Bayly effected a junction at Alnwick, where the Royalists had made a pretence of defending the bridge with the guns of a Dutch flee-boat. Sir Thomas Glenham collected masons and workmen to cut Felton Bridge, but, frightened by the execrations of the country-women, while he went into a house to refresh himself they all ran away. Warkworth Castle surrendered at the first shot, though it had, it would seem, a garrison of seventy soldiers, seven pieces of brass ordnance, and a year's provisions. The Scottish leader told Bemerton, the Governor, that if he had fought as well as he danced, it would never have been taken. Leslie remained four days at Morpeth, and though the castle was 'a ruinous hole, not tenable by nature and far less by art,' he left Lieutenant-Colonel Somerville with 500 men in it to deter the garrison of Newcastle from plundering the country. On February 3 the Scottish army appeared before Newcastle. The Marquis of Argyle's trumpeter was sent with a letter to the Mayor, explaining that, though their 'appearance in that posture, through mis-informations and misunderstandings, might occasion strange thoughts,' they were ready to treat for 'the preservation of Religion, the King's true Honour and Happinesse, and the publick Peace and Liberty of his Dominions.' Sir John Marley and the Common Council replied that they would not 'betray the trust reposed in them, or forfeit their allegiance to His Majesty, for whose honour and preservation, together with the Religion and Lawes of the Kingdome, they intended to hazard their Lives and Fortunes.' Meanwhile the Scottish musketeers drove the English out of a small sconce about a quarter of a mile from the town, near the stone bridge leading into the Shieldfield. A stronger fort near a wind-mill, within half a musket-shot of the walls, is said also to have been taken after a severe struggle. A sortie of horse proved ineffective, the number of coal-pits making charging difficult work. The Sandgate, a straggling suburb by the river-side, was set on fire by the Scots, and burnt for two days.

No serious attack could be made on the town till the arrival of the 'murthering pieces,' which were brought by sea to Blyth's Nook. Even then nearly a fortnight was passed in inaction, the Scots being fully persuaded that the town would surrender. Perceiving that the Marquis of Newcastle and Sir John Marley were made of different metal than Lord Conway and Robert Bewick, they determined to approach it from the south. The

ford at Newburn was now fortified not only by the river-
side, but above, near the hilltop; so they despatched some
regiments of horse to secure the fords higher up the Tyne.
On February 19 Sir Marmaduke Langdale and Colonel
Fenwick of Hexham attempted to surprise those quartered
at Corbridge, under Leslie's son Lord Balgoney, and
Lord Kirkcudbright, but a timely warning had drawn
them out into the field. Colonel Ballantine charged the
Royalists twice with his lancers, and had taken 100
prisoners, when, charging a third time, he approached
too near their musketeers. Sir Marmaduke rallied his
men and routed the Scots, who had 'a very narrow retreat
through a gap.' Balgoney was shot through the shoulder,
and among the many prisoners was Major Agnew, dangerously hurt. In their flight the Scots found themselves
face to face with Colonel Dudley's dragoons, who had
crossed the river from Prudhoe that morning and surprised several of their quarters. Colonel Brandling, who
had the chief command, rode out impetuously before his
troops, and exchanged pistol-shots with a Scottish lieutenant named Elliot. Both wheeled to draw their swords,
but Brandling's horse stumbled, and Elliot pulled him out
of the saddle. His misadventure threw the English into
disorder. Dudley, conceiving himself outnumbered, retreated across the river, losing those of his dragoons
whose horses were too weak to follow. The fortunes
of the day were thus equally divided.

Shortly afterwards, a snowstorm having abated, General
Leslie, leaving six regiments under Sir James Lums-
dale before Newcastle, led his main army to Heddon-
on-the-Wall for the night, and then into quarters along
the river between Ovingham and Corbridge. The English horse fell back in front of them, and abandoned
Hexham at midnight, leaving Major Agnew there to protect the house of Colonel Fenwick, who had used him
courteously. After another drifting storm, the Scots
passed the Tyne on February 28 at Ovingham, Eltring-
ham, and Bywell, the foot wading very deep; indeed, the

flood had so risen in the Derwent by the time they reached it, that they had to march single file over a tree-bridge near Ebchester. They successfully occupied Sunderland, and stormed a fort at South Shields. In April the Marquis of Newcastle marched South to York, where he was besieged by Leslie and Fairfax.

On May 10, 1644, Montrose, and the Scottish noblemen and gentry with him in Newcastle, resolved ' to ferret out their rebellious countrymen, who had nested themselves in the castle of Morpeth.' Having himself effected a reconnaissance of the Royalist advance, Somerville, the Governor, backed the castle-gate with earth and sods, to prevent its being blown in by a petard. As his garrison was more numerous than his arms, he divided it into three eight-hour companies. At dawn the next morning Montrose delivered a furious assault; this, however, was repulsed, so he pitched his camp, and invested the castle with a trench. He was soon disturbed by the news of fresh troops advancing from Scotland; these he drove back, though he was unable to overtake them. Somerville devoted this interlude of five days to destroying Montrose's breastwork and the houses near the castle, but spared a great barn which had been just built by the Lord of the Manor. Montrose, on his return, placed his cannon in this barn, and battered down the battlements of the castle, without, however, making much impression on the walls. A successful sally set on fire the rye-straw thatch of the barn, so Montrose raised two batteries nearer the castle. These began to play at daybreak, and by four in the afternoon a breach was effected. Somerville closed this with feather beds; but in the general bombardment that followed a musket-ball entered his neckcloth and went out at the crown of his hat, ' taking off some of the hide and hair of his head.' After some deliberations a white flag was displayed, and an honourable capitulation agreed upon. The garrison marched out at ten o'clock on the morning of May 29; they had lost only about twenty men, the besiegers two hundred.

At Marston Moor Newcastle's 1,000 Whitecoats, raised chiefly among his Ogle tenantry, scorned to yield or flee. All, except thirty, were 'slain in rank and file as they stood.' The coats which they had begged the Marquis, in his want of scarlet cloth, to give them undyed as they were, promising to dye them in the enemy's blood, were now all red with their own. The surrender of York to the Parliamentary forces followed. After this the Earl of Callendar, who had entered England with a reserve of 10,000 Scots and had taken Hartlepool and Stockton, made himself master of Gateshead, and so threatened Newcastle from the south. The Mayor, Sir John Marley, now proved himself no 'carpet-knight from a tap-house.' Although he had with him only 800 train-band soldiers, and about an equal number of volunteers and pressed men, he conducted the defence with extraordinary spirit. In order to leave no foothold for scaling-ladders, the ditch round the town was dug deeper close into the walls, which were underpinned with clay. The embrasures of the battlements were closed with stone and lime, only narrow slits being left for sharp-shooters; the cap-stones of the merlons were lifted and balanced on little stones, so as to fall with any of the enemy who should attempt to mount them. In the castle, with a view to securing the river and the Quayside, heavy guns were laid on the Half Moon (the round tower at the south end of the old Moot Hall), while great ordnance planted on the keep essayed to silence the five batteries established by the Scots on Gateshead Banks. At the north-east corner of the town, the Shieldfield fort and its four bastions, with shipmasts laid along the outworks, 'commanded champion-like the fields.'

During the second week of August, Leslie returned from York with the main Scottish army. Passing the Tyne on a bridge of keels above Newcastle, he sat down on the north side of the town. His common soldiers constructed huts of turf, clay, straw, and wattles; the officers were provided with round tents. Three thousand countrymen were ordered to bring mattocks, spades, and shovels, and labour in the trenches. The Earl of Callendar crossed the Tyne, also by a bridge of boats, to the east of Newcastle, and completed the ring of investment which had hitherto been broken by the Shieldfield fort. No provisions could now enter the devoted town. At great jeopardy the loyal burghers issued from the posterns, and engaged the Scots in the flanking trenches. The siege grew daily hotter and hotter. A Scottish battery in the Sandgate beat down the upper part of the Carpenters' Tower. Undistracted by the bombardment, the garrison discovered a mine that was being driven at the time between this tower and the river. Lord Callendar himself, who was directing the excavation, thrust a pick into the countermine. To prevent his own mine being drowned, he had it sprung the next morning. The explosion overthrew a strong horn-work, which now became a shelter for the attacking force.

Imagining that Sir John Marley was buoying up his people with false hopes, the Scots threw letters over the walls, giving their version of the state of affairs. On Michaelmas Day, General Bayly's batteries 'brashed down' part of the town wall near St. Andrew's church, to within two feet of the ground. Ten men might have marched in abreast at this breach, but the royalists, under cover of canvas, speedily barricaded it with timber and rubbish. St. Andrew's church suffered considerably from the cannonade; the beautiful spire of St. Nicholas might, it is said, have been demolished, if Scottish prisoners had not been purposely confined under the lantern. The church bells rang all one night to celebrate the discovery and destruction of three Scottish mines.

Montrose's rising in the Highlands made Leslie anxious to bring matters to an issue. Negotiations for a capitulation were begun, but Marley imagined he knew enough of the Scots' character to buy them off with a good sum of money, while Leslie did not allow sufficient time for deliberation. Marley at last pretended that Leslie must be dead, as he had not been seen for some time before the town. Accordingly he sent a letter to be delivered personally to him by a drummer, charged to see if he were really alive. This 'base derision' made a peaceful solution impossible. On the morning of October 19 Leslie determined to storm the town. By ten o'clock his different regiments were under arms in their positions round the walls. They were subjected to the taunts of the guards on the ramparts, who kept calling 'Come on, you cowardly rogues, if you dare.' Yet it was not till three o'clock in the afternoon, when the besieged had nearly succeeded in blowing up with their countermines the chambers in which the Scots kept their mining powder, that the general assault was actually delivered. Under the direction of John Osborn, 'a false Scot,' the colliers of Elswick and Benwell successfully sprang one mine near the White Friar Tower, and another at the Sandgate. The batteries effected four great breaches. These, however, were very steep and difficult to mount, and the townsmen did great execution on the Scots who entered them with the iron spikes of their hand grenades. The death of Colonel Hume at the breach near the Andrew Tower was 'involved' in the quaint epitaph:

> 'Woe to that breach beside Black Bessie's Towre,
> Woe to itselfe, that bloudy butchering bowre !
> Where valiant Home, that sterne Bellonaes blade
> And brave commander fell : for there he stay'd
> Arraign'd by death.'

Nothing was left undone by Marley and his garrison that might repel the fury of the assault. A desperate fire poured from the castle on the breaches, while volley on volley of scattered shot was discharged from the flanking towers of the walls. For a long hour the thunder of the opposing artillery continued to peal amid a driving hail-storm of musket-balls, drowning, except at rare intervals, the clang of the swords and the 'brangling' of the pikes. The attack had lasted two hours, when Loudoun and Buccleugh's regiments poured in at a breach near the

Close Gate.   Even after their entry they were thrice
charged in the narrow street by Marley's horse.   In their
rage they set a house on fire, while Captain Andrew
Abernethy launched a whaler's boat, all in flame, with
the intention of burning the vessels which lay along the
Quay.   Lord Callendar had now passed over the breach
made by the mine in Sandgate.   Marching rapidly to the
Sandhill, with colours flying and drums beating, he gave
orders to check any further conflagration.   He despatched
Lords Livingston and Kellhead with their two regiments
to clear the royalists off the walls on the east side of the
town.   Pilgrim Street Gate, with its long barbican, was
bravely defended by Captain George Errington and nine-
score tradesmen.   They would hold no parley with the
enemy without; but finding themselves attacked in the
rear, they surrendered to Colonel Sinclair, by whom they
were honourably treated.   The Bigg Market was soon
choked with fugitives from the walls, crying for quarter,
and throwing down their arms.   All noise and tumult
suddenly ceased.   The soldiers of the garrison vanished
behind the closed doors of the houses; the more crafty
'sat down by their fathers' firesides' as though they had
never had a musket or pike in their hands.   The Scottish
regiments patrolled the streets unmolested, and refrained
for the time being from pillage and rapine.   Sir John
Marley and the three loyal Scottish lords, Crawford,
Reay, and Maxwell, took refuge in the castle with 500
men, and held out for three days longer.   The plague
having broken out in Tynemouth Castle, it, too, yielded at
the end of the month.

In an age of indiscriminate massacres like those of
Magdeburg and Drogheda, the mercy shown by the
Scots to a town taken by storm, with the loss of 1,000 on
their own side, was, as far as human life was concerned,
absolutely without parallel.   Against this must be set
their complete sack of Newcastle.   At their first entry, a
dozen of them burst into a house where a christening party
were drinking 'Confusion to the Scots rebels,' rifled their

pockets, and stripped off their clothes. The town was now deliberately given over to be plundered by the whole army for twenty-four hours. Bedclothes, table-linen, skins and leather, coats and dresses, pots, plates, and pans, all found their way across the Tweed. With singular lack of the power to see themselves as others saw them, the Scots subsequently bewailed the 'ignorant negligence and careless omission' they had shown on this occasion, 'as illustrating their own old proverb'—it must indeed have been an extremely old one—that 'Scottish men are aye wise behind the hand.'

In memory of the heroic resistance she offered to Leslie, Newcastle adopted at the Restoration the proud motto :

FORTITER DEFENDENDO TRIUMPHAT.

This—'She glories in her brave defence'—being considered too loyal, has been altered by the Corporation to the meaningless

FORTITER DEFENDIT TRIUMPHANS.

King Charles, who had fled from Oxford to the Scottish camp at Newark-on-Trent, was brought to Newcastle in the beginning of May, 1646. It was here that, soon after, a Scottish minister, preaching insolently before him, gave out the fifty-second psalm :

> ' Why dost thou, tyrant, boast thyself,
>   Thy wicked works to praise ?'

The King stood up, and called instead for the fifty-sixth,

> ' Have mercy, Lord, on me, I pray,
>   For men would me devour,'

which the people accordingly sang. Charles appears to have been lodged in the Elizabethan mansion called Anderson Place. He attempted to escape in disguise by the passage of the Lortburn, and is said to have got as far as a grate in the middle of the Side, when he was apprehended. After this he was deprived of the liberty of playing golf on the Shieldfield, and strictly watched by a guard of soldiers, who annoyed him by continually smoking. The English Parliament, who had sent Captain Robert Batten to occupy Holy Island, ultimately agreed to pay the Scots £200,000 for the costs of their campaign. Subsequent negotiations stipulated that the King should be handed over to his English enemies. Having completed this ignominious transaction on January 28, 1647, the Scots marched off home.

In the spring of 1648, Sir Marmaduke Langdale, commissioned by the Prince of Wales, seized Berwick. In June, leaving Colonel Grey there, he advanced into Cumberland to await the arrival of the Duke of Hamilton's army, but was driven into Carlisle by General Lambert. From Carlisle he sent 700 horse under Colonel Tempest to meet Colonel Grey near Alnwick, a move that forced the Northumberland horse of the Parliament and Major Sanderson's troops, who had been watching Berwick, to draw towards Sir Arthur Haselrig at Newcastle. They were joined at Newburn by Colonel Wren's newly-raised Bishopric regiment of horse, and advanced to Chollerton Edge to prevent the Cavaliers encamping there on their march west. At Capheaton they were reinforced by fifty dragoons from Newcastle, but although Grey and Tempest were afraid to attack them, they judged it prudent tactics to fall back on Hexham. Colonel Lilburn now reached Haydon Bridge with three troops from the west. At eleven o'clock at night, on June 30, the Roundheads all marched from their rendezvous at Chollerford to Harterton, where they baited their horses for two hours. At Tosson a Royalist lieutenant and his six dragoons were surprised in bed by Major Sanderson and the 'forlorn hope.' Colonels Grey and Salkeld were seized at Callaley. Of all the Royalist quarters, Cartington Castle, where Sir Richard Tempest and Sir Francis Radcliffe were in command, was the only place that offered resistance, and that only for two hours. Three hundred prisoners, mostly officers and gentlemen, were driven on foot to Morpeth, their horses having been promptly sent off for sale at Newcastle. Sir Richard Tempest contrived to escape the next morning.

On August 10, a week before Cromwell's defeat of Hamilton at Preston, Colonel Henry Lilburn, who had been a devoted Parliamentarian, suddenly pulled up the drawbridge of Tynemouth Castle, where he was Deputy-Governor. Setting the prisoners, many of them taken at Cartington, at liberty, he declared he would pistol every soldier that would not be for him and King Charles. A corporal who refused to give up his arms he ran through the body. Many seamen from Shields flocked to his assistance. Sir Arthur Haselrig, the Governor of Newcastle, immediately despatched Colonel Ashfield with a large force of infantry and 100 dragoons to recover the castle. Between one and two in the morning Major Cobbet led the 'forlorn hope' to the storm. Lilburn welcomed them with four cannon. As they mounted by their ladders, they were pushed down with pikes and 'gunners' ladles.' Forced to expose themselves, however, on the battlements, the garrison were picked off by the soldiers underneath. Lilburn was among those shot dead ; the escalade proved at last successful, and the castle was won.

Sir George Munro, in his retreat through Alnwick with the remnants of Langdale's force, swept everything out of the country. Berwick surrendered to Cromwell on September 30. Although the Earl of Northumberland took the Parliamentary side, Warkworth Castle was ordered to be 'sleighted,' a word to which Pye, the Governor, gave the widest interpretation, not restricting himself to destroying the military works and removing the doors.

The officers and men in garrison at Newcastle, Tynemouth, and Holy Island were especially eager for Charles's execution. Nothing else, they urged, could be 'an acceptable sacrifice to the justice of God while Agag was spared.' Colonel Hewson's regiment deplored, in addition, the great increase of lawyers as being 'a Pathognomonical Symptom of a Cachectic Commonwealth.' The fanatical misuse of the Old Testament gave rise to a great campaign against witchcraft at Newcastle. Those whose skin was insensible to the pin of the witch-trier were condemned forthwith; a wizard and fifteen witches were executed on one day on the Town Moor. A far more terrible episode in the 'Reign of the Saints' followed. Six thousand of Cromwell's prisoners from Dunbar were penned in the inner ward of Alnwick Castle. After eight days' starvation, 3,000 survived. These were turned into a large walled garden at Morpeth. The raw cabbages they devoured, leaves and roots, brought on a plague, from which scores died by the roadside on their march to Newcastle and in the church of St. Nicholas, into which they were huddled for the night. Out of the 6,000 brought to Alnwick, not more than 1,000 escaped alive from their final privations at Durham.

On the whole, religious matters were kept fairly quiet at Newcastle, through the eloquent ministrations of Silver-tongue Sydenham, an ejected prebendary of Wells. The more extreme sectaries at Hexham allowed themselves to be thoroughly imposed upon by a Scotsman named Ramsay, who variously pretended to be a Benedictine emissary of the Pope, and a Mantuan Jew of the tribe of Judah.

When at length the hour struck for the comparative restoration of civil and religious liberty, General Monk, who had secured Berwick in the autumn, crossed the Tweed with his army at Coldstream on the New Year's Day of 1660. His first night's quarters were at Wooler. Lambert, who was suspected of being a Roman Catholic, and of wishing to make himself King, immediately abandoned Newcastle. His soldiers, though superior in number to Monk's, were a pampered and delicate company, weary of being quartered among a coarse and hardy people. Their pay was in arrear, and they were driven to desperate courses; some of the dragoons actually surprised Chillingham Castle, in the hope of seizing Lord Grey's rents. No wonder, then, that the church bells everywhere welcomed Monk's advance. The snow lay too deep to permit of his march from Wooler to Morpeth in one day. He broke the journey at a vicar's house, probably at Edlingham, where he met with only cold entertainment. Next day he fared better, for in passing Long Horsley Tower the honest old knight, Sir Thomas Horsley, though he made no secret of his sympathies being with Lambert, received the General and his train very kindly and nobly. At Morpeth the High Sheriff and principal gentry of Northumberland waited on his Excellency, in company with the sword-bearers of London and Newcastle. Tynemouth Castle alone had the effrontery to declare against him.

The impending Restoration of Charles Stuart was not altogether in harmony with the old Border feeling still latent in Newcastle. 'What!' exclaimed Margaret Dixon, 'can they find no other man to bring in than a Scotsman? What! is there not some Englishman more fit to make King than a Scot?' Nor did the extravagant expenditure of the King tend to allay this incipient discontent. 'What can have become of all the money collected in the country?' asked Thomas Busby, as he was walking near Alnwick with Henry Elder. 'What should become of it?' rejoined Elder; 'there is none to destroy it but a company of ranting fellows; and as for his Majesty, he has taken up the bones of an honester man than himself, and there will be no quietness till he goes the way his father went.' There were constant rumours of plots against the new Government; on one alarm, Sir James Clavering, the Mayor of Newcastle, caused the trained bands to be called out into the market-place; on another, a lantern was ordered to be hung out of every house till the morning. The 'drum ecclesiastic' continued to be a potent factor in politics. Standing at the stairhead, outside a secret prayer-meeting at Newcastle one night, Thomas Story, the Quaker, was disgusted to hear no word of Christian doctrine from the famous Presbyterian preacher, but only suggestions of jealousy and dislike of the Government, delivered in a highly objectionable strain. For holding weekly meetings of this kind under the cloak of mutual assistance and improvement in religion, some young men were denounced to Judge Jeffreys at the Newcastle Assizes of 1684. 'Can you read, sirrah?' he contemptuously demanded of one of them named Verner, who had but a mean aspect at the best. 'Yes, my lord,' was the reply. 'Reach him the book.' The clerk of assize handed his Latin testament to Verner, who began at the first place that struck his eye. This was Matt. viii. 1. 'Construe it, sirrah!' roared Jeffreys. Verner did construe it: 'Judge not, lest ye be judged; for with what judgment ye judge, ye shall be judged.' Jeffreys took this text so much, for him, to heart, that, after Verner and his companions had remained in prison for a year, he dismissed them at the next assizes with the Scriptural caution, 'Go, and sin no more, lest a worse thing come unto you.'

Ambrose Barnes, a Puritan alderman of Newcastle, found the blind side of James II., and attained to considerable influence at Court. The cause of religious liberty brought about strange acquaintances; Barnes had one day two Jesuits and a Capuchin at his table in the Close. It is not to be wondered at that many looked on the Alderman himself as a Jesuit in disguise. Harry Wallis, a mastershipwright, who had taken more beer than was good for him, indulged in open abuse of Barnes, and for this was confined in the tower on the Tyne Bridge. A quantity of malt happened to be stored there; Wallis amused himself by shovelling it into the river, to the tune,

> 'O base mault,
> Thou didst this fault,
> And into Tyne thou shalt.'

Sir Francis Radcliffe, the third baronet of Dilston, used to call Barnes his 'honest Whig.' He actually conveyed his estates to him in secret trust, when he himself was in danger of being involved in the Popish Plot. Notwithstanding the losses of his family under the Commonwealth, when their estates were ordered to be sold for the use of the Navy, and only saved in consequence of the heavy settlements upon them, Sir Francis had been able to buy out his wife's sisters, the other co-heiresses of the Fenwicks of Meldon. The retired life he led at Dilston, owing to his having been received into the Latin Church, increased both his wealth and local popularity. Frequent doles to the poor, and visits from the neighbouring gentry, were the chief events in his household. Sir Cuthbert Heron of Chipchase would send his keeper with a fallow deer, and Mr. Errington's man bring great rolls of brawn and ' other civilities ' from Walwick Grange. In winter, players from about Blaydon and Stella came and acted the comedy of ' Mucedorus, the King's Son of Valentia.' The tuner of the virginals and a poet who came out of Scotland also received their guerdons. There were few postal facilities: Tom the footman had to go all the way to Newcastle on the Saturday night, to put in the letters and wait till the Monday morning for the down mail. Sir Francis kept in touch with the yeomen and farmers through having a large amount of land in his own hands: one winter an express arrived from Alston Moor to say that the snow lay deep, and that the hay for the cattle at Tyne Head would not last another week; during another long storm, the steward at Spindleston lamented that the sheep had all to be hand-fed. In 1688 Sir Francis married his eldest son to Lady Mary Tudor, a natural daughter of Charles II., and attained the goal of his ambition in being created an Earl. The Radcliffes were not an old Catholic family. Sir Francis had the mal-address to ask James II. for a revival of the Earldom of Sussex, a dignity borne by Thomas Radcliffe, who suppressed the Catholic Rising of 1569. He had to be content with the romantic title of Derwentwater. The pleasure his elevation to the peerage afforded was soon damped by the landing of William of Orange. A troop of 250 horse, raised by the new Earl, was refused admission to Berwick, and Derwentwater himself thought it prudent to ride away to the seclusion of Whitton Shield. Declaring 'for the Protestant religion and a free Parliament,' Newcastle threw open its gates to Lord Lumley, while Colonel Billingsley seized Berwick and made prisoner the Lieutenant-Governor, Sir Thomas Haggerston. At Newcastle Colonel Heyford took upon himself to attach Sir John Fenwick of Wallington, on suspicion of being in communication with King James, and sent his soldiers with a hired rabble to pull down the equestrian statue of the unfortunate monarch which had been erected on the Sandhill.

Sir John Fenwick's loyalty to James II. led him to enter into conspiracies for his restoration. Finding that these had been betrayed to the existing Government, he endeavoured to escape to France, but was arrested and beheaded on Tower Hill, January 27, 1697, by virtue of a special Act of attainder which made the evidence of one informer sufficient proof of his guilt. This unconstitutional proceeding roused an intense feeling of indignation throughout Northumberland, and embittered the relations of political parties. During the assizes at Newcastle in 1701, the greater part of the grand jury of Northumberland were dining together in convivial fashion at the Black Horse. John Fenwick of Rock came in singing the popular ballad, 'Sir John Fenwick's the flower among them.' This gave umbrage to Ferdinando Forster of Bamburgh, one of the knights of the shire. A violent altercation took place, which was appeased by some of the company. Next morning, however, Fenwick and Forster happening to meet near the White Cross, drew their swords on each other, and Forster fell. Fenwick was immediately indicted for murder. In spite of the popular feeling in his behalf, which found expression in the doggerel,

> ' Noble squire Fenwick, he must be put down,
> For killing squire Forster of Bamburgh town,'

he was hung during the following month. The gates of the town were shut for fear of a rescue by the miners in his employment at the Kenton collieries.

The accession of George I. extinguished all hope of the Jacobites in a Restoration by constitutional means. In August, 1715, Captain John Shafto, a half-pay officer, and Captain John Hunter of North Tyne, who had received a commission from Queen Anne for raising an independent company, but was better known as a smuggler, came down to Newcastle to prepare an armed rising in the North. About the end of September, the young James Radcliffe, third Earl of Derwentwater, who had been brought up at the Court of St. Germain's, and had just lived long enough at Dilston to make himself universally beloved, received warning from an upholsterer at Newcastle that the Secretary of State had issued a warrant for his apprehension. The three messengers who brought this down took with them four of the trustiest bailiffs of John Johnson of Bebside, the Sheriff of Northumberland, and watched Lord Derwentwater enter Dilston Hall at seven o'clock in the evening. When they searched it at six the next morning, the Earl was nowhere to be found. He had escaped to the house of his neighbour, Mr. Bacon of Styford, who, though a justice of the peace, did nothing to persuade him to surrender. From Styford he proceeded to quarters more secluded and less suspected, at Mr. Lambert's of Newbrough. His horses at Dilston were seized by the bailiffs and messengers, and committed to the custody of Mr. Coatsforth, a rigid Whig magistrate.

Thomas Forster of Edderston, the younger, one of the county members and a Protestant, was also in danger of being attached. The Government described him as ' of middle stature, inclining to be fat, fair-complexioned, his mouth wide, his nose pretty large, speaking the Northern dialect.' He had taken refuge with Mr. Fenwick at Bywell. The State messenger stopped at a village half a mile off to call a constable to his aid, and when he reached Bywell, Forster was flown. Fearful of being all taken up to London, and doubtful as to what the result of an inquiry there might be, Derwentwater, Forster, and the rest resolved, at a conference held at Nafferton, to openly declare for James III., and to meet in arms the next morning at Greenrig, on Watling Street, between Reedsmouth and Sweethope Lough. Fenwick, Tate, Green, Allgood, and other of their Tory neighbours, urged this course, and promised to join them. Acting, as he said, on Cromwell's maxim, that he could gain his ends anywhere with an assload of gold, Lord Derwentwater got back his horses from Coatsforth, and early on October 6 rode out from Dilston with the whole of his servants and a few friends, all armed to the teeth. After marching through Corbridge with drawn swords, the party halted at Beaufront. Mr. Errington, who had served with credit in the French army, was induced to join them, through his many obligations to Lord Derwentwater. Several other gentlemen followed his example. At the top of a hill near the Waterfalls, a little to the south of Greenrig, Forster and twenty more were waiting for them, bringing the whole number of insurgents up to sixty. After a hasty council of war, they decided to proceed to Plainfield Moor, on the north bank of the Coquet, near Sharperton. Here they were met by Lord Widdrington, who had come away at short notice accompanied by a few of his family armed with ordinary fowling-pieces. Mad Jack Hall of Otterburn, as he was called, presently rode up. He had been sitting on the bench at the Alnwick Quarter Sessions when he first heard of the rising, and set off in such haste as in the first instance to forget his hat. He endeavoured to persuade the insurgents to swoop down on his brother justices and the county clerk and his books. Instead of this they marched to Rothbury for the night. On reaching Warkworth the next morning, their chaplain, Mr. Buxton, took possession of the church, and prayed for King James, Mary the Queen-mother, and all the dutiful branches of the Royal Family. Forster, disguised as a trumpeter, proclaimed King James III. at the market-cross. Having received considerable reinforcements at Alnwick and Felton Bridge, the Jacobites entered Morpeth 300 strong, all on horseback, as they refused for the present to enlist any foot, though large numbers proffered their services. Meanwhile, Lancelot Errington and others had surprised the castle on Holy Island, and hoisted the Stuart standard. They were speedily dispossessed by the garrison of Berwick, while Robert Lisle, who went to prepare a rising in Newcastle, found the Whigs on the alert, and had the misfortune to be made prisoner on entering Pandon Gate.

Disappointed at Newcastle's not opening its gates, the insurgents marched across country to Hexham, and then encamped on a moor near Dilston, expecting every moment that Sir William Blackett would join them with his keelmen and lead-miners. Sir William, however, was being closely watched at Wallington by the Sheriff's officers; the militia and trained bands were mustered on Killingworth Moor, and the Earl of Scarburgh, Lord-Lieutenant of Northumberland, had arrived in Newcastle. The Jacobites therefore returned to Hexham. After remaining there three days, hearing that General Carpenter and his troops had reached Newcastle, they set out to support their friends from the West of Scotland, who had accomplished a difficult march from Jedburgh to Rothbury. On the eve of their departure from Hexham they again proclaimed King James, Forster careering in the market-place on his fine black horse. The proclamation remained on the cross several days after they had left, a good indication of the popular sentiment.

Robert Patten, Vicar of Allendale, who acted as Forster's chaplain, lagged behind the main cavalcade. He chanced to overtake a party of keelmen in Rothbury Forest. One brave young fellow among them boldly told him: 'We are Scotsmen going to our homes to join our countrymen, now in arms for King James. I'll drink his health just now !' And, dipping his bonnet in a runner, he cried, ' Here is King James's health !' In this he was followed by his comrades. Patten enlisted them each with a shilling, and they all spent the night in Rothbury, after taking the precaution to secure the head-constable in his own house. Next day they came up with the English and Scottish horse at Wooler. The whole little army then moved on to Kelso to effect a junction with the advancing Highlanders.

During the fatal march southwards, Forster opened at Brampton his commission to act as General of the Stuart forces in England. He had never seen an army in his life, and his appointment was due to the mistaken idea that the selection of a Protestant would rally a multitude of Tories to the Cause. As it was, William Craster and two others were the only recruits brought in through Forster's influence. At Preston the Stuart army was surprised in front by General Wills, while its retreat was cut off by Carpenter's advance from Newcastle. Forster, who, though no soldier, was no coward, allowed himself to be persuaded to a miserable surrender at discretion by Colonel Oxburgh, who was fitter for a priest than a field-officer, and Lord Widdrington, who could not travel, it was said, without strong soup in a bottle. Lord Derwentwater, who had signally distinguished himself, working in the trenches with his coat off, bitterly reflected on the broken promises of his Tory neighbours. Remorselessly chosen to be the scapegoat of the whole movement, he was beheaded on Tower Hill, February 24, 1716, ' for loyalty to his lawful Sovereign.' Baron Bernstoff offered Lady Cowper, the wife of the Lord Chancellor, to let Forster, who was her cousin, escape on his way up to London. Whether or not the Government felt they were under a debt of gratitude to Forster on account of his bad generalship, there is little doubt that his final escape from Newgate was connived at in high quarters. According to the genuine traditions of the countryside, his sister Dorothy rode up to London in the company of John

Armstrong (whom, as a matter of fact, she soon afterwards married), and obtaining an impression of the master-key of Newgate, had one made like it, with which she let her brother out. Charles Radcliffe, Lord Derwentwater's youngest brother, also escaped from Newgate. William Sanderson of Highlaws and the brave young John Talbot of Cartington were equally fortunate at Chester. Lady Cowper prevailed on the Government to forego the prosecution of her near relation, John Clavering of Callaly; and Thomas Errington was also set at liberty. The only Northumbrian gentlemen who were executed were George Collingwood of Eslington and John Hall of Otterburn; but the fate of two young Swinburnes was particularly sad—Edward dying in Newgate, and James going melancholy mad.

In violent contrast to the influence exercised by the '45 on Scottish literature, the '15 produced nothing more romantic in Northumberland than Thomas Whittle's ballad of 'The Midford Galloway':—

> 'The routing the Earl of Mar's forces,
>   Has given their neighbours supplies;
> They've stock'd us with Highlanders' horses,
>   Like kileys for madness and size:
> The whirligig-maker of Midford
>   Has gotten one holds such a stear,
>   *   *   *   *   *
> The devil ne'er saw such a gelding
>   As this to be foal'd of a mear.
>
> 'It had been so spoil'd in up-bringing,
>   It vext his poor heart every day;
> Sometimes with biting and flinging,
>   And sometimes with running away.
>   *   *   *   *   *
> Perhaps it was brought up a Tory,
>   And knew the poor man for a Whig.'

The quest of his Jacobite pony gives the whirligig-maker a long lesson in Northumbrian geography. After searching all Rothbury Forest, he accompanies Fortune, the clothier of Heslyhurst, to Tom Fawdon, the fuller's, at Brinkburn, where they regale themselves heartily, He has the 'galloway' 'cried' in Whittingham church-yard after morning service on the Sunday, and ultimately recovers it at Earle, near Wooler.

A serious riot, occasioned by a pretended scarcity of corn, broke out in Newcastle in 1740. Many of the merchants' apprentices formed themselves into the White Stocking Regiment of volunteer militia The mob was pacified for the moment by the announcement that the corn-factors had agreed to moderate their prices. This they did, but closed their shops. The populace proceeded to plunder the granaries. The militia was forbidden to assemble, owing to the Mayor's jealousy of their commander, and on a rioter being killed by a shot from the Guildhall, the rabble broke into the building, destroying the glass and pictures and robbing the town's hutch of more than £1,000. They threatened to set fire to the town, when three companies of foot, under the command of Captain Sowle arrived after a forced march from Alnwick, and soon succeeded in restoring order.

Viscount Radcliffe, the only son of the third Earl of Derwentwater, died in 1731. Dilston and the other estates which had been saved to him under his mother's marriage-settlement reverted to the Crown, and were bestowed by King George on Greenwich Hospital. His surviving uncle, Charles Radcliffe, who was living abroad, assumed the title of Derwentwater. He had the misfortune to be taken on board a French privateer during the Stuart rising of 1745, by which Northumberland was little affected, owing to the prompt measures taken for the defence of Berwick and Newcastle. The Government resolved to proceed against him on his previous attainder after the rising of 1715, but had some difficulty in proving his identity. At last two witnesses were procured from Northumberland: Abraham Bunting recognised him as the same brother of Lord Derwentwater who had marched out from Hexham in 1715 at the head of 500 of their tenants and other insurgents; Thomas Mozley, living within two miles of Dilston, had often noticed the white scar on the right side of his face that looked like the mark of a scald.   A bravado at his trial, a saint on the scaffold, Charles, Earl of Derwentwater, suffered on Tower Hill, December 8, 1746.

CHAPTER XI.

NEWCASTLE-UPON-TYNE.

FOUGHT like the battle of Mons Grampius in the Far North, Culloden finally accomplished that pacification of Britain which had been the dream of Julius Agricola. No longer was there any fear of Caledonian ravages, and Northumberland lost the Border character that had distinguished it for so many centuries. Its history, which at the beginning forms an integral part of that of the Roman Empire, and then contributes a most important chapter to the annals of Christendom, becomes henceforward a mere miscellany of declarations of polls, long runs with fox-hounds, failures of turnip-crops, eccentricities of old families, and pretensions of new ones, little differing from that of any of the other thirty-nine counties of England. During the last century and a half, its main feature is the development of the coal-mines in the south-eastern corner of the county, and the consequent growth and expansion of Newcastle-upon-Tyne.

In the reign of Henry IV., when Newcastle became a county of itself, the population is said to have numbered about 4,000, less than that of Morpeth at the present day. It had increased sevenfold by the beginning of this century, and cannot now be put at much under 200,000. Including the thickly-inhabited district on the north bank of the Tyne down to its mouth, it is considerably over a quarter of a million. If Gateshead and the whole district which forms with its pall of smoke one continuous town be brought in, that figure may safely be doubled.

In Northumberland proper, the populations of the towns of Morpeth, Hexham, and Alnwick have long remained almost stationary at 5,000, 6,000, and 7,000 respectively. The population of the country districts has been distinctly retrograde, probably being now only half what it was when the century opened. Since 1873 the quantity of land under the plough has decreased by a third, while proportionately fewer hands are employed on that still left under cultivation. After the '45, Newcastle lost its character of a Border fortress, and became more than ever the county town of Northumberland; all Northumberland is now rapidly becoming a suburb of Newcastle.

The surrender of Carlisle to Prince Charles Edward, in 1745, was attributed largely to the inability of General Wade to advance to its relief from Newcastle, owing to the want of a good road. This was remedied by the construction of the Military Road between the two towns in 1748. The route chosen between Newcastle and Sewinshields was the line of the Roman Wall, which was for the most part levelled for the purpose. Fortunately, John Horsley, a learned Presbyterian minister of Morpeth, who died in 1731, had left a careful description of the Wall in his ' Britannia Romana.' From a military point of view, the Carlisle road may have been well planned, being probably only a resuscitation of the Roman road that preceded the Wall. It certainly attracted at the time a considerable amount of trade and traffic to Newcastle, and it has proved of great service to those anxious to visit the portions of the Wall and Four Dykes which were spared by the Hanoverians. For ordinary purposes there is not a worse engineered road in the kingdom.

The fatal news from Culloden broke the heart of Lancelot Errington, the hero of the capture of Holy Island in 1715, but the hopes of the Jacobite party were not entirely crushed. The attachment of the working classes to the Stuart cause was much deeper than might now be supposed. General Wade issued warrants to impress all vagrants into his ranks The celebrated piper, Jimmy Allan, a native of Rothbury Forest, was arrested while playing at a ' widow's merry night,' for the benefit of a poor family at Otterburn, but soon made his escape. During a seven weeks' strike of the keelmen, in 1750, some of them actually proclaimed Charles III. from a stile in Elswick fields. The ' young Gudeman of Ballengeich,' as he was called, still had his emissaries in the district. These the rough squires of North Tyne, 'disdaining the superficial formalities of the new school of manners,' received with ' the old undisguised gentleman-like welcome.' In other words, they fuddled them with drinking the King's health ' over the water' and ' under the rose,' a rose and oak leaf being purposely cut on the bowls of their Venetian glasses. Even after George III. was prayed for in the Catholic Church at Hexham on the relaxation of the penal laws about 1780, Jacobite spinsters would rise and walk out at the first mention of his name.

Northumbrian society of all ranks was pervaded by a love of feasting and good cheer. Chicken, in his ' Collier's Wedding,' has preserved a somewhat coarse picture of what was the great occasion of merry-making at a time when

> ' The colliers and their wives
> Liv'd drunken, honest, working lives.'

The customs he describes are so diametrically opposed to those of the ' miners ' at the present day, who often keep their marriages secret as long as possible, that the story forms a valuable *conte de mœurs*. Jenny, a collier's daughter, wins the ' smock ' at the Benwell ' hopping ' by dancing to the tune of ' Jockey's lost his fellow-swain.' Tom pays her attentions, and, after a brief but warm courtship, they go to obtain her mother's consent. They find the old woman seated on a ' cracket ' by the fire, the 'rock' just spun off her wheel, and an earthern pot of 'humming beer' on a little table beside her. Tom is received with 'Hout, lad, get hame, ye're nought but fash.' He reveals his passion for Jenny, and her mother comes out with, ' De'il rive their sark gans hame to-night.' Jock and Doll, two old neighbours, are called in; 'gray-beard' is washed, and after plenty of strong beer and tobacco, the old lady reels up to Tom with her consent. The wedding-day is fixed, and all prepare to 'mense' the bride. Jenny determines that the dinner is to be at her mother's house. On the fated morning Tom and a jolly train of collier lads ride into Benwell with whips cracking and bagpipes playing. After a refection of ale, cakes and cheese, all set out for the church at nine o'clock:

> 'Two lusty lads, well dress'd and strong,
> Step out to lead the bride along ;
> And two young maids of equal size
> As soon the bridegroom's hands surprise.
> The pipers wind and take their post,
> And go before to clear the coast.'

The crowd in church—

> ' Some perhaps that were threescore
> Were never in a church before '—

climb and break the pews in order better to see the cere-mony. The collier lads seize the bride's garters and carry them round the church in triumph. The pipers, as the procession leaves, strike up ' I'll make thee fain to follow me.' At the 'church-stile' four rustics kiss the bride, and then, mounting their cart-horses, ride as hard as they can to her mother's house in order to secure the ' kail,' or broth with currants and raisins in it. After the banquet and dance, the bride is solemnly put to bed with a ' posset ' of currant-cakes swimming in ale.

No less than 5,000 people, most of them from the country, and mounted on pillions, attended the wedding of William Weatherburn, a miner of Heaton, at All Saints', Newcastle, in 1754. At the marriage of William

Donkin, a Tosson farmer, 500 men and women partook of 120 quarters of lamb, 44 quarters of veal, 20 quarters of mutton, and 12 hams, not to mention the poultry and other viands. The punch required four ankers of brandy, and the beer was brewed from ninety bushels of malt. These were supplemented by twelve dozens of cider and a great many gallons of wine. Among the twenty-five fiddlers and pipers were Jimmy Allan and his father, who, on his son's complaining of his playing out of tune, rejoined, 'Who learnt ye? I'll shiver the back-lill'—the highest or thumb note on the small pipes—'with you or e'er a piper in Breaton!' The completion of the water-mill at Alnwick in 1768 was celebrated by the consumption of an enormous currant dumpling, eight feet in circumference. To surpass this the housekeeper at Howick built a game pie nine feet round the base and twelve stones in weight, which was sent up by sea to Sir Henry Grey in London, provided with a case on wheels for rolling it up to each guest.

The ruin of the Radcliffes, whose barrack-like mansion at Dilston was finally pulled down in 1768, was not a greater blow to the Stuart cause in Northumberland than the return of the Percies as friends of the Government in power, after an absence of nearly two hundred years. Algernon Seymour, seventh Duke of Somerset, the grandson of Joscelin Percy, the eleventh and last Earl of the house of Ragnar Long-neck, and himself created Earl of Northumberland in 1749, died in the following year. He left only a daughter, who, before her brother's death, had insisted on marrying Sir Hugh Smithson, fourth baronet, of Stanwick, in Yorkshire, a country gentleman of good family. This match was not altogether to the fancy of her grandfather, the proud Duke of Somerset. He devised the great Percy estates in Yorkshire, Cumberland, and Sussex to his nephew, Sir Charles Wyndham, so that Sir Hugh and Lady Elizabeth Smithson, on succeeding to her father's Earldom of Northumberland, only received those situated in that county. They very properly took the name of Percy, which owed its chief glory to its previous assumption by the descendants of Joscelin of Louvain. It was easy for Horace Walpole to sneer at the young Earl and Countess ' living by the etiquette of the ancient peerage.' The Countess, no doubt, had very exalted ideas, but they all tended to the advantage of Northumberland. It is, perhaps, to be regretted that her husband was not content with the time-honoured title of Earl of Northumberland. It is certainly fortunate that when he was made a Duke, it was by the style of Northumberland, and not, as he wished, by that of Brabant, though the bestowal of a title taken from the Austrian dominions might have been justified as a retort for the creation of Essex's son, Robert Dudley, Duke of Northumberland, by the Emperor Ferdinand II. In addition to being 'one of the handsomest men in the kingdom' and ' most courteous in his demeanour,' the first Percy Duke of Northumberland was the possessor of exceptionally high intellectual qualities. He was, in fact, in every way superior to the first Percy Earl. The value of the family estates in Northumberland increased enormously under his good management, and to the great contentment of his tenantry. He restored the castle of Alnwick (which was almost as much a ruin as Warkworth or Prudhoe) in the true Strawberry Hill style of Gothic. The plaster decorations of this had at any rate the advantage of interfering comparatively little with the medieval work they concealed, and there was no mistaking the one for the other. Thomas Percy, Bishop of Dromore, acted as the historian of the revived house. His work, though directed mainly to attempting to connect his own family with the race of Hotspur, was well done for those days, and has never received the appreciation it merits. He owes his popular reputation to the ' Hermit of Warkworth,' a base plagiarized doggerel that fully deserves the severe condemnation passed on it by Dr. Johnson; the dedicatory lines to the Duchess of Northumberland alone display any of that good taste which rescued for us so much of our ancient minstrelsy.

The Duke's endeavour to raise the character of the peasantry by granting them small portions of land at a reasonable rate won for him a high encomium from Thomas Bewick, who has left us a series of highly-finished verbal vignettes of Northumberland in the eighteenth century. Bewick's skill as an autobiographer is almost more remarkable than that which has gained him world-wide celebrity as a wood-engraver. He was born in 1753 at Cherryburn, on the right bank of the Tyne, a little to the west of Prudhoe. The house and byres stood close to a little dene in which grew a number of cherry and plum trees, while nearer the river were some remarkably tall ashes and an oak, supposed to be one of the tallest and straightest in the kingdom. Indeed, at that time the whole country between Wylam and Bywell presented the appearance of a continuous forest, now long since stubbed up. The obstreperous boy broke the shins of the old schoolmaster at Mickley with his iron-hooped clogs, but made good progress with his less morose successor. Although he had seen no other paintings than the King's arms in Ovingham Church, and the signs of the village inns—the Black Bull, the White Horse, the Salmon, and the Hare and Hounds—he began to draw by natural instinct, and as soon as the blank spaces in his books were filled, he betook himself with a piece of chalk to the gravestones and floor of the church porch. A friend gave him some paper and pens and ink; the juice of the brambleberry made a great change, a camel-hair brush and shells of colours a still greater. His love of animal life was encouraged by fox-hunting, coursing, and badger-baiting; by looking after his long-legged, black-faced sheep on the fell, by 'mucking' the byre and milking the cows, and by watching the rarer birds in the dene. During the hard winter of 1765 he was employed in 'creeing' the tender shoots of the whin-bushes with a wooden 'mell' for the horses. After flogging had lost its effect as a punishment for fighting with other boys, he was locked up in Ovingham Church, where he hid himself by climbing the pillars. 'Silky' and the 'Hedley Cow' had lost their terrors for him; but one night, after playing at cards—those 'devil's books'—he fled from a man going 'a-guising to a kirn-supper,' whom he mistook for the author.

The health and happiness of the peasantry who kept a few sheep or a Kyloe cow on the beautiful wild common adjoining Cherryburn were at this time unbounded, though their daily fare consisted of rye-bread, potatoes, oatmeal-porridge and milk, varied with meat-broth on Sundays. Honest and independent, they still greatly respected the gentry, and were equally respected by them. There were many original characters among them:—Will Bewick, who would discourse 'largely' on the stars and planets; Anthony Liddell, wearing a large curled wig of the seventeenth century, a great reader of Josephus and Bunyan's 'Holy War,' and a poacher on principle, through his belief in the inalienable rights of man, but so bad a shot that he had always to rest his fowling-piece on a hay-fork; Thomas Forster, who amassed wealth by keeping a secret stock of bees in a 'whin rush'; and John Cowie, who had been under fire at Minden in the ranks of Napier's grenadiers, and whose shot-riddled uniform did duty at last as a scarecrow on a corn-rigg. Most of these had received or inherited from their Border ancestry sobriquets of the Red Indian order, such as the Hawk, Steed, Falcon, Fox, Wolf, Bloodhound, Raven, or Crow-foot. The farmers were not of so intelligent a cast of mind as their labourers, their minds being exclusively occupied with their farms; and this has long remained the case in Northumberland. The lairds who lived on their own lands were mostly grossly ignorant and offensively proud, attributes that soon forced them into the oblivion of the towns, while the 'ha' houses,' that had been in their families for generations, gradually mouldered away.

In the same parish of Ovingham, but on the opposite bank of the Tyne, about three miles lower down, was born, in 1781, the man who did more than all others to destroy that beautiful old world in which Bewick took such keen delight. George Stephenson, too, derived an early love of birds from the tame robins and blackbirds that flew in and out of the one room in the High Street house in which he was brought up with three or four brothers and sisters; but, earning only twelve shillings a week, his father could not afford to send him to any school, and the surroundings of his home, with the Wylam waggon-way running close in front, were very different from those of Cherryburn. Horses were at that time employed to draw the chaldron-coal waggons on rails of beechwood to Lemington Staith, a distance of five miles. In 1808 Mr. Blackett of Wylam replaced the wooden tramway with iron rails—an improvement that doubled or trebled the efficiency of the line. A locomotive, with lots of pumps, cogwheels, and plugs, bought in 1812, proved a failure. The first one constructed at Wylam was not much more successful, but it was now found that sufficient friction could be obtained for an engine to run on a smooth rail, instead of having a toothed driving-wheel working on a rack-rail; and the second Wylam locomotive answered better. It was not, however, till George Stephenson, then engineer at Killingworth, let the waste steam into the chimney of his locomotives to increase the draught, in 1815, instead of letting it blow out to the terror of any horses near, or pass into a special condenser, that the success of steam was assured. Even in 1824 a Newcastle paper scornfully asked: ' What person would ever think of paying anything to be conveyed from Hexham to Newcastle in something like a coal-waggon, upon a dreary waggon-way, and to be dragged for the greater part of the distance by a roaring steam-engine?' It was not until 1835, ten years after the completion of the Stockton and Darlington line, that a railway was opened between Blaydon and Hexham, then lit with gas for the first time. The following year other sections between Hexham and Haydon Bridge, Greenhead and Carlisle, and Blaydon and the Redheugh, were finished;

but for two years more a coach ran between Haydon Bridge and Greenhead. The journey by steamboat to the Redheugh was only dispensed with in 1846, when the railway actually entered Newcastle for the first time.

It was considered wonderful that letters could be taken from Newcastle to London by steamer for eightpence in 1835; three years later a mail came round by Carlisle in twenty-six hours, delivering the London morning papers at one o'clock on the day after publication, instead of on the morning of the second day. In 1844 a railway was opened from Darlington to Gateshead, and Newcastle was reached in nine hours and a half, by way of Rugby and Derby. In 1847 the line from Tweedmouth to Newcastle was finished, and temporary wooden viaducts were thrown over the Tyne and the Tweed in the two following years, thus completing the last links in the East Coast route to Scotland. The permanent High Level Bridge at Newcastle, with its subway for carriage traffic, was not finished till three or four months before the Queen's visit to Howick in 1849, when the royal train drew up on it for ten minutes. The other principal railways in Northumberland—the North Tyne, Wansbeck Valley, and Alnwick and Cornhill—were opened in 1858, 1864, and 1887 respectively.

Mr. Hodgson Hinde, one of the members of Parliament for Newcastle, and the author of a short general history of Northumberland, had from the beginning urged on the Government the necessity of laying down a comprehensive scheme of railway communication for the whole country, and then granting concessions for the construction and working of the various sections. Northumberland would have gained immensely if this excellent advice had been followed.

As if for the express purpose of vaunting modern progress at the expense of the historic past, the East Coast route was carried relentlessly through the castles of Newcastle and Berwick. Quite recently the Norman keep of the former has had a narrow escape of being

18

practically turned into a signal cabin. After having been advertised as suitable for a mill in the last century, it was fortunately acquired by the Corporation of Newcastle and leased to the Society of Antiquaries, which, founded in 1813, is the oldest provincial institution of the kind in England. By this it was restored, too thoroughly as regards the Norman ornamental work, while its venerable outlines were utterly spoilt by the addition of poor unmeaning battlements. The magnificent collection of Roman altars and other inscribed stones, long immured in its dungeons, was removed in 1884 to the Black Gate, the main entrance to the castle, built in the middle of the thirteenth century, which was acquired by the Society on similar terms with the keep, and repaired more judiciously. The stones can now be seen, but they are in greater danger of fire. It is a matter of much regret that the memory of Mr. John Clayton and Dr. Collingwood Bruce, the two great antiquaries of the Roman North, has not been enshrined in a museum that would allow of a systematic arrangement of the treasures of the Wall on the lines so magnificently developed in the Provincial Museum of Treves.

The Pilgrimage conducted along the Wall by Dr. Bruce in 1849 proved a most powerful incentive to the study of its remains. Three years later the meeting of the Archæological Institute at Newcastle opened out the numerous other antiquities of Northumberland, especially the medieval castles, towers, and peles. The restoration of Alnwick Castle by Algernon, fourth Duke of Northumberland, followed. This might have been conducted on more conservative principles, but the architectural adaptations were clever and the workmanship excellent. Archæological specialists were to blame if early fourteenth-century windows were inserted in walls built some fifty years later.

The project of a canal to connect the Tyne and Solway was mooted early in the last century. Formal plans of it were prepared in 1794, but the scheme was abandoned in consequence of the open opposition of the owners of Close House and Beaufront, and the fear the coal-owners near Newcastle had of competition from mines further inland. The navigation of the Tyne itself has been greatly improved by the piers at its mouth, begun in 1853, as well as by the removal of the bar and by dredging operations. The river commissioners lacked courage to cut through the great bend between Newburn and Lemington, a work which would have opened out the upper portion of the tideway and kept the lower portion efficiently scoured. The Albert Edward Dock cut out of the hillside at Coble Dene, near Shields, at an enormous cost, in 1884, has been little needed, except for a few vessels of exceptional size. The question of forming a harbour of refuge on the rock-bound coast of north Northumberland (the scene of the heroic rescue of the survivors of the *Forfarshire* by Grace Darling and her father in 1838) has ended, after great expenditure, in the construction of a small harbour at North Sunderland by Lord Crewe's trustees. The most remarkable change along the Northumbrian littoral has been that effected by the improvement of Blyth Harbour, thanks to the energy of Sir Matthew White Ridley. This has now diverted a very considerable portion of the Northumberland steam-coal exports from the Tyne. The quantity shipped at Blyth has risen from 146,264 tons in 1883 to 2,643,778 tons in 1894, while the growth of the town has also been phenomenal.

The output of the Northumberland collieries was estimated at 1,053,274 tons in 1794. It was 6,463,550 tons in 1874, and 9,541,199 tons in 1894. A much greater number of men are employed, as recourse is had to thinner seams. The system of bonds or yearly agreements with a bonus of £5 was established in 1809. Severe riots occurred in 1831, when a body of 1,500 miners stopped the pits working in the Bedlington district, throwing the corves (or baskets in which coals were then drawn to the surface) down the shaft of the Glebe Pit. A great strike occurred again on the expiration of the bonds in 1844, when the men demanded that they should be assured wages of 15s. for every week in the year, but on no account be required to earn more than 3s. a day. The annual bonds were solemnly burnt in 1862, and a simple fortnightly agreement substituted. Although there were long strikes in 1877 and 1887, and arbitrations, sliding scales and conciliation boards have proved futile to satisfactorily regulate wages, the relations between the miners and their employers have been generally good. This has been largely owing to the influence on both sides obtained by Mr. Thomas Burt, M.P. for Morpeth, and Mr. Charles Fenwick, M.P. for the Wansbeck division of Northumberland.

The most famous contest in the Parliamentary annals of Northumberland was that of 1826, when the poll remained open at Alnwick for more than a fortnight, and the Hon. H. T. Liddell and Mr. Matthew Bell were elected knights of the shire, in opposition to Mr. Beaumont and Lord Howick. The Reform Bill of 1832 split the county into a northern and a southern division, each with two members. It took one of its representatives from Morpeth, and gave a member to Tynemouth. The Reform Bill of 1868 endeavoured to preserve Morpeth as a pocket-borough, by adding to it the district of Bedlingtonshire. The result was that Sir George Grey did not stand again, and Mr. Burt was elected by the mining vote. The by-election held in South Northumberland in 1878, in consequence of Lord Eslington, the popular Conservative member, succeeding to the Earldom of Ravensworth, ended in a tie between Mr. Edward Ridley and Mr. Albert Grey, but the former was returned on a scrutiny.

Berwick-upon-Tweed made a vain protest against its Parliamentary absorption in Northumberland under the provisions of the Redistribution Act of 1885, on the ground that it was entitled to separate representation as a distinct member of the United Kingdom. The northernmost division of Northumberland was called after it, to the disappointment of Alnwick. The western portion of the county was formed into a fairly satisfactory division, with its centre at Hexham. The manufacturing district on both sides of Newcastle made another homogeneous constituency, to which the name of the Tyneside Division was stupidly given, as, except in parliamentary geography, Tyneside includes Hexham. In consequence of the retention of the fictitious borough of Morpeth, an irregular nondescript tract was now left stretching from the Coquet right over the Tyne, without any common interest or common centre. For this no name was forthcoming until Sir Charles Trevelyan suggested it should be called the Wansbeck division, after the river flowing past Wallington.

The great increase in the population of Newcastle after 1745 was naturally accompanied by important changes in the aspect of the town. In making these the authorities showed, perhaps, that the character given them in the local ballad was only too true :

> ' Their foolish pride there's none to stop,
>   Improvement's all the go ;
>   Unseemly's everything that's old,
>   So all that's old's laid low.'

The steeple of St. Nicholas' was the only landmark left absolutely untouched. In 1763 the great wall of the town along the quay was removed, and this was followed by the erection of Mozeley Street and Dean Street. The rage for innovation led St. Nicholas' to be made into ' a sort of cathedral,' to the destruction of its ancient monuments. All Saints', one of the most interesting of the churches, was entirely pulled down, and replaced by a circular Doric structure with fine mahogany pews. The Guildhall was shorn of its principal features, and recased with plain stonework. One after another the gates of the town, Pandon Gate, Sand Gate, Pilgrim Street Gate, and West Gate were removed. New Gate, which had served as the prison of Newcastle since it became a separate county, was respited till a new castellated gaol was finished in 1823.

During the wars of the French Revolution the now un-walled town was on several occasions the scene of a panic. In 1793 the sailors at South Shields endeavoured forcibly to release their comrades from the press-gang. The alarm they caused spread to Newcastle; the Earl of Fauconberg sounded to arms, and marched his North York militia through the town to the house of detention for impressed seamen, when the danger proved to be imaginary:

> ' From Newgate down to the Broad Chare
>   They march'd with might and main ;
> Then gallantly they turn'd them round,
>   And so march'd up again.'

Soon after some practical joker sent a letter to William Yielder, the Mayor of Newcastle, in the name of two Northumberland magistrates, to say that a party of French had landed near Bamburgh. Once more Lord Fauconberg's drums were futilely beat :

> ' Lo ! scarce were Tuesday's terrors past
>   And calm'd our perturbation,
> When news from Bambro' came post-haste,
>   Reviving consternation.
> For Fauconberg and Yielder too
>   Then felt their blood run cool ;
> And thinking both the tidings true,
>   Both chose to play the fool.'

A yet more serious alarm was occasioned throughout Northumberland in 1804, by some whins burning on Lammermoor being mistaken for a beacon to announce a French invasion.

The real improvement of Newcastle, and that on a plan which, if it had been adhered to, would have given it the stamp of a true city, began in 1834, with Richard Grainger's purchase of Anderson Place, which still occupied the centre of the town with its gardens. As it is, Grey Street, rising gently in a curve, past the fine façade of the Theatre Royal, to the monument of Earl Grey, who carried the

Reform Bill of 1832, is one of the finest streets in the kingdom, in spite of the discordant shop-fronts and the intrusion here and there of impurer styles. The Butcher and Vegetable Markets, opened in 1835, are of excellent design. If the original elevation had been carried out, the Central Station would have possessed a Roman grandeur. Even as it is, the carriage portico is one of the best pieces of architecture in the town.

In 1836 the reformed Corporation signalized themselves by deciding to abandon the historic Mansion House in the Close, and selling off their furniture, books, pictures, and plate. Since then, her Majesty's judges and other visitors of distinction have been entertained in a very genteel residence in an upper street. There is now no fear of their falling into the Tyne like Baron Graham, the Lord 'Size of John Shield's humorous ballad. The keelman describes at the inquest how he found Lord 'Size in the river, and fished him out, dead to all appearance :

> ' " Aw was setten the keel, wi' Dick Stavers an' Mat,
>   An' the Mansion-hoose Stairs we were just alangside,
>   When we a' three see'd sumthing, but didn't ken what,
>   That was splashing and labbering aboot i' the tide.
>   ' It's a fluiker !' ki Dick ; ' No,' ki Mat ; ' it's owre big.
>   It luik'd mair like a skyat when aw furst seed it rise ;'
>   ' Kiv aw'—for aw'd getten a gliff o' the wig—
>   ' Odd marcy ! Wye, marrows, becrike it's Lord 'Size !'" '

On the conclusion of his evidence,

>   ' the Jury, for close consultation, retired.
>   Some " Death accidental" were willing to find ;
>   Some " God's visitation " most eager requir'd ;
>   And some were for " Fell in the river " inclin'd.
>   But ere on their verdict they all were agreed,
>   My lord gave a groan, and wide open'd his eyes ;
>   Then the coach and the trumpeters came with great speed,
>   And back to the Mansion House carried Lord 'Size.'

The Town Hall, the foundation-stone of which was laid in 1853, is in an awkward situation, and shaped like a grand piano. The corn-market held underneath is, in the present state of agriculture, of quite secondary importance to the cattle market. This is conveniently situated to the west of the Central Station.

Northumberland, especially Tyneside and Glendale, was long noted for good farming. The cultivation of turnips was introduced at Rock so early as 1727. Mr. Proctor brought there for the purpose one Andrew Willey, who afterwards settled as a gardener at Lesbury, and sowed turnips broadcast on horseback for the farmers in that neighbourhood. In 1770 Mr. Ilderton taught the boys and girls at Hawkhill to hoe turnips, leaving a certain number in each given square. The present system of drill-culture was introduced about twelve years later. The first threshing-machine in the county was one invented by Mr. Gregson, in 1765. He took the idea from a small mill that a Scotsman carted from farmhouse to farmhouse, to 'swingle' the flax then grown for home use. His machine was worked by a man who had hard work to thresh twelve bushels of wheat in the day. Mr. Oxley, of Flodden, soon afterwards constructed a horse machine. Lime had long been used, even to abuse, on the land in Bamburghshire; James Hall, of Thornington, in 1757, was the first to cart a load of it west of the Till. The great progress that Northumbrian agriculture made in the latter part of the century was due mainly to the example set by the Culleys of Akeld and Fowberry. Thomas Bates laid the foundation of his celebrated shorthorn herd at Halton Castle and Ridley Hall, and used a primitive form of reaping-machine to cut the thistles in Haughton pastures.

The commissioners of Greenwich Hospital did much for the improvement of their estates in the early part of the present century. The good which ultimately resulted from their profuse expenditure has been unduly ascribed to John Grey of Dilston by the filial partiality of his biographer. An honest and popular Receiver of the Hospital estates, John Grey destroyed some of the most beautiful scenery on the Tyne through his hatred of hedgerow timber; he was no friend of small holdings, and paid little attention to the cottages of the agricultural labourers, who had then no votes. In 1865 an extraordinary character, wearing long ostrich feathers, and styling herself 'Amelia, Countess of Darwentwater,' appeared on Tyneside, and laid claim, in spite of all rhyme and reason, to the Radcliffe estates. Half monomaniac, half impostor, she contrived to attract considerable public sympathy, especially when, after being ejected from the ruins of Dilston, she encamped for forty days by the roadside, and when, in a fit of romantic exaltation, she drew 'the sword of her ancestors' on the Hospital officials. After a whole series of adventures, she died in 1880, without anyone ever finding out who she really was. It has been surmised that she was a lady's-maid from Dover, of the name of Burke, who had lived in a family at Schwerin, and had had her imagination fired by reading a novel, written about forty years previously, in which Viscount Radcliffe, the son of Lord Derwentwater, instead of dying in 1731, settles in Germany after a mock funeral. Her career served to show the strong affection in which the memory of the Radcliffes was still held, and the little idea most people have of what constitutes historical accuracy and legal proof. It directed the attention of the Government to the cost of administrating the Hospital estates, and the greater portion of them have since been sold by auction. The prices obtained for Dilston and Thornbrough in 1874, during what was a regular land-hunger in Northumberland, amounted to about fifty years' purchase. Quite recently the great national fortress of Bamburgh, the seat of the charities of Lord Crewe and Dr. Sharpe, has been privately sold by the Charity Commissioners to Lord Armstrong.

The fatal subjection of the country to the town, which has become the ruling feature of modern English life, was emphasized on the partition by Parliament of the ancient diocese of Durham in 1882. Instead of a see of the first rank being established in Northumberland, where the origins of English Christianity still throw a halo round Lindisfarne, and where the priory church of Hexham, with its nave rebuilt, would form a real cathedral, the ambition of Newcastle to rank as a city was gratified by a bishop's stool being set up in a typical parish church under the patronage of St. Nicholas of Myra, a saint in no way connected with Northumbrian history.

Agriculture has suffered comparatively less in Northumberland than in many other counties; still, the problem of how to keep any population on the land is none the less pressing. It is harrowing to see in many districts the ruins of what until recently were smiling homesteads, where stalwart families were brought up in health and happiness. What will occur in the not distant future, when the coalfields will be exhausted, it is difficult to foresee. History is no more concerned with prophecy than it is with geology—Sir Thomas Gray and the Sibyl did not mount the fifth round of the ladder—but the hope may be expressed that the hard-headed Northumbrian character, formed by centuries of Border vicissitudes, and perhaps in some degree the outcome of strange crosses, introduced by settlers and soldiers of various nations and periods, will prove equal to the crisis, and that the blessing called down by Aidan on the hand of Oswald may rest equally on Bernicia :

'NUNQUAM INVETERASCAT !'

' Length of days be in her right hand, and in her left riches and honour.'

INDEX.

* The notation followed is that of the ancient pedigrees at Alnwick Castle.

THE END.

ERRATA.

Page 14, line 12, *for* 'with its' *read* 'and their.'

Page 18, line 12, *delete* comma.

Page 28, line 7, *for* 'one vestige' *read* 'one positive vestige.'

Page 29, line 14, *for* 'During Agricola's' *read* 'During this Agricola's.'

Page 42, line 4 below table, *for* 'estates' *read* 'states.'

Page 43, line 21, *enclose* 'Carrawburgh' *in brackets.*

Page 48, line 3, *for* 'Grampius' *read* 'Graupius.'

Page 59, line 31, *delete* 'out.'

Page 88, line 1, *for* 'portions' *read* 'portion.'

Page 142, line 17, *for* 'by' *read* 'through.'

Page 152, lines 25 and 26, *for* 'missing' *read* 'stolen.'

Page 187, at bottom of page, *read:*

> 'Then the Percy out of Bamburgh came,
>   With him a mighty many,
> With fifteen hundred archers bold ;
>   They were chosen out of shires three.'

Page 231, line 30, *for* 'night' *read* 'day at night.'

Page 264, line 1, *for* 'Grampius' *read* 'Graupius.'